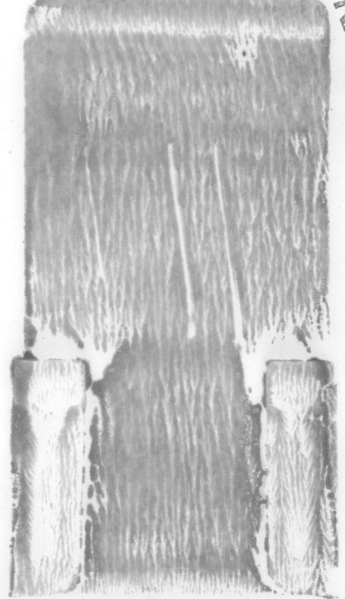

REASON AND AUTHORITY IN THE EIGHTEENTH CENTURY

REASON AND AUTHORITY IN THE EIGHTEENTH CENTURY

BY

GERALD R. CRAGG

Professor of Historical Theology in the
Andover Newton Theological School
Newton, Massachusetts

CAMBRIDGE
AT THE UNIVERSITY PRESS
1964

PUBLISHED BY
THE SYNDICS OF THE CAMBRIDGE UNIVERSITY PRESS

Bentley House, 200 Euston Road, London, N.W. 1
American Branch: 32 East 57th Street, New York 22, N.Y.
West African Office: P.O. Box 33, Ibadan, Nigeria

Printed in Great Britain
by Spottiswoode, Ballantyne & Co. Ltd.
London and Colchester

CONTENTS

PREFACE

Reason and authority were two of the chief preoccupations of eighteenth-century thought. Other issues, of course, also commanded attention, but most of them were related, in one way or another, to the dominant interests of the age. I have therefore used reason and authority as focal points around which to arrange the materials for a study of eighteenth-century thought in England. I have not attempted to write an exhaustive history of all the intellectual movements of the age, but, on the other hand, I have been concerned to provide more than an intensive examination of two isolated concepts.

I have found that reason and authority provide a useful approach to the problems of the period. As the seventeenth century closed, it was apparent that reason was displacing many of the authorities which an earlier generation had accepted. But the nature of its claims required careful study. Locke laid down the lines along which such an examination would proceed; Newton profoundly affected the atmosphere in which it would be conducted. Few were disposed to challenge the primacy of reason, but the extent and character of its authority remained a matter of vigorous debate. Was it an all-sufficient source of truth? Or did revelation provide a necessary supplement to what man's unaided powers could discover? Around this issue the Deistic controversy raged, and for nearly half a century it profoundly affected the character of English thought. But the exaggerated claims advanced on behalf of reason provoked a reaction. Scholars and thinkers of great eminence contended that its powers were much less extensive than its champions had claimed. Hume argued that reliance on reason led, not to absolute certainty but to complete scepticism. John Wesley insisted that an adequate account of human experience will allow reason a valid but a very restricted

vii

role, and will assign to faith the principal part in integrating the scattered forces of man's personal life. This radical and twofold challenge to the supremacy of reason seemed to presage the end of an era, but reason, though shaken, continued to be one of the controlling concepts of eighteenth-century thought. Even in the days of its undisputed power, reason was not the only claimant to man's intellectual obedience. A number of issues concurrently demanded attention, and in the context of each the nature of authority was carefully reassessed.

Many of these matters are still highly pertinent. Modern thought is affected at many points by assumptions derived from the eighteenth century. But is there any need to retell the story? In recent years there have been many excellent studies of particular figures or of specific issues; relatively few works have attempted to trace the course of eighteenth-century thought. Perhaps this is partly due to the continuing authority of Sir Leslie Stephen's classic work on *English Thought in the Eighteenth Century*. For nearly ninety years it has held the field. In many respects it is unlikely to be superseded. Stephen knew the period with an intimacy which few of his successors will duplicate. His two massive volumes allowed him a scope which a modern writer might envy but would hesitate to emulate. But Stephen's work has certain characteristic faults. It suffers from defects of arrangement and emphasis. As Sir George Clark pointed out in *The Later Stuarts*, 'Stephen's mind was neither very acute nor capable of wide sympathies: he praises his authors in proportion as they approximate to a rather ingenuous Victorian agnosticism.' I have tried to expound with accuracy, and I hope with reasonable sympathy, the thought of the period. I have not felt entitled to dictate what the various authors could or should have said.

I have deliberately restricted myself to British thought. Intellectual history can seldom be confined within national frontiers, but in this case the nature of the subject makes the limitation possible, and considerations of space make it necessary. M. Paul Hazard's works provide a recent and detailed study of European

Preface

thought, and consequently a fully comprehensive work is less necessary. In any case, the eighteenth century is a period in which it is possible to study English thought in relative isolation from continental influences. It has often been pointed out that most of the revolutionary ideas of the Age of Reason originated in England. Even in the second half of the century, when the originality of English thought had so obviously declined, most thinkers were preoccupied with issues which had been raised at home. William Godwin, it is true, acknowledged his debt to Holbach, Rousseau and Helvetius, but Godwin was a nonconformist in almost every respect. Priestley's sympathies might suggest a certain kinship between himself and continental thinkers, but the account, in his *Memoirs*, of his visit to Paris makes it clear that his thought was definitely English both in origin and character.

With some hesitation I have omitted any detailed discussion of ethics. The subject invited treatment, and originally I devoted a chapter to it. But this allowed insufficient scope, while more than one chapter would have upset the balance of the work.

It is a privilege to acknowledge my obligations to the Syndics and to the secretaries of the Cambridge University Press. Librarians in many places have patiently put their resources at my disposal; in particular I would like to thank the staffs of the British Museum, the Cambridge University Library, the Widener and Houghton Libraries at Harvard University, the Andover-Harvard Library of the Harvard Divinity School, and the Library of Andover Newton Theological School. I am grateful to my colleague, Professor C. G. Rutenber, for advice on the section on Bishop Berkeley. My wife has helped me in so many ways that the customary formulae of appreciation seem more than usually insufficient.

G.R.C.

Andover Newton Theological School
1 December, 1963

THE NOTES

Superior figures in the text refer to the
appendix of notes beginning on p. 298

CHAPTER I

THE LEGACY OF LOCKE AND NEWTON

THE closing years of the seventeenth century saw a change of revolutionary proportions in the complexion of English thought. Richard Hooker and Launcelot Andrewes belong to one period, John Locke and Isaac Newton clearly belong to another. Men began to ponder in a new spirit the perennial problems which engage their attention in every age. For deduction from arguments they substituted observation of facts. Assumptions which had been accepted for centuries were abandoned as obsolete. New principles began to govern human thought. There had, of course, been harbingers of this momentous change. For some time the pioneers of modern science had been steadily pushing back the frontiers of knowledge. Bacon had shown that experimentation is the key which unlocks the mysteries of nature. Descartes had inaugurated a new approach to basic philosophical problems. Hobbes had boldly challenged traditional views about man and society. The Cambridge Platonists had exemplified a religious position which was mystical yet reasonable, and which showed itself to be both humane in outlook and charitable in spirit. The way had thus been carefully prepared. The resultant change was in large measure the product of a series of celebrated works which appeared as the seventeenth century was drawing to a close. This revolution proved to be European in scope, but it was largely English in origin, and in the ensuing period this fact was noted by Englishmen with pardonable pride. 'So true it is,' wrote Hume, 'that however other nations may rival us in poetry and excel us in some other agreeable arts, the improvements in reason and philosophy can only be owing to a land of toleration and liberty.'[1]

I

As the eighteenth century opened, the significance of the new developments in thought became increasingly apparent. The new age inherited the results achieved by Locke and Newton; it accepted as its primary enterprise the task of deducing the consequences which followed from the impregnable certainties now available to man. But the character of eighteenth-century thought was determined by reaction as well as by appropriation. It responded to the new science and the new philosophy, but there was much in the recent past from which it recoiled. It was shocked by the violence which had formed so large an element in the political and intellectual life of the seventeenth century. It was repelled by controversy; men had wrangled about religion as well as about many other things, and by reducing matters of belief to the status of ingredients in a debate, they had undermined the certainties of faith. The new age hoped to escape from the dust of contention into the clear air in which reasonable men could see clearly the truths which they could then willingly embrace.

Thus all forms of traditional authority were suspect. In both the moral and the political spheres the new age subtly shifted the grounds of confidence. Nothing was to be taken on trust. Men were to be taught to rely on the evidence provided by nature or reason, not on the arguments supplied by tradition. Indeed, the history of eighteenth-century thought is largely concerned with the problem of authority. The previous age had vacillated between a number of claimants to men's intellectual allegiance. The Laudians had stressed tradition and the place of the Church. The Puritans had relied on Scripture. The Quakers had listened to the promptings of the Spirit. The early Deists had insisted on the unique pre-eminence of reason, and this was an emphasis which would become increasingly popular as the new century progressed. But even this latter alternative failed to carry complete conviction; it was a partial answer and therefore in the long run it was to prove an untenable one as well. The problem of authority, reappearing in one guise after another, would exercise the finest minds of the eighteenth century. It is well to notice the characteristic form in which Locke posed it for his successors. He insisted that the traditions both of the philosophers and of the churchmen must be set aside. Neither in speculation nor in belief should the past control the present. He turned to new sources of certainty. In philosophy he found his starting-place in experience. In religion he turned to the Bible, but he proposed to treat it like any other book. Indeed, he insisted that religion itself must be approached in the same spirit as any other subject. In his *Essay Concerning Human Understanding*, he repeatedly emphasised the mischief which had been wrought by an indolent submission to traditional authorities. 'So much as we ourselves consider and comprehend of truth and reason, so much we possess of real and true knowledge. The floating of other men's opinions in our brains makes us not one jot the more knowing, though they happen to be true.'[1] Thus the philosophy of the new age was launched on the tide of a vigorous protest against any disposition 'to take men off from the use of their own reason and judgment and put them upon believing and taking upon trust without further examination'.[2] This antipathy to authority fitted well with the other qualities which marked Locke's work and which form part of his bequest to the next age. He showed that a man who claims a new freedom must be careful, patient, and tolerant, with a generous confidence in the power of reason.

Freedom, beyond any question, was one of the chief preoccupations of the eighteenth century. Intellectually, men felt that they had escaped from an oppressive confinement into a world of liberty and light. The restraints imposed by a mysterious universe were lifted by the discovery that order and intelligibility embraced its most minute particles and its most remote spaces. In all Locke's writings we can detect a determination to be free and self-sufficient, and this, too, became part of the outlook of the new age. Without 'freedom of enquiry', said Bishop Lowth, there can be no 'advancement of religious knowledge'. Truth has always gained from free enquiry. So has Christianity; its fortunes fluctuate with those of learning and liberty. 'It is therefore of the utmost importance to the cause of true religion, that it be submitted to an open and impartial examination; that every disquisition concerning it be allowed its free course; that even the malice of its enemies should have its full scope and try its utmost strength of argument against it. Let no man be alarmed at the attempts of atheists or infidels. . . .'[1] But at the same time even the unbeliever could feel secure against any attack which placed undue reliance on tradition. Both the new science and the new philosophy encouraged the belief that truth can be established only by the verdict of the enlightened and emancipated mind. The caution and sobriety of the new age, its tolerant outlook and its faith in reason united to discredit all reliance on ancient forms of authority.

Impatience with the past had a good deal to do with this reaction against the old and cherished certainties. And new influences, varied in kind but powerful in appeal, were beginning to modify the intellectual outlook of the new age. Geography was making known the character of continents which had hitherto barely been names, and it became apparent that customs, cultures and beliefs were more varied than anyone had dreamed. The narratives of returning travellers were often naïve as well as inexact; and when the genuine explorers had exhausted the resources of experience, the armchair travellers showed how fertile the imagination can be. A new type of literature emerged, designed to afford more than amusement. As *Gulliver's Travels* proved, an account of fictitious lands and imaginary civilisations could provide social criticism of a particularly cogent kind. The virtues, genuine or imagined, of the Egyptian, the Persian, the Chinese, even of the wise but untutored savage, were invoked to undermine the confident certainties of traditional beliefs. Comparative religion had barely begun to emerge, but already it was challenging the exclusiveness which had always been associated with the true faith. Biblical criticism was still in its infancy, but it was beginning to prompt some very disconcerting questions about Holy Scripture. Chronology had suggested that man's history was neither as brief nor as simple as an earlier day had imagined; apparently the records of revelation provided an inadequate framework for the story of human life on this planet. A wide variety of influences had thus begun to refashion the intellectual climate. In due course it will be necessary to examine the general temper of this new age; first we must consider the contribution of the men who determined the lines along which speculation would advance. Wherever we turn we encounter the authority of Locke and Newton. They shaped the legacy which the eighteenth century received from the seventeenth, and their influence was all-pervasive and supreme. The new direction given to philosophy and the strong interest awakened by science promised that new concerns would dominate the new period. The picture of the universe supplied by Newton and the interpretation of the human mind proposed by Locke rapidly modified the outlook of the educated man; they provided the presuppositions which governed the thought of the new era. As d'Alembert remarked in his introduction to the *Encyclopédie*, Locke was the creator of scientific philosophy and Newton the originator of scientific physics. Yet the claims of religion and morality were by no means eclipsed. Men carefully studied the bearing of science and philosophy on belief and practice, and here Locke and Newton themselves showed the way. They examined, with devout interest, the religious implications of their speculations and discoveries. This set the pattern for the coming century. The prevailing emphasis on morality is also reflected in the authoritative place conceded to the sermons of John Tillotson. He may seem a feeble third beside his two great contemporaries, but unquestionably he exerted an influence of considerable significance. The popularity of his works indicates the powerful appeal exerted by a prudential ethic, moderately conceived, reasonably expounded, and expressed with a felicitous ease which delighted the Augustan Age.

Locke, beyond any other writer, was to be the moving spirit

of the eighteenth century. He summed up all that the previous period had achieved. He anticipated all that the new generation would attempt. In every branch of intellectual endeavour his influence was supreme. 'Locke', said Warburton, 'is universal'; he is 'the Hercules of metaphysics', declared Voltaire.[1] The measure of his authority can be gauged by the asperity with which Lowth, a distinguished ornament of the Tory University of Oxford, defended himself against the dangerous insinuation that he held opinions condemned by Locke.[2] Even those who initially objected to the details of Locke's system found themselves imperceptibly affected by his all-pervasive influence. He expounded with unparalleled persuasiveness the views which seemed most important to the generations which succeeded his own. The characteristic caution of his mind made him an ideal preceptor to an age repelled by even the faintest suggestion of spiritual daring. His *Essay Concerning Human Understanding* achieved unprecedented popularity because its teachings seemed so relevant to the issues uppermost in the moral and religious life of the age. Some people considered that the solutions which he offered to traditional problems were subversive, but his fundamental contribution was to gather into one system all the beliefs about God and man and nature which the majority of his contemporaries were ready to accept. He had the happy faculty of making philosophy speak the language of daily life. 'He appealed', said Bolingbroke, 'to the experience and conscious knowledge of everyone, and rendered all he advanced intelligible.'[3]

In striking contrast with the range of Locke's influence was the modesty of his professed objective. He was content, he said, 'to be employed as an under-labourer in clearing the ground a little and removing some of the rubbish that lies in the way of knowledge'.[4] The first step in the right direction was to ask a few fundamental questions. What are the problems with which we can profitably be concerned, and what are the subjects which we would be wise to ignore? 'If by this enquiry into the nature of understanding, I can discover the powers thereof: *how far* they reach: to what things they are in any degree proportionate: and where they fail us, I suppose it may be of use to prevail with the busy mind of man to be more cautious in meddling with things exceeding its comprehension; to stop when it is at the utmost extent of its tether: and to sit down in a quiet ignorance of those things which, upon examination, are found to be beyond the reach of our capabilities.'[1] In deciding what questions can profitably engage our attention, Locke believed that a simple test was to ask how far they are related to our daily lives, for 'our business here is not to know all things, but those things which concern our conduct'. This restriction of our enquiry will be an advantage rather than a handicap. 'We shall not have much reason to complain of the narrowness of our minds, if we will but employ them about what may be of use to us.'[2] The notable feature of Locke's method was that it gave full scope to his great gift of raising the questions which would be important for the future. By focusing attention on the problem of knowledge, Locke determined the course which European philosophy has been following ever since. But the skill with which he analysed the powers of the human mind directed popular attention to the things we can know rather than to the ones we cannot. He himself was quite aware of the metaphysical and theological mysteries about which we dare not be dogmatic, but his very success in explaining the human understanding created the impression that man's reason is sufficient to unlock all the treasures of knowledge.

Locke's explanation of how we acquire knowledge was simple; his method had far-reaching effects. He repudiated innate ideas. With the exception of our intuitive awareness of our own existence, he believed that everything we know is derived either from sensation or from reflection upon sensation. These two constitute experience, which is the source of all ideas. Locke's use of the crucial term *idea* is beset with ambiguities, and this is only one example of the difficulties in which his system abounds. His successors spent a disproportionate amount of time trying to resolve his inconsistencies; they disliked the details of his argument, but they could not ignore the general pattern which he had laid down. In particular they could not escape from the pervasive rationalism of his thought. Locke did not restrict knowledge to the things which the human mind can grasp; he acknowledged that some truths are above reason—though never contrary to it. He allowed a place for the supernatural order and for divine revelation. But he was a rationalist in that he insisted that all truths must ultimately be judged by reason, and he viewed with deep distrust any attempt to override its verdict.

'Reason', said Locke, 'must be our best judge and guide in all things',[1] and his historical importance is largely due to his share in determining the meaning to be attached to this crucial term. He claimed that knowledge is derived from 'outward sense and inward perception'. Is this not enough? 'What need is there of *reason*?' We need it, he answered, 'for the enlargement of our knowledge and regulating our assent'.[2] The fact that Locke's detailed analysis of reason is open to criticism is, for our purposes, beside the point. The importance which he attached to reason and the general character of his treatment of it were authoritative for the eighteenth century. He taught his successors the value of reflecting on ordinary experience and the necessity of subjecting it to careful scrutiny. This seemed to him much more important than framing ingenious theories. The common sense which he exemplified sometimes degenerated, in the hands of others, into an exposition of the prudential wisdom of the average man. But this was not what Locke commended; he urged upon his contemporaries the need of careful reflection on ordinary experience.

For the new age 'Nature' would prove to be a concept almost as important as reason itself. Here, again, Locke's influence was decisive. His political writings taught men to believe that rights and obligations are rooted in the proper constitution of human existence, and are regulated by a law which we ignore at our peril. As the seventeenth century ended, it seemed that regularity was everywhere displacing confusion. Nature's order seemed so clear that men were tempted to forget its ambiguities. Its laws were simple, authoritative and apparently universal. The intelligent person found within himself a testimony which responded to what Newton told him about the universe and to what Locke told him about men and society. Natural law was normative for man's life and thought; natural order demonstrated the existence of God, and suggested the pattern of an acceptable service of him. 'For so far as we can know by natural philosophy what is the first cause, what power he has over us and what benefits we receive from him, so far our duty towards him as well as towards one another will appear to us by the light of nature.'[1]

Reason and nature combined to indicate the kind of religion which would be most congenial to man and most acceptable to God. The authority claimed by natural religion and the universal respect accorded it were among the most characteristic features of eighteenth-century thought. To that assured and self-confident period it seemed clear that man's intelligence had traced God's handiwork in creation, and had detected the divine purpose both in the structure of the universe and in the operation of man's mind. Locke did not devise this new pattern of belief. It could claim an ancient lineage, and its place had been conceded—though often with reservations—in most periods of the Christian era. But Locke and Newton conferred on natural religion an unchallenged prestige. Latent in Locke's epistemology was a scepticism which in due course emerged, but initially men observed only his own strong faith in a rational form of religion. He insisted that Christianity can be both clear and simple. Moral and religious truths can be lifted above the assaults of doubt. The authority of the cosmological proofs of God's existence seemed secure. Locke commended to his contemporaries the kind of deity presupposed in the reconciliations of science and religion which were already fashionable. God could be established by argument; he could be approached through logical demonstration. For Locke Christianity seemed to be exclusively a matter of intellectual conviction. Human reason can both discover and expound the fundamental religious beliefs. What cannot be proved is conjectural and consequently unimportant. This religion, based on reason, and buttressed by testimony from the natural creation, was immensely popular. Its implications for the thought of the new age were no less extensive than its influence. It supplied a system of belief which seemed entirely compatible with the principles of the new science. The faith which Locke expounded was the one which Newton commended. But the emphasis on reason's place in religion implied a reassessment of man's inherent capacities. Perhaps the corruption wrought by the Fall had been exaggerated; a growing confidence in man's powers suggested that he should rely more exclusively on his native capacities.

A faith which placed its trust in reason was naturally suspicious of anything which threatened the supremacy of man's intellect. The seventeenth century had seen enough of opinionated fervour. 'Enthusiasm' was the accepted term for doctrinaire fanaticism. 'It arises', said Locke, 'from the conceits of a warmed and over-weening brain'; it weakens the valid supports of religion and 'substitutes in the room of them the ungrounded fancies of a man's own brain, and assuming them for a foundation both of opinion and of conduct'.[1] It supports foolish claims to special inspiration. It sweeps the susceptible into excited reliance on intuition and emotion. Locke was not the first to expose the perils of ground-less zeal, but he invested a general and growing antipathy with the authority of his prestige. To the eighteenth century he trans-mitted an almost pathological fear of religious emotion. Samuel Clarke felt it wise to insist that the candid student of Christ's moral teachings 'cannot without the extremest malice and obstinacy in the world charge him with enthusiasm'.[2] David Hartley described with some care the nature and consequences of this aberration. 'Enthusiasm', he said, 'may be defined as a mis-taken persuasion in any person that he is a peculiar favourite with God; and that he receives supernatural marks thereof.' Naïve and impressionable people, 'of little experience in divine things and narrow understandings', are peculiarly exposed to its con-tagion and suffer most from 'the great flattery and support which enthusiasm affords to pride and self-conceit'.[1] In the new age worship was marked by a subdued propriety and theology by a sober rationalism. The spiritual exultations of the past were stringently exorcised, and men were encouraged to put their trust in the decorous propriety of a rational belief.

Because he magnified the place of reason, Locke was obliged to define with some care the role of faith. Hume subsequently argued that Locke had virtually identified the two. 'Locke', he said, 'seems to have been the first Christian who ventured openly to assert that *faith* was nothing but a species of *reason*, that religion was only a branch of philosophy, and that a chain of arguments, similar to that which established any truth in morals, politics or physics, was always employed in discovering all the principles of theology, natural and revealed.'[2] It is true that Locke's aim was to establish the truths of religion on as firm an intellectual foundation as possible, and he believed that this could best be accomplished by avoiding any confusion between faith and reason. Undoubtedly both produce conviction; knowledge issues in certainty, while faith 'is a settled and sure principle of assent and assurance and leaves no manner of room for doubt or hesitation'.[3] 'Faith', he added, 'cannot be afforded to anything but upon good reason, and so cannot be opposite to it.'[4] The difference between them is largely a matter of the alternative routes by which they lead us to conviction. The truths which are mediated by reason are based on evidence supplied by sensation or reflection; those which we owe to faith result from our acceptance of any proposition 'upon the credit of the proposer as coming from God in some extraordinary way of communication'.[5] The distinctive feature of faith is its reliance on revelation.

In the new age progressive thinkers were generally agreed that though reason and revelation were both sources of religious knowledge, a distinction must be drawn between what they offer and the ways in which they function. Locke defined this distinction so clearly that he provided one of the normative principles of eighteenth-century thought. In describing the relation between faith and reason, he was particularly careful to maintain a proper balance between them. *'Reason'*, he said, 'is natural *revelation*, whereby the eternal Father of light, the Foundation of all knowledge, communicates to mankind that portion of truth which he has laid within the reach of their natural faculties. *Revelation* is natural *reason* enlarged by a new set of discoveries communicated by God immediately, which reason vouches the truth of, by the testimony and proofs it gives that they come from God'.¹ Locke denied that there is any incompatibility between the two. To repudiate reason in order to rely upon revelation is as foolish as to put out your eyes in order to benefit from using a telescope. But in assessing Locke's various statements on this subject, it is clear that he placed his reliance primarily on reason. He suggested that men of understanding can usually apprehend the essential truths of natural religion by the use of their own intelligence. Those less richly endowed—'the multitude'—perforce depend on revelation. We can rely on revealed truth only if we are persuaded that it has indeed been revealed, and it is obviously the task of reason to provide this assurance. And so, even when Locke admitted that revelation can convey to us truths which are beyond the reach of our unaided intelligence, he added that 'it still belongs to reason to judge of the truth of its being a revelation, and of the significance of the words wherein it is delivered'.² It might seem that in this Locke set the stage for the subsequent debate about the relative authority on the one hand of the religion which appeals to Scripture and on the other of the religion which relies solely on the resources which man's own capacities provide. The Deists claimed, with a degree of plausibility, that Locke's prestige reinforced their position. And yet Locke, it appears, was a rationalist who exalted reason but did not put his final faith in it. 'This apparently paradoxical attitude of his is the outcome of a prudent realization of human limitations. Reason alone is inadequate. It is inadequate in the sphere of religion, just as it is inadequate in the sphere of natural science.'³

On the problem of reason and revelation, Newton powerfully

reinforced Locke's general position. The development of science had made the relative prestige of natural and revealed religion a matter of crucial importance. For Wilkins and Boyle the created universe bore impressive witness to God's wisdom and power, and man's mind could grasp these truths and from them fashion a system of belief. But both these men carefully maintained the superior value of revealed religion. Newton, however, represented a more advanced position. He, too, was concerned to preserve both the due rights of reason and the essential doctrines of the Christian faith. He believed that their competing claims could be reconciled by judiciously reducing religious doctrines to a minimum on which intelligent men could agree. An elementary system of belief and a correspondingly simple code of ethics would be enough to satisfy the basic requirements. In its true and original form religion was a universal morality which the reason of man devised. 'Thus you see there is but one law for all nations, the law of righteousness and charity dictated to the Christians by Christ, to the Jews by Moses, and to all mankind by the light of reason, and by this law all men are to be judged at the last day.'[1] In effect, Newton ignored the claims of revelation, and pointed in a direction which many eighteenth-century thinkers would willingly follow. His native diffidence restrained him from publishing many of the theological works on which he spent so much time and care, but his contemporaries were able to infer the drift of his speculations even though he declined to print them. The prestige of the new science was thus enlisted to confirm the growing conviction that the authority of reason vindicated the superior claims of natural religion. Here was a challenge which the champions of Christianity could not ignore.

Newton, of course, had no intention of repudiating Christianity; he merely proposed to reinterpret its truths, but his rationalistic restatements left few of its traditional doctrines untouched. In this respect he epitomised, even though he did not publicly express, an attitude which was congenial to many of his contemporaries. Locke openly published the views which Newton covertly held. He believed that Christianity was basically simple in character and ought to be expounded with appropriate clarity. In *The Reasonableness of Christianity*, he undertook to explain to his age the irreducible essentials of the faith. He addressed himself to the understanding of sensible men; the authority to which he appealed was the Bible, and in interpreting it he relied on reason. We are unjust to the Scriptures when we search their pages for abstruse principles; the obvious sense is the true one, and is 'therefore generally to be understood in the plain, direct meaning of the words and phrases'.[1] When he examined the substance of revelation, he was amazed at its directness and simplicity. Its demands can be reduced to a single requirement: to be saved a man need only acknowledge Jesus as the Messiah. Belief in God, of course, is a precondition and amendment of life a necessary consequence of man's right relation to God, but basically 'salvation or perdition depends upon believing or rejecting this one proposition'.[2] Locke somewhat obscured the simplicity of his doctrine by his exhaustive marshalling of proof texts, but even the most casual reader is aware that what he propounded is far removed from the historic formulations of the Christian faith. The familiar phrases of theological discussion have been eliminated because Locke felt no need for the concepts to which they refer. In the course of his book he returned repeatedly to the one point: the essentials are few and simple—'these two, faith and repentance; believing Jesus to be the Messiah and a good life; are the indispensable conditions of the new covenant'.[3] This was to prove a highly acceptable gospel in the new age. It was a discreet combination of a simple religious position and the new philosophy. It was suitably deferential to Christianity, even though it ignored its traditional doctrines, and it could readily be adjusted to the demands of the new science. Locke claimed that what he commended was thoroughly reasonable, and he proved that it could be held in conjunction with a humane and tolerant outlook.

The extent of Locke's influence was determined by the variety of points at which he touched the intellectual life of his age. He wrote about government at a time when revolutionary movements had invested the subject with absorbing interest. In his *Two Treatises of Government*, he claimed that natural law is the foundation on which society rests, and this was an emphasis entirely consistent with prevalent trends in theology, philosophy and science. He showed that the protection of property is a primary duty of government, and this became one of the undisputed axioms of the eighteenth century. Locke's general position strongly appealed to a generation which found its distinctive task in stripping from truth the accretions of tradition. The 'phantasm of the imagination' had to be swept aside; reason had to be liberated, that its clear, cool pronouncements might have free course in the world. The result, of course, was a divorce of thought from feeling. The Age of Reason would be as suspicious of emotion as it was enamoured of logic.

Locke seemed to be the apostle of common sense and the harbinger of a supremely self-confident period, but there was another strain in his legacy and it must not be ignored. Though most of his contemporaries rejoiced at the assurance with which he had laid bare the secrets of the world of thought, some were assailed by doubts. Locke's theory of knowledge disturbed the traditional patterns of thought. Bishop Burnet, who found many of Locke's views peculiarly congenial, was disturbed by his treatment of conscience and by his rejection of innate ideas. Bishop Stillingfleet was not alone in detecting in Locke's system an insidiously sceptical tendency.[1] Locke claimed that ideas are the only immediate objects of understanding, and he encountered difficulties when he tried to establish the real existence of external bodies. It is here that Locke's epistemology raised doubts about the status of natural science. In this respect also he anticipated future developments, for even the scepticism of Hume is a highly original elaboration of elements latent in Locke's thought. Locke's great gift, of course, was his ability to raise questions in a way which provoked further investigation, and the eighteenth century seldom got beyond the programme which he bequeathed to it.

In epitomising the convictions of the seventeenth century he imposed them, by his authority, on the eighteenth. But he transmitted a series of problems as well as a set of assumptions. Yet even his most vehement critics unconsciously absorbed his ideas, and Locke stands forth as the source of convictions which are woven into the intellectual heritage of the western world.

At many points, as we have already seen, the impact of the new science reinforced the influence of Locke; in certain respects it went beyond it. As Samuel Clarke realised, the altered conception of the universe had revolutionary implications for philosophy and theology. The remarkable extension of man's horizon had been the work of many men, but in the eyes of the educated public Sir Isaac Newton's achievements eclipsed all others. He had discovered a single principle which explained both the falling of a pebble and the movements of the stars. In one dazzling synthesis he had bound together the smallest and the vastest elements in the universe and he had made them amenable to a single law.

> O unprofuse magnificence divine!
> O wisdom truly perfect! thus to call
> From a few causes such a scheme of things,
> Effects so various, beautiful and great,
> An universe complete! And, O belov'd
> Of Heaven! whose well-purged penetrative eye
> The mystic veil transpiercing, inly scanned
> The rising, moving, well-established frame.[1]

His authority was equalled only by Locke's. Samuel Clarke called him 'the incomparable Sir Isaac Newton'; to Hume he was 'the greatest and rarest genius that ever rose for the ornament and instruction of the species'. Voltaire claimed that Newton, to a greater extent than any other man, had broken up the old conception of the universe and had substituted for it a cosmology appropriate to modern man.[2] His contemporaries were heartened to observe that the high priest of the new science was apparently satisfied that its laws could be reconciled with the substance of the old faith. John Jackson claimed that Newton 'was the greatest philosopher that ever lived on earth, and also was a true believer of the Christian religion and was confirmed in his belief in the truth of it from the prophecies of Scripture'.[1]

Newton approached the problems of physics with certain presuppositions which he had derived from his faith. He believed that religion was more important than science; it was more rewarding to search the Scriptures than to scan the stars. He regarded faith as perfectly compatible with knowledge; he began with this conviction, and it sustained him through all his enquiries. He showed that the universe is an ordered cosmos. This did not surprise him: in its structure God's creation naturally reflected its divine origin. He revealed his assumptions so clearly in everything he wrote that his contemporaries drew certain conclusions about the enterprise on which he was engaged. In spite of the uneasiness which prevailed in some quarters, it was apparent that science was really a beneficent—even a pious—undertaking. It was absorbed in the study of God's handiwork, and it brought to light, with impressive consistency, the evidence of the Creator's wisdom and power. Theology had seemed to offer a devious and uncertain road to God; science brought its devotees face to face with his works. It was possible to look 'through Nature up to Nature's God', and the conviction that science declares the glory of God became so firmly entrenched that it was seldom challenged.

Gradually, but with impressive results, Newton modified the outlook of his contemporaries. He created the impression that science had produced a conclusive demonstration of the existence of God. The evidences of order and design could be found throughout creation—even at points where their minute scale or their extreme distance had hitherto made them inaccessible to man. Philosophy had relied on abstract arguments for the existence of God; Newton had apparently come forth with irrefutable proof. From whatever angle you approached the created universe, the conclusion you could draw seemed equally gratifying.

You could argue that the world is good and therefore it must be governed by God; or you could claim that the world is manifestly governed by God and therefore it must be good. This highly satisfactory result had unforseen consequences. Newton showed that the rule of law is universal; as men gradually appropriated the implications of this vast unifying force, they subtly modified their views about God and man and nature, and about the relations of each to the others. Newton denied that natural laws alone can account for the universe, though 'being once formed it may continue by these laws for many ages'.[1] Apparently the natural world bears all the marks of a machine. Every effect in nature can be attributed to a material cause; is there any need—indeed, is there any room—for supernatural agents? The Great Machine, of course, presupposed the Great Mechanic. God was still necessary; who else could maintain his creation in efficient operation? But this line of thought imperceptibly substituted a first cause for a personal God. Our Father in Heaven faded 'into a metaphysical projection of creation'.[2] The difficulties which the scientists faced were admittedly acute. Could they afirm the rule of natural law and still believe in providence? Could the mechanical order permit such exceptions as miracles, or could the operation of cause and effect be modified to allow a place for prophecy? Newton was unable to deny the rule of law; he was unwilling to limit the operation of providence. He bequeathed the problem, unsolved, to the eighteenth century.

As the new era opened, the rise of science promised to check the spread of intolerance. After much inconclusive strife about matters which could not be proved, the clear certainties of the new disciplines seemed to offer an assured basis of agreement. But this new attitude modified the prevailing intellectual outlook in a variety of ways. Man had at his command a vast increase in factual information about the physical universe. This was the result of his own endeavours; it was a disclosure of his latent powers. The temptation to intellectual arrogance was strong. Ancient traditions had been discredited and old forms of authority were being challenged. The new age would question the certainties which had satisfied its predecessors; it would examine, one by one, the grounds of confidence. The whole nature of the intellectual enterprise was thus affected. Was it still necessary, men asked, to pursue the quest for first principles? God seemed more remote; his providence became less assured and less immediately relevant to human problems. Relatively few denied his existence, but it seemed possible to acknowledge it in a formal and conventional way. Consequently the triumphs of science deflected the interests of many intelligent men into new enquiries. They were less concerned than in the past to master metaphysical questions or to comprehend the niceties of speculation. The mysteries of the physical universe could be fathomed; its laws could be successfully deciphered. Man's reason promised to unlock a new world in which everything would be clear and simple. Comets, which had once seemed to be the playthings of mere chance, were shown to be subject to the very same laws which preserved the stars from harm; their courses could be exactly charted and the date of their future return could be predicted with perfect precision. Familiarity breeds contempt, and a universe which harboured no secrets awakened no awe. The sense of wonder had little place in the intellectual outlook of that cool and reasonable age. Pragmatic evidence, it appeared, rightly carried the greatest weight with human minds, and this conviction was primarily the consequence of the new forces released by the new science.

> . . . Newton, pure Intelligence! whom God
> To mortals lent, to trace his boundless works
> From laws sublimely simple.[1]

This was part of the spirit of the times. What Newton did in science, others attempted in their various fields of investigation—Pufendorf and Montesquieu in law, Simon in biblical criticism, Locke in philosophy, Shaftesbury in ethics. The transcendental was losing its appeal, and men turned instead to the visible and the concrete.

19

If the philosophers and the scientists were intent on stripping mystery and wonder from life, the theologians were not behind-hand in doing the same thing. The general tone of religious discussion had altered. The measure of the change is found in Archbishop Tillotson's sermons. The next generation welcomed them as an exceptionally persuasive exposition of a moderate and reasonable faith. The moral standard which they inculcate is so unheroic in its prosaic worldliness that it seldom rises above a pedestrian common sense. Even Tillotson's style—so simple and elegant, so candid, rational and clear—exemplifies the qualities which the eighteenth century valued most highly in its religion. At every point he quietly confirmed prevailing trends. He taught that institutional religion was necessary; he never inferred that it might in any way encroach on natural religion.[1] Those who advocated a faith based on nature and acceptable to reason could henceforth invoke the high authority of an Archbishop of Canterbury. Tillotson discussed the attributes of God—his perfection, his unchanging constancy, his wisdom in creation, in redemption and in providence[2]—with a sedate rationality which eighteenth-century thought would appropriate as its norm. Occasionally his sermons are lit up with flashes of unexpected insight. He noted, for example, the disconcerting injunction 'to enter in at the strait gate', and he preached on *The Difficulties of a Christian Life Considered*.[3] Much of his ablest work is a careful apologetic for the Christian faith. He did not state his case too boldly, and he consistently stressed the arguments most likely to convince his contemporaries. If the next age treated religion either as an exercise in logic or as an invitation to be upright on the most advantageous terms, it was because Tillotson had taught it the lesson. But Tillotson was not the only culprit. Archbishop John Sharp was a churchman acceptable to many who detested Tillotson and all he stood for, but Sharpe preached sermons which, but for a less polished style, are indistinguishable from those of Tillotson.

This restrained religion, so careful to guard against unruly zeal, was ardent only in commending the practical advantages of Christianity. 'He is not a wise man', said Tillotson, 'that doth not take care of himself and his own concernments. . . . As self-preservation is the first principle of nature, so care of ourselves and our own interest is the first part of wisdom'.[1] Religion promotes the well-being of societies and the advantage of the individuals who comprise them. Whoever faithfully obeys the commandments of Christianity will find that he benefits both inwardly and in 'the outward man'. Religion will improve his understanding because it will subdue the eruptive power of lust, and so it 'tends to the ease and pleasure, the peace and tranquillity of our minds'.[2] It promotes man's material advantage by guarding his health, improving his estate, increasing his reputation and benefiting his relations. 'What reason then can any man pretend against religion when it is so apparently for the benefit not only of human society but of every particular person?'[3] This is typical of much of the preaching of the times. In his sermon on *The Profitableness of Godliness: or the Advantage of Piety for the Promoting all a Man's Interests in this World*, Archbishop Sharp was no less explicit in delineating the benefits which accrue to the Christian. 'I begin', he said, 'with the conduciveness of religion and godliness to improve our outward fortunes; the advantages of it for the getting or increasing an estate.'[4] Wealth, of course, is not necessarily entailed upon religion, but the upright man is very likely to prosper. His religion promotes diligence in his calling; it encourages frugality and good husbandry; it establishes a good reputation; it helps him to 'thrive in the world' because it keeps 'a good correspondence with all those in whose power it is to hinder or promote our affairs'.[5]

The strength of this school lay in its emphasis on moral obligation. 'Doing good in our lives', said Sharp, is 'everyone's duty', and he carefully set forth 'rules for the government of life'.[6] Two of Tillotson's most characteristic sermons are *Of Doing Good*[7] and *Of the Great Duties of Natural Religion*.[8] There are obligations, said he, from which no man of intelligence and good will should try to escape. Beneficence on the part of God should be matched by benevolence on the part of man. This was doctrine acceptable to the Age of Reason, and it was effectively reinforced by the conviction that happiness is the reward of morality. The claims of righteousness were fortified by strong inducements and by even stronger sanctions. According to Tillotson, the justice of God is most clearly seen 'in the distribution of rewards and punishments';[1] few beliefs were more prevalent in the next age, and it focused its attention chiefly on the rewards. The unabashed hedonism of this complacent period acknowledged few limits. 'Our chief end and highest interest is happiness', said Tillotson. '. . . Now religion designs our greatest and longest happiness.'[2] This had not yet been fashioned into a comprehensive ethical theory, but it was already a very popular attitude. The upshot of such preaching was the benign good will reflected in Addison's essays. It issued in a widespread belief that faith merely adds an extra inducement to the practice of virtue and moderation.

The authority attached to certain names and the pre-eminence assigned to certain strains of thought profoundly affected the character of eighteenth-century speculation. But the specifically intellectual interests of the period were a part of a much wider general background. They influenced the general outlook of the age; in turn they were modified by many forces which were at work in society at large. The character of the eighteenth century is reflected with unusual distinctness both in its literature and in its thought. Good sense and sound reason were the qualities most highly esteemed; if they could be set forth with wit and brilliance, the gain was great, but at least they must be presented with incisiveness and point. Clarity was more highly esteemed than profundity; precision and definiteness were desired both in ideas and in their expression. A manly vigour, a robust directness, a straightforward common sense characterised the best thought and the best writing of the period. Samuel Johnson was their most successful exponent, but they are equally the marks of Tillotson at the beginning of the century and of Paley at the end. They represent the types of thought which prose transmits more successfully than poetry; they point to the specific qualities which made eighteenth-century prose so polished a medium for its thought and so exact a reflection of its standards. The lucid and harmonious style in which men wrote was the counterpart of the balanced pattern and the classic quality of their thought. The progress of science accentuated the drift towards prose; but the philosophy of Locke and the theology of Tillotson suggest that the atmosphere of the new age pervaded all areas of thought, and found its appropriate expression in a prose style of conspicuous clarity and exactitude.

This was an age, however, which harboured at the centre of its life strange and unexpected contradictions. Generalisations about the Age of Reason are easy; they are always dangerous and are often wrong. Courtliness laid a veneer of civility over a society which was still turbulent at heart. An age of refinement countenanced and even encouraged unmeasured abusiveness in debate. Dr Johnson's overbearing dogmatism was more than a personal idiosyncrasy; it was an accurate reflection of what the age expected from, and even encouraged in, its intellectual mentors. Bishop Warburton's coarse and noisy contradiction was accepted as the badge of his primacy in criticism and scholarship. A man who could shout down all his opponents might claim to be victor in the mêlée of abuse. 'The manners of the ruffian here betray the morals of the savage.'[1] Yet it was an age which prided itself on its tolerance, and its leading figures often adopted towards minorities a conciliatory attitude in sharp contrast with that of their predecessors and even of their immediate successors. The best way of dealing with sectaries, said Archbishop Secker, is not to render them 'railing for railing' nor to indulge in ridicule and contempt.[2] He insisted that the claims of religious liberty ought not to be obscured by religious contention.[3]

The eighteenth century was a period at once callously brutal and self-consciously humane. The outward pattern of certain aspects of its life has been immortalised by Hogarth. The other side of the picture is represented by Bishop Lowth's tribute to the philanthropic impulse which established new hospitals in such numbers. 'Among the many humane and pious institutions of public charity, various in their designs, all beneficial in their effects, which of late years have greatly increased in this nation, covering, we hope, in some degree the multitude of sins of a vicious age; none hath more generally prevailed, none hath been found more universally useful, than the establishment of public infirmaries for the relief of the sick poor. This species of charity addressed itself at once to reason and religion, to humanity, to policy.'[1]

The Age of Reason abhorred all 'enthusiasm', but it had its own characteristic dogmatisms. Philosophic rationalism had many of the marks of an accepted orthodoxy, and it was a more serious threat to religious beliefs than the licentious spirit which had invaded both literature and fashionable life. The moralists, of course, were not inclined to underestimate the threat posed by dissolute behaviour. They were aware that men pleaded the promptings of nature in extenuation of the eruptions of vice. From Addison at the beginning of the century to Paley at the end, the custodians of morality were busy buttressing the feeble wills of their contemporaries against the blandishments of sin. And though the age rings with the complaints of those who saw iniquity on every hand, few centuries placed such consistent emphasis on morality. Probity was the mark of the upright man; a sober integrity was the pattern of his days. 'He thought himself bound', wrote Porteus of Archbishop Secker, 'to labour for the glory of God and the good of mankind, and that all indolence and self-indulgence which interfered with these great objects was in some degree criminal.'[2]

The eighteenth century was an intensely secular age, yet many of its most representative figures were sustained by a deep and genuine religious conviction. In many quarters the practice of Christianity had become a matter of form. Even its professed defenders sometimes felt that it should be advocated 'without heat, passion or dogmatism'. A shrewd and calculating cleric warned his young nephew at Cambridge to avoid at all costs a topic so indiscreet as the Holy Trinity. 'Say, you have not considered such weighty matters enough—Or, may it not be thus? Or, what if we should suppose so and so. . . . Your thoughts proposed in some doubting way will be most inoffensive.'[1] The free thinkers set no bounds to their speculations, though they were careful not to discuss their theories in the presence of the servants. Collins sent his domestics to church, that they might learn not to rob him or cut his throat. The sophisticated treated 'all religion as a matter of policy, to influence the common people and keep them in order'.[2] Early in the century, Swift remarked that 'it will be granted, that hardly one in a hundred among our people of quality or gentry appears to act by any principle of religion; that great numbers of them do entirely discard it. . . . Nor is the case much better among the vulgar.'[3] Complaints about the decay of religion are a constant ingredient in the literature of the age. They run like a refrain through episcopal sermons; they appear in the prefaces to most serious works, whether written by the champions of the traditional faith or by Latitudinarians balancing on the edge of Deism. This explains the sombre note which so many thoughtful bishops struck in their episcopal charges. 'It is impossible for me', said Butler, '. . . to forbear lamenting with you the general decay of religion in this nation; which is now observed by everyone and has been for some time the complaint of all serious persons.'[4] This is one side of the picture. The evidence on the other side is equally extensive and it cannot be lightly dismissed. Samuel Johnson was as typical a figure as the age produced, and his prayers are the reflection of a deep and genuine religious faith. More surprising, because more un-expected, are the signs of real piety to be found in the diaries and letters of statesmen. Viscount Percival and the Duke of Newcastle were absorbed in the complex and sometimes dis-creditable intricacies of politicial intrigue, but they discharged their duties as members of the Church with a devotion which was due to more than habit.

This was an age at once supremely self-confident and strangely diffident. Addison, who set the tone of the succeeding period in so many ways, carefully inculcated maxims which would sustain a buoyant outlook on life. 'A man', he wrote, 'who uses his best endeavours to live according to the dictates of virtue and right reason, has two perpetual sources of cheerfulness; in the consideration of his own nature and of that Being on whom he has a dependence.' He felt that it was his duty to 'engage my reader to consider the world in its most agreeable light', and he believed (with Locke's encouragement) that even evil can contribute to the achievement of a happy life.[1] In developing this complacent optimism the new science played its part. It cleared the universe of mystery; it provided man with a home which was ruled throughout by laws which his mind could decipher. It was reassuring to live in a world so thoroughly rational, so fully and finally explained by man's intellectual powers. At last the truth had been unveiled, and this confident generation believed that ahead stretched a broadening highway which led to a golden future. Throughout the century apostles of progress were preaching the twin duties of gratitude and expectancy. The cult of the coming golden age never developed in England as fully as it did in France; the *philosophes*, to whom Voltaire communicated the new gospel, accepted it with greater zeal and pressed it to greater extremes than any of its originators. But even in England the succession was never completely broken. Priestley and Godwin proclaimed the better day which was coming, and transmitted their confidence to the philosophical radicals of the next century. And yet persistent doubts would not be silenced. Even science seemed at times a questionable blessing. If the universe was ruled throughout by the uniformity of law, if indeed it chiefly resembled a Great Machine, what was to become of man? Must he accept the humble status of a cog in that Machine? Was free will an illusion, and immortality an idle dream? As time passed, some men accepted with equanimity and even with zest the uninviting verdict implicit in these questions.

Priestley was a mechanist and a necessitarian; so was Godwin. Both showed the ardour of the new convert. But many felt that a chill draught had blown through their secure and comfortable dwelling place. Optimism was shadowed by a lurking doubt. Melancholia beset even the most buoyant minds. Death was an intractable mystery which the rationalism of the age could neither dispel nor forget. An enlightened century believed that 'light is come into the world'; on the strength of the available evidence, a contemporary concluded that men nevertheless preferred darkness to light.[1]

This was not the uniform and simple age which has often been depicted. Cross-currents of thought swept the unwary in unforeseen directions and often to unexpected destinations. It was a period when great men were perforce concerned with great questions. Man and his nature, his mind and its powers, his common life and its guiding principles—these are problems as important as they are perennial. And with these issues the eighteenth century was persistently concerned.

CHAPTER II

THE AUTHORITY OF REASON
CONFIRMED BY REVELATION

THE seventeenth century had magnified the claims of authority. The leaders of various groups and factions had fought bitterly but inconclusively on behalf of truths which they could neither persuade nor compel their opponents to accept. The natural result was a reaction against dogmatism. The Cambridge Platonists, the early Latitudinarians, the founders of the Royal Society all helped to foster a new mentality. Locke and Newton gave it its distinctive form and stamped it with their own prestige. By the beginning of the eighteenth century the assumptions which would govern subsequent thought had clearly emerged.

The supremacy of reason was universally accepted. The powers of the human mind were variously conceived, but the differences dividing men of similar outlook proved relatively unimportant. In some quarters reason was regarded as the foundation of faith, in others as its substitute. As Mark Pattison pointed out in a celebrated essay, rationalism 'was a habit of thought ruling all minds, under the conditions of which all alike tried to make good the peculiar opinions they might happen to cherish'. It took complete possession of the field of theology: argument became the method, proof became the goal of everyone who discussed religious topics. 'Yet the rationalism which is the common character of all writers of this time is a method rather than a doctrine; an unconscious assumption rather than a principle from which they reason.'[1] Such an approach assigned particular authority to certain intellectual disciplines. Theology was eclipsed by ethics (which had obvious practical values) and by metaphysics (which promised to succeed in 'proving the truth'). The greater the skill of the metaphysician, the more abstract became his treatment of religious truth. Samuel Clarke's works established a new standard of clarity and cogency; in discussing God he reduced the divine nature to wholly abstract terms. 'The self-existent being, must of necessity be but one. This evidently follows from his being necessarily-existent. For necessity absolute in itself is simple and uniform, without any possible difference or variety: and all variety or difference of existence must needs arise from some external cause and be dependent upon it. . . . Whatsoever, therefore, exists necessarily is the one simple essence of the self-existent Being; and whatsoever differs from that is not necessarily existing. Because in absolute necessity there can be no difference or diversity of existence.'[1] Abstract thought finds its ideal in the scientific and mathematical disciplines, and eighteenth-century writers consciously set this austere pattern before them. Locke had claimed that the evidence for the existence of God was 'equal to mathematical certainty'.[2] William Whiston, appealing to the example and authority of Newton, argued on mathematical grounds for the validity of religious belief, and used astronomy to establish the major truths of both natural and revealed religion.[3] Clarke, in expounding his ideal of perspicuity combined with economy of words, explained that he relied on 'one only method or continued thread of arguing, which I have endeavoured should be as near to mathematical as the nature of such a discourse would allow'. The ideal might seem severe; Clarke believed it would prove effective: the triumphs of science were already working 'to the shame and confusion of atheists'.[4] When Warburton epitomised his paradoxical defence of revelation, he claimed that it fell 'very little short of mathematical certainty', and that 'nothing but a mere physical impossibility to the contrary' could be opposed to it.[5] Many were perforce content to work in a less rarefied atmosphere and with less exacting standards, but the influence of the dominant intellectual disciplines was everywhere apparent. Clarity of thought and simplicity of expression became established norms. 'Scholastic jargon' was dismissed with contempt; the pattern to which Christians were committed, and with which they should be content, was 'the plainness and simplicity of the Gospel'. The essence of religion, it was felt, can be condensed into a few elementary propositions: there is a rule of life; man is free to observe it; there is a governor of the universe.[1]

A reasonable outlook encouraged a moderate temper. 'Enthusiasm' was the *bête noire* of the age.[2] The previous century had left, as its abiding legacy, an ineradicable fear of fanaticism in any form. Zeal without knowledge, said Wake, had a disastrous effect upon its devotees: 'it was a furious, blind erroneous zeal; and such, notwithstanding their good intention, would end in nothing less than damnation at the last'.[3] Throughout the century the episcopal mind was particularly sensitive to any claims to special inspiration. That was the point of Butler's famous rebuke to John Wesley about that 'very horrid thing', enthusiasm.[4] Warburton, discarding for a moment the truculence he usually displayed towards critics, wrote a long and patient letter to a young Oxford don who had shown a dangerously envangelical spirit: it was necessary, he told his friend Hurd, to 'soften and humanize a little this atrocious virtue'.[5] In order to escape the perils of misguided zeal men ought to cultivate a calm and rational approach to intellectual and religious problems. In this the bishops faithfully reflected their age. Horace Walpole, in his account of a sermon preached by Wesley, remarked that 'there were parts and eloquence in it; but towards the end he exalted his voice, and acted very ugly enthusiasm'.[6] Wherever we turn we encounter this subdued ideal. As his legacy to the new age, Bishop Wilkins had commended 'a mind free from violent prejudices and a desire of contention'[7]; the bequest was gratefully accepted. Hoadly found the secret of Clarke's amazing success in 'a certain strength and coolness of head, which could not easily be surprised or deceived'.[8] A greater tolerance was the natural consequence of this sober outlook. Those who did not claim a monopoly of truth were less disposed to exclude their opponents from grace or intellectual integrity. With certain notable exceptions, a more conciliatory attitude and a greater willingness to compromise mark the controversies of the eighteenth century. 'I do not urge authority to the persons I am at present speaking to', said Clarke; reason and calm discussion would be enough to bring them to a better mind.[1] Objections must be faced in an honest and candid spirit; it was wrong to intimidate opponents with the threat of coercion; they should be met with patience and understanding. 'It seems incumbent on our parts', wrote Sykes, 'as lovers of men and friends to truth, to examine fairly and without bitterness the objections which are brought against the religion which we profess; and to take care that those who produce their difficulties should be by no means molested or any ways injured on that account.'[2] The use of constraint is an admission of weakness. This implied no disposition to avoid controversy; Bishop Gibson regarded few duties as more imperative than that of meeting the challenge of error, but in the great debates of the age the participants were usually willing to do justice to their opponents' position.

Eighteenth-century writers generally accepted certain basic assumptions; they held in common certain convictions which gave to the thought of the age its distinctive quality. A large measure of essential agreement was compatible with considerable variations of belief. Before considering the principal emphases of the Age of Reason, it is necessary to notice the pattern of the unfolding thought of the period.

The supremacy attributed to reason involved intense preoccupation with the problems which the reign of reason inevitably raised. Throughout the first half of the century debate raged around the sufficiency of reason to serve as the sole interpreter of existence. Deism will be examined in detail in a later chapter; meanwhile we should remember that there were many thinkers who, while making generous concessions to the claims of reason, remained (as they believed) on the safe side of the frontiers of heterodoxy. Here, indeed, we have the best example of the willingness of the eighteenth-century writers to argue from the presuppositions of their opponents. They conceded the pre-eminence of reason; they were prepared to test revelation, as well as its evidences in miracle and prophecy, by the standards which reason suggested. Since *The Reasonableness of Christianity* (the title of Locke's influential work) 'may be said to have been the solitary thesis of Christian theology in England for the greater part of a century',[1] most of the prominent authors participated in the discussion of the issues Deism raised, and some of them conceded so much that it is difficult to determine their exact position. William Wollaston regarded himself as a loyal—but enlightened—son of the Church. *The Religion of Nature Delineated* examined the extent to which reason and nature alone can lay bare the foundations of religious truth. He did not believe that his conclusions in any way constituted an endorsement of Deism. Churchmen had no more intention of repudiating revelation than of abandoning natural religion to their foes. But the general tone of Wollaston's argument unquestionably encouraged those who relied chiefly on human reason. 'And, then', he wrote, 'since there is *religion*, which follows from the distinction between moral good and evil; since this distinction is founded in respect, which men's actions bear to the truth; and since no proposition can be true which expresses things otherwise than as they are in nature: since things are so, there must be religion which is founded in nature, and may upon that account be most properly and truly called the religion of nature or natural religion.'[2] Conyers Middleton also illustrates the ambiguous position which a prominent churchman might occupy. Opponents sarcastically remarked that he must still consider himself a Christian since he had not disavowed his ministerial orders, and he certainly believed that he was entitled to a far greater share of the emoluments of the Church than had come his way. Gibbon remarked that Middleton 'rose to the highest pitch of scepticism in any way consistent with religion'; he saw whither his principles led, but he refrained from drawing the obvious inferences.[1] He had the detached outlook which could see both the defects of orthodoxy and the weaknesses of Deism. He considered religion necessary for the masses; he was less explicit in affirming its truth. He could argue with vigour, learning and persuasiveness for that enlightened interpretation of the Scriptures which he considered necessary in the modern age,[2] but many observers, noting the implications of his treatment of miracles, felt that religion had been grievously assaulted in the house of its friends.

If orthodoxy trembled on the frontiers of Deism, it was in equal peril of subsiding into Arianism. Here, too, the effects of an age enamoured of reason could clearly be seen. Late in the seventeenth century the doctrine of the Trinity had come under review. In the decade from 1690 to 1700 a number of pamphlets —none particularly able or profound—had questioned the validity of the doctrine. But it was the defence, rather than the attack, which did the damage. Both Robert South and William Sherlock upheld the dogma but fell furiously upon each other. The public, though unable at times to follow the argument, were in no doubt that two of the leading churchmen of the age could neither agree about doctrine nor disagree in charity. The controversy widened in scope and increased in bitterness until Archbishop Tenison issued a directive that the subject be no longer discussed. The leaders of the eighteenth-century church had no illusions about the unprofitable character of the debate. 'I abhor every tendency to the trinitarian controversy', wrote Archbishop Herring. 'The manner in which it is always managed is the disgrace and ruin of Christianity.'[3] Nevertheless few subjects engrossed so much attention.

It was known that Locke and Newton had wished to clarify belief in the interests of simplicity, and this fact alone made it impossible to stifle debate. One of the most indefatigable agitators was 'the pious and learned, but unfortunate Mr Whiston',[4] a disciple of Newton, and his successor in the Lucasian chair of

3

Mathematics at Cambridge. With a fearless devotion to the truth as he saw it, he combined a naïve assurance of—almost an obsession with—his own infallibility. Without a trace of diffidence he informed his friends what they must do—on the basis of his own discoveries and convictions—and if they hesitated to act accordingly, he put the worst construction on their attitude. It is little wonder that his correspondents were incensed. 'I think you have already shown that you can err', wrote the Bishop of Norwich, 'and that a little more coolness would do you no hurt.' 'And I likewise believe you to be a sincerely honest, undesigning man', wrote the Archbishop of York. 'But then give me leave to add . . . that if you have any weakness it is this: that you are too fond of new notions, and oftentimes lay too great stress upon them.'¹ In a series of works, Whiston advocated his views, recorded his discoveries, and narrated the marvellous triumphs and the undeserved reverses of his version of the truth. His purpose was to re-establish the simple faith of the early Church. To do so, he would have to overthrow the evils of the Athanasian position, and restore the Arianism which he found in the earliest records of the faith.

A quixotic strain in Whiston circumscribed his influence; he was an irritant rather than a menace. Samuel Clarke, on the other hand, was a personal and intellectual force of the first magnitude. He was recognised as Locke's true successor. He was considered the foremost metaphysician in England. The precision of his thought commanded universal respect. Warburton quoted with approval Voltaire's verdict: Clarke was 'a reasoning engine'.² As rector of St James's, Piccadilly, he occupied one of the leading pulpits in England; as friend and confidant of Queen Caroline he had access to the highest circles. Hoadly believed that Clarke's sermons would be immortal; they 'must last as long as any language remains to convey them to future times'. Hoadly was neither a self-effacing nor an inconspicuous man; yet he declared, 'I shall think myself greatly recommended for the want of any other memorial if my name may go down to posterity thus closely joined to his, and I myself thought of, and spoke of, in ages to come under the character of "The Friend of Dr. Clarke"'.[1] The opinions of a man like Clarke carried great weight, and it was apparent that his opinions were scarcely orthodox. In 1712 he published his *Scripture Doctrine of the Trinity*. The results of an exhaustive examination of all pertinent biblical texts were condensed in fifty-five propositions. There is, he said, one Supreme Cause, one simple, uncompounded, undivided, intelligent Agent who is the author of all being and the source of all power. From the beginning there has existed with the Father his Word or Son—and with both the Holy Spirit. Unqualified worship is due to the Father alone, and all reverence accorded to Son or Spirit must satisfy this primary condition. Clarke insisted that for the metaphysical Trinity of the creeds he was substituting a Scriptural Trinity. He believed that the Athanasians were guilty of Sabellianism, but that both the Arians and the Socinians were also unsound. Yet the strong rationalism which marked his position unquestionably fostered the trend toward Arianism, and prominent Churchmen considered him a very dangerous man. Bishop Gibson felt obliged to block his elevation to the bishops' bench. Bishop Robinson accused him of being under 'the strong delusions of pride and self-conceit'.[2] But Clarke had many and ardent supporters. John Jackson assured Clarke that when he began to study the meaning of the Trinity he 'was presently able to discern that your scheme was much more agreeable to itself throughout and to Scripture interpreted by itself and the plainest and most undisguised Reason' than any alternative view. He was satisfied, therefore, 'that the doctrine you maintain should be tried by the Scripture and the Scripture only; being at the same time persuaded that as it is most agreeable to reason, so the notions defended in opposition to yours are contrary to it'.[3] Jackson's support of Clarke's position steadily assumed a more Arian tone. He believed that 'the first and principal article of all religion, both natural and revealed, [is] the unity of God'; he was satisfied that 'the Scriptures of the Old and New Testament

35

everywhere teach and inculcate it, as a principle known by the light of natural reason'.[1] Similar in outlook and emphasis was Arthur Ashley Sykes, and the position adopted by these men was consistently represented within the Church of England. It was strongly challenged by Daniel Waterland, one of the most vigorous defenders of orthodoxy. Waterland was an able rather than a distinguished writer; he reaffirmed the Anglican position in a way which commanded the reluctant respect of a rationalistic age.

The forces affecting Anglican thought were also at work among the nonconformists. Here their effects were even more pronounced. Though the dissenters had not been directly involved in the great Trinitarian controversy, their own contentions had deepened the cleavage dividing the stricter Calvinists from those who claimed a greater latitude. Some of the younger ministers had studied in Holland and had there learned a more flexible approach to doctrine, but unquestionably Dr Clarke's works were the strongest single influence in encouraging Arian tendencies. His *Scripture Doctrine* convinced James Peirce that traditional theology was unsound. Peirce, a minister at Exeter, had earned a distinguished reputation as a defender of nonconformity. When the dissenting congregations in Exeter became embroiled in controversy, Peirce made his position clear: he was opposed to speculative theology, he was not an Arian, and he promised to preach only plain Christianity. It was obvious, however, that he was moving in an heretical direction, and it soon became apparent that the controversy would spread far beyond Exeter. The crux of the debate was the degree of doctrinal latitude which congregations should allow their ministers, and when the question was referred for decision to the leaders of London nonconformity, the central issue became the desirability of theological tests. At the Salters' Hall Synod (1719), the nonconformist ministers began to divide into two parties; the more conservative demanded subscription to a Trinitarian formula, the more progessive argued for credal affirmations couched in strictly scriptural terms. A series of votes, while revealing the even balance between the two sides, did not indicate the complexity of the situation. The one party believed it was resisting the onset of heresy; the other was equally certain that it was opposing the spirit of persecution. Yet some who were perfectly orthodox voted against the imposition of any test, and many who contended for liberty had clearly not forsaken orthodoxy. Independents and Presbyterians were to be found on both sides, but the latter were usually against subscription, and in due course their name became a synonym for freedom of thought, even for laxity of opinion. Arianism steadily gained ground among them. By 1770 barely half the Presbyterian congregations were Trinitarian in belief; thereafter they rapidly veered toward Socinianism, and in due course became explicitly Unitarian. Thus the Presbyterians passed from Calvinism to Arminianism, then to Arianism and so to Socinianism. Many of the ablest dissenters became Arians. Nathaniel Lardner was one of the most learned apologists for Christianity, but though he argued cogently for *The Credibility of the Evidences*, he sat very loosely to some of the historic doctrines of Catholic Christianity. John Taylor, who left a distinguished ministry at the Octagon Chapel in Norwich to become the principal of Warrington Academy, affirmed the right of unfettered enquiry in a way which is both characteristic of many of the Arians and indicative of the temper which prevailed in the dissenting academies.

The academies unquestionably played an important role in modifying nonconformist thought. Early in the century a 'progressive' outlook pervaded many of these institutions. Doddridge gave an interesting account of John Jennings' academy at Kibworth. Jennings, though orthodox, encouraged free enquiry. In his teaching he did not restrict himself to a single theological position; he would defend in turn Calvinist, Baxterian and Arminian views, and he always insisted that the Scriptures provide the only satisfactory standard of faith. Doddridge himself was orthodox in theology and progressive in educational theory, but he held his views in so moderate a spirit that he did little to arrest the drift to Arianism. Meanwhile, both in the west and in the north many of the academies were becoming distinctly heterodox. Priestley was a student at Daventry and a tutor at Warrington, and in his *Memoirs* he described in some detail the life of these academies. At Daventry, the principal was orthodox but the tutor distinctly less so, and in theological debates they usually took opposite sides. The doctrine of the Atonement was one of the contentious issues, and most of the students accepted it at least in a modified form. A few were already Arian in their Christology; many became so after they left. A few years later, when Priestley went to Warrington, the views of his fellow tutors reflected the erosion of orthodox convictions which had been taking place. His own beliefs had changed considerably. At Warrington all the tutors were Arians; some of them were far advanced on the road to Socinianism. The academy encountered serious difficulties and soon disbanded, but while it survived its intellectual distinction made it the most vigorous of the forces working for the spread of Arianism.

The Congregationalists were less affected by prevailing influences than the Presbyterians. Many of them adhered faithfully to Calvinism; many others showed that they could be both orthodox in theology and liberal in outlook. The best examples of the latter point of view are provided by the two greatest names in eighteenth-century nonconformity. Isaac Watts reflects the anxious preoccupation of the age with the doctrine of the Trinity, and the frequency with which he returned to the subject suggests that he found it hard to frame a satisfactory statement. His initial attempt, *The Christian Doctrine of the Trinity*, condensed his views into twenty-two propositions, briefly elaborated and defended. Watts accepted the doctrine which the Athanasian Creed affirmed, but he was painfully aware of its metaphysical problems and he felt that these were aggravated—if not created—by the unscriptural language which the creed employed. He kept clearly in mind the unity of the divine nature and the richness of communion characteristic of its life. 'I have often asserted, and I repeat it again, that when I express the doctrine of the Trinity by three persons being one God, I mean no more than that there "are three who have sufficient communion in one Godhead to have proper divine names, titles and attributes ascribed to them, and sufficient distinction from each other to maintain the various characters and offices that are assigned to them in scripture".'[1] 'Person', in effect, becomes 'character' or 'office', yet Watts found it an unsatisfactory and confusing term. The essential truth seemed to be as follows: if Son and Holy Spirit share in the divine nature, then the same true Godhead which is in the Father is in the other two Persons also. Watts was in no danger of exaggerating the distinctness of the Persons—here 'arithmetic and reason' were sufficient safeguards. He was in much greater danger of slipping into Arianism. He accepted a subordinationism of the Son, but it was of his *human* nature only; he stoutly maintained the full equality of Christ's *divine* nature.

Like Watts, Doddridge believed that English Calvinism, in its traditional form, had to be modified, but he was anxious to conserve its essential truths. Its distinctive terms needed to be reinterpreted; if expressed in scriptural language they would gain a new incisiveness. He defined the Trinity in a way which safeguarded the insights of evangelical faith and satisfied the demands of the Christian conscience, but avoided the difficult question of the relations of the Persons in the Godhead. There are some truths, he said, which we can believe without wrangling about their precise expression. Realities are more important than definitions, and faith transcends words and phrases. Doddridge was 'reasonable' and practical in his approach to contentious matters, and he had a gift for retaining the friendship of men who were not unduly charitable to dissenters. One of the most unexpected documents of that disputatious age is the letter which Warburton wrote to Doddridge during the latter's fatal illness: '. . . you will have the prayers of your friends, as conquerors have the shouts of the crowd. God preserve you; if he continues you here, to go on in his service; if he takes you to himself, to be crowned with glory. Be assured the memory of our friendship will be as durable as my life.'[1] Doddridge was not an Arian, but the restrained tone of his teaching apparently made it easier for many of his students to forsake the orthodoxy which he himself upheld.

The cult of reason, which made Deism popular and Arianism attractive, exposed orthodoxy to other temptations as well. Latitudinarianism reflects both the strength and the weakness of a rationalistic faith. From Tillotson to Paley, most of the leading theologians in England can, with essential justice, he included within the ill-defined limits of the Latitudinarian school. These were the men who sustained the running battle with the Deists and who met the challenge of the Arians. The writers of genius— Law, Berkeley, Butler—cannot be embraced even by so elastic a term, and they will be considered separately. There was little uniformity among the Latitudinarians, but they held in common certain basic principles which merit detailed examination and to which we shall return. The Boyle lectureship gave them their favourite platform, and the series of volumes which the foundation encouraged represents rational orthodoxy in its most coherently formulated guise.

Two other leading figures, Sherlock and Warburton, typify the trend of eighteenth-century thought. Thomas Sherlock was involved in most of the famous controversies of the age. Even at Cambridge, he and Hoadly—able rivals in one of the smaller colleges—had been at odds, and in the Bangorian controversy Sherlock found an unequalled opportunity to display his ability and his animosity. He met the Deist challenge both to prophecy and to miracle, and in both cases his works were conspicuously successful. As he climbed the ladder of promotion, his discourses and sermons reflected the outlook of many of the leaders of the Hanoverian church. He was authoritarian but not dogmatic. He conceded the importance of natural religion, and proved its close affinity with Christianity. He admitted the supremacy of reason, and though he subjected it to criticism, he was in danger of granting it too much latitude rather than too little. The rationalist spirit, it is clear, had gained admission to Christian theology; increasingly it permeated the whole life of the church. In the lucidity of his thought and the measured sobriety of his language Sherlock was typical of his age, yet he recognised the peril of reducing religion to prudential morality and of so defining ethics that it excluded revelation. The laws of morality, he insisted, are subject to the will of God. 'All powers are the gift of the creator and every being subsists not by the law and authority of nature but by the law and appointment of God, who is master of his own laws and appointments, and can change them whenever he pleases; and Nature will follow and obey his command, and ever be what he intends it should be.'[1]

In William Warburton the eighteenth century produced a figure at once typical and unique. He would be inconceivable in any other age, yet he deliberately stood apart from his contemporaries. He claimed to be the arbiter of taste. He posed as a dictator in the realm of letters; in many circles his pronouncements were accepted as law. In *The Divine Legation of Moses* he produced a theological work avidly read by his contemporaries and virtually forgotten by posterity. In its own day it was a book difficult to ignore. Warburton was fascinated by the paradoxes of human thought and history, and he pressed novelty to its utmost limits. Everyone assumed that a belief in immortality was an essential element in religion; the Hebrew religion, said the Deists, lacked this necessary ingredient, and therefore it could not be a divinely inspired faith. Warburton admitted the justice of the charge; he denied the validity of the inference. Only a faith providentially maintained could have survived a defect fatal by all human standards. The argument could be condensed into a syllogism;[2] its proof was expanded to three large volumes and was never finished. Into his book Warburton poured the learning amassed by years of intensive study. Few subjects fell outside his scope. He dealt, said Gibbon, with 'the ancient world, eighteen centuries

41

and four hundred authors, genuine and apocryphal'. Omniscience is a dangerous foible, and Lowth pitilessly exposed its full absurdity. *The Divine Legation*, he said, 'includes in itself all history, chronology, criticism, law, politics, from the law of Moses to the late Jew-bill, and from Egyptian hieroglyphics to modern rebus-writing; and to it we are to have recourse, as to an infallible oracle, for the resolution of every question in literature'.[1] Yet the comprehensiveness of the work was only one of the qualities which commended it to contemporaries and made it a faithful reflection of the age. There is no doubt as to the vigour of the author's thought or the robustness of his mind. His judgments are often acute and his insights highly original, even if he sometimes displays them in perverse and futile ways. His style is forcible; his meaning is always clear. He writes with wit, though never with subtlety. He marshals great masses of material with authority and success. His ingenuity is immense, and his store of illustration inexhaustible. In an unhistorical age he perceived, dimly perhaps but none the less surely, that the story of man's religious development is one of growth. He saw the fact, though he missed its full significance. But it was a signal merit to realise that 'the Holy Spirit, quite throughout God's grand economy, from his first giving of the Law to the completion of it by the Gospel, observed the same unvarying method of the GRADUAL COMMUNICATION of Truth'.[2]

It might seem that a work of such varied merits deserved a less ephemeral fame. Its assured self-confidence impressed contemporaries but has alienated posterity. The eighteenth century was a disputatious age; Warburton's arrogance made him a particularly truculent brawler. 'I did not care', wrote Lowth, '. . . to question your investiture in the high office of Inquisitor General and Supreme Judge of the opinions of the learned, which you had long assumed and had exercised with a ferocity and despotism without example in the republic of letters, and hardly to be paralleled among the disciples of Dominic; exacting their opinions to the standard of your infallibility, and prosecuting with implacable hatred everyone who presumed to differ from you.'¹ This was severe but not unfair. Warburton himself described the treatment he intended to mete out to one of his critics. 'I shall hang him and his fellows as they do vermin in a warren, and leave them to posterity to stink and blacken in the wind.'² More serious were the limitations of his outlook. He showed little interest in doctrinal issues. He believed that religious matters could be exactly proved; he committed himself to the appropriate method and he restricted his attention to questions which lent themselves to logical treatment. His training and his prejudices kept obtruding themselves. He argued theological issues as a sharp attorney might argue a brief, and apparently forgot that to wrangle is not necessarily to reason. And the results of applying legal concepts to religious problems are often grotesque. But in spite of its defects, *The Divine Legation* was one of the important works of the century. It attracted immediate attention. Concern over the decay of religion was general. Warburton believed that he had discovered a new and powerful argument for the defence of the faith, and even those who disliked his methods felt compelled to consider seriously their results.

The general drift of thought in the first half of the century is indicated, as we have seen, by the principal figures who fashioned it. When we turn from the course of speculation to its contents, we face a large measure of agreement on major issues and considerable divergence on minor ones.

The cardinal article of Latitudinarian belief was the existence of God. In the symmetrical and overarching structure of its thought, he was the keystone which held all other elements in perfect unity. It is entirely reasonable, they claimed, to believe in God; the testimony of all history encourages it and the wisdom of the profoundest philosophers confirms it.³ The structure of the universe and the nature of everything within it point to an almighty and all-wise Creator. 'Indeed, there is no account to be given, how such a glorious and regular frame of things, as the world that is now before us should come to be, without

43

supposing a God; that is an infinitely wise and powerful Being, that was the great and wise creator, and is the governor of it.'[1] From the stars in outer space to the minutest forms of life beneath our feet, everything testifies to beauty and order, which point in turn to purpose and power. Thus 'the plain signatures of wisdom and good sense in those parts of the world with which we are best acquainted' are proofs of its being 'the effect of some wise and intelligent being'.[2] But so grave a certainty could not be reached in a single step. From stage to stage the argument advanced. God's existence is possible; it is even probable; it is actually certain.[3] So we reach the conviction that one Supreme Being must exist, and the strenuous logic of Samuel Clarke and his associates in the Boyle lectureship was intended to put this assurance beyond the shadow of a doubt. From an examination of God's nature men could advance to an investigation of his attributes, which show him to be 'infinite in power, wisdom, justice, goodness and truth'.[4] So the interminable discussion continued—arguments to confirm the existence of God, inferences to indicate his nature, conclusive evidence to expose the folly of unbelief. It was the controversy with the atheists which in part explains the character of Latitudinarian thought. Acknowledged infidels were relatively rare, but the apologists did not believe that they were simply demolishing men of straw. In their less argumentative moments they realised that proof and demonstration were not synonymous with religious faith. Mere belief in God's existence, said Bishop Leng, is not sufficient ground for religion unless it is supported by trust in God's providential care.[5] Essentially, however, the deity of eighteenth-century speculation played a crucial part in a tightly integrated system. The Latitudinarians may have divorced him from life; they never isolated him from the other elements in their thought.

The world is God's handiwork and provides the surest testimony to his wisdom and power. It includes 'all things visible and invisible, material and immaterial, except . . . God',[6] and consequently it embraces the whole universe. At times the Latitudinarians blandly assumed that the world is derivative in character; they were equally prepared to prove, by ingenious and intricate arguments, that it could not be self-existent. In either case, the inference which they drew from it was the same: the world must be the product of divine will. Under whatever guise we consider the created order, it is clearly the effect of God's goodness. It is true that the symmetry of the universe is broken by irregularities which it is hard to explain. Land and water are unequally distributed; so are mountains and valleys. The structure of animals suffers from strange defects. But a triumphant answer could be found to every doubt,[1] and the Latitudinarians were satisfied that the world is indeed governed by God's wisdom. Its existence presupposes his existence, and at every point its structure illustrates his creative power. The argument from design became the stock-in-trade of every apologist; it was popularly accepted as the sure support of religious faith. What scores of writers were expounding with painstaking care Samuel Clarke expressed with characteristic cogency:

> 'Yet the notices that God has been pleased to give of himself are so many and so obvious; in the constitution, order, beauty and harmony of the several parts of the world; in the form and structure and our own bodies, and the wonderful powers and faculties of our souls; in the unavoidable apprehensions of our own minds, and the common consent of all other men; in every thing within us and everything without us: that no man of the meanest capacity and greatest disadvantages whatsoever, with the slightest and most superficial observation of the works of God, and the lowest and most obvious attendance to the reason of things, can be ignorant of him; but he must be utterly without excuse.'[2]

Within the created order, man occupies a position at once pre-eminent and unique. It was natural for the new age to turn with particular fascination to the study of human nature. The universe, revealed in its wonder by Newton, provided a setting that

45

enhanced man's native dignity. Locke, by unfolding the workings of the mind, gave a new impetus and a new direction to psychology and morality. 'The proper study of mankind is Man', and Pope's epigram was 'the Shibboleth of the new anthropocentric movement'.[1] The Biblical evidence was not entirely ignored; at points, indeed, it proved particularly useful, but increasingly the picture of man was defined by observation and argument. The Latitudinarians did not forget that man is a creature; to regard him as the product of mechanical forces or of mere chance would degrade him in the scale of nature. He is the supreme proof of God's creative power. His soul, no less than his body, is most marvellously made. 'We have enough to fill us with admiration of the munifence [sic], power and wisdom of the Infinite Creator, when we contemplate the faculties of this our superior part, the vast reach and compass of our understanding, the prodigious quickness and piercingness of its thought, the admirable subtlety of its invention, the commanding power of its wisdom, the depth of its memory, and in a word its divine nature and operations.'[2] Man was made perfect in both mind and body. He was designed for happiness, and he was surrounded by every circumstances that could promote it. He was so constituted that he found his felicity in acting at the behest of reason.[3] Why, then, is he so often a prey to passion and blind impulse? The answer is simple: man's misery is the consequence of his Fall. He is now indisposed to obey the divine will; he has forfeited salvation and he cannot regain it by his own endeavours.[4] Yet human nature, even in its ruin, retains the traces of its former grandeur. Man has not completely lost his freedom nor has his reason been wholly corrupted by the Fall.

Man remains essentially a free agent. In spite of all that Hobbes and Spinoza had said, the Latitudinarians contended that daily experience provides evidence which we cannot ignore. As to the liberty of human actions, 'let us any of us . . . try whether we must not be conscious to ourselves that we can make a thousand spontaneous motions, and think of as many things, how or

46

when, or as we please'.¹ Free thought in its proper sense—the exercise, that is, of private judgment in matters of religion—is more than a possibility; it is 'not only every man's right . . . but 'tis every man's duty'.² Obedience to truth ought to be the law of human action; but we can only know and accept the truth if we are free agents, and consequently freedom is the condition of the moral life. But since moral obligation is beyond question, the reality of freedom should be beyond doubt.³ To complete the chain of reasoning, a further link is necessary. Man's freedom 'consists in choosing upon reason'; it follows, therefore, that 'the more reason we have for the choice of anything, as our choice is the more rational and perfect, so it is likewise the more free. And, by consequence, when our wills choose nothing but what is reasonable to be chosen, and those things most that are most reasonable, and when our actions are exactly conformable to our wills, then we are in a true state of rational and perfect freedom.'⁴

Reason, like freedom, has been tarnished by the Fall; its lustre has been dimmed but not destroyed. It has been further 'weakened by evil customs and habits', themselves the products of 'superstition and immoral wickedness'.⁵ What survives defectively in us exists perfectly in God. This is the ground of the essential kinship between man and his maker. 'We must conclude', wrote Warburton, 'that it was the faculty of reason which made the resemblance.'⁶ Because reason links man with God it provides the means by which we can discover the divine nature, and come to know God as he is.⁷ The splendour of man's highest endowment inspires the sustained enthusiasm with which the Latitudinarians always spoke of 'that brightest and most glorious ray of the divine, and the perfection of human, nature'.⁸ It is easier, of course, to praise reason than to define it with precision. Its perfection, said Harris, 'seems to consist in these two things: 1. In knowledge and wisdom in the understanding faculty. 2. In rectitude or righteousness in the will.' 'By reason', said Burnet, 'we usually mean a principle of thought, which, according as it exerts itself differently, is conceived under different names of

understanding and will.'¹ Its possession lays an inescapable constraint upon every man: 'what our reason approves or condemns . . . we are commanded to do or not to do by God himself
who gave us such a nature'.² Its more ardent champions admitted
no limits to its capacity; the more cautious conceded that some
things lie beyond its power. It cannot reform the world's corruption. It is too weak even to restrain the evil impulses which
custom has made natural to man.³

The task of reason is to disclose the truth, and the fulness of the
truth is embodied in religion. Religion is an original and ineradicable characteristic of human life. Consequently it is related
to the essential structure of our nature and discloses its true
character to the scrutiny of reason. It 'is a chain of principles,
which being received as true, are the reason obliging us to the performance or non-performance of such and such actions'.⁴ The
element of obligation, as we shall see later, resulted in the emphasis
which the Latitudinarians laid upon morality, but it is well to
remember that it was a fundamental ingredient in their understanding of religion itself. 'For certainly', said Wollaston, 'to
obey the law which the author of his being has given him is
religion; and to obey the law which he has given or revealed to
him by making it to result from the right use of his own natural
faculties, must be to him his natural religion.'⁵ Intelligent beings
are required to follow virtue and to govern themselves by the
rules of truth. But this means that the idea of God is brought into
immediate relation with the pattern of human life, 'and then we
have a new set of arguments, more encouragements and stronger
motives to do what is right than we can possibly have without
such a principle'. Religion, therefore, 'consists in the belief or
practice of anything that is right, from the consideration of God'.⁶
This view was marked by a simplicity and a clarity which seemed,
to its proponents, to lift it above criticism. 'It will not, I think, be
denied', said Sykes, 'that by the religion of nature we are to
reverence and adore God, to believe in him and to hope in him;
and that we are likewise to have an universal love and benevolence

to all men. Wherever we can know any particular relation which we can stand in to any person, the voice of reason shows us our duty in those circumstances.'¹ So modest and practical a view of religion led to the belief that there is available to every man an important—if not, indeed, a wholly sufficient—guide to truth. 'The reasonableness and the credibility of the principles of natural religion'² became the favourite theme of a whole generation of writers. It was generally admitted that unless you began with the truths which natural religion supplied, you could not 'argue with any consistency about the origin of things, their order, regular motions, ends, cause: and with them there is a perfect harmony of the whole'.³ Christianity may add to natural religion or go beyond it, but it rests firmly on the foundation of its basic principles, and this is responsible, in no small measure, for 'the truth and excellency' which are its distinguishing marks.⁴ It also accounts for the reasonableness which so greatly impressed the Latitudinarians when they contemplated the Gospel. They regarded it as 'the true original religion of reason and nature'; 'though not indeed discoverable by bare reason, yet, when made known by revelation [it] appears very consistent with right reason'; all its doctrines are agreeable to reason, and there is nothing, even in the preaching of the Cross, 'that ought to shock our understandings'.⁵ 'What cannot be compounded or understood cannot possibly be a matter or object of faith',⁶ and it was this approach to Christianity which gave to most of the writings of the period their argumentative tone. But if it stripped them of every trace of mysticism it saved them from any suggestion of 'superstition'. An uncompromising utilitarianism pervades Latitudinarian thought. 'The great end of religion is future happiness', said Bishop Sherlock, and his contemporaries entirely agreed. But the benefits are not restricted to another world. Christianity is immediately advantageous to society and to the individuals who compose it.⁷ The reasonableness of true religion is also the surest safeguard against superficial attacks on God's perfect justice. 'In short, either reason is sufficient to guide men in matters of religion, or else there has been a defect in God not giving his creatures sufficient aids to direct them to their duties.'[1]

At this point a rift appears in Latitudinarian thought. A few enthusiasts claimed that natural religion can meet all men's essential needs. Christianity 'then was not necessary in respect of the absolute insufficiency of human reason', but it offers additional incentives and inducements. It provides 'a more powerful means of promoting the practice of true religion and godliness, by strengthening the obligations of natural religion'.[2] But the great majority took exception to what they could only regard as extreme and sweeping views. Bishop Hurd maintained the two elements involved in belief in delicately balanced equipoise. 'The religion of nature is the law of God speaking by the voice of reason; the religion of the Gospel is the law of God speaking by the revelation of Jesus. Each of these laws is deservedly called a great salvation: the former as the basis of all true religion: the latter, as the consummation of all God's religious dispensations to mankind.'[3] Bishop Gibson, while emphasising the importance of reason, warned his people that by itself it 'is an insufficient guide in matters of religion'.[4] The 'light of nature', said William Berriman, provides natural religion with its truths, but this light is synonymous with reason, and experience exposes its defects. It can supply elementary ethical insight, but it cannot instruct us in the more searching duties which the Gospel inculcates. Its account of evil is defective, and its explanation of its origin is at best misleading, at worst fatally wrong. It offers no assurance of pardon, and so holds out an insufficient hope to those who have failed or fallen. It provides motives to obedience, but these are both weak and misleading.[5] Bishop Sherlock is an excellent example of the divine who was rationalistic in emphasis yet firmly orthodox in belief. His criticism of natural religion was based on an appeal to history and experience. If nature could 'instruct us sufficiently in religion', we should submit to her tutelage and look no further. But when we abandon speculation and appeal to fact, we discover that unaided reason always fails its devotees. Countries which have relied on natural religion have been engulfed in superstition. 'No antiquity affords an instance of any people great or small who served God upon the principles of natural religion.'[1] All save the stoutest rationalists admitted that man stands in need of some source of truth which will supplement what his native faculties can discover. Reason and revelation belong together, and one of the tasks incumbent on the leaders of thought was to consolidate the relatively weak foundations of revelation. 'The truth of natural religion', remarked Sykes, 'is not much controverted; but revelation has met with many adversaries; the great point therefore was to prove that there had been a revelation given to mankind.'[2]

Revelation supplements reason, but there is no conflict between them. Natural and revealed religion are both 'strictly rational' and equally 'worthy of every serious man's attention'. Those who sincerely accepted the one form of religion would concede at once that it was a reasonable expectation that it would be supplemented by the other. Gibson, so careful to warn of the insufficiency of natural religion, concurred in the 'universally acknowledged' view that 'revelation itself is to stand or fall by the test of reason'. 'Destroy the principles of reason,' said Sherlock, 'and there is no room left for revelation.' He visualised an interrelation so intimate that the one could not survive without the other: '. . . 'tis impossible that any true revelation should contradict or evacuate any clear dictates of natural religion, which stands at least upon as good a bottom as any revelation can do, . . . and therefore the principles of natural religion must be supposed for the foundation of revealed'. When our reason tells us to expect revelation, it is also able to demonstrate its sufficiency and its truth. It is apparent that God has not restricted himself to a single method, and those which he uses are complementary one to another. It is folly to assert the superior merit of different forms of truth when God himself has made them interdependent. Therefore 'whoever maintains the reality and dignity of revelation

at the expense either of natural religion or of morality highly
injures and weakens all three'.[1]

Surely the wisest course is to regard revelation as a consequence
of belief in God. Anyone who accepts the truth of God's providential care must enquire if God has actually disclosed himself.
Reason will then assess the truth of what reason has prompted
him to expect.[2] But what, we may reasonably ask, is the precise
meaning which we may assign to revelation? In a general sense,
it simply points to the disclosure of something which has hitherto
remained a secret. 'In a religious use of the word', said Bishop
Williams, 'it is God's making known himself, or his will, above
what he has done by the light of nature.' A definition of this
kind might be useful, but in that disputatious age it was necessary
immediately to defend the concept which you had defined. So
Williams pointed out that religious knowledge falls into three
categories: what nature affords, what revelation can supply, and
what nature haltingly suggests but which revelation must confirm. It can then be shown that the divine disclosure of special
truth is at once possible, expedient and certain. A variety of
considerations can be adduced to prove the reliability of what
revelation supplies. Natural proofs go a certain distance, the
testimony of experience (tradition) carries us farther, moral
evidence and the Scriptures take us beyond the reach of doubt.
If we demand assurance that particular statements can claim the
authority of revelation, we have ready to hand standards which
we can readily apply: revelation must be authenticated by convincing signs, it must be inherently worthy of God, and it cannot
contradict the canons of morality.[3] In keeping with the temper of
the age, revelation was conceived in terms of propositions, and the
book in which they were communicated was the Bible. Some
writers claimed that the truth of the Gospel should be set forth
in the very words of Scripture. This would safeguard its simplicity, it would exclude the theological niceties which bewilder
the ignorant and entangle the learned.[4] Most were content
to 'prove that the Scriptures of the Old and New Testament

contain the matter of divine revelation, and have upon them the characters belonging to it'.[1]

We have noted that in spite of the high estimate of reason's powers, it was conceded that reason by itself was not enough. In defending revelation it seemed necessary to specify the points at which it made good the defects of natural religion. Sin has corrupted man's nature; since the Fall reason has been so impaired that it has forfeited its original sufficiency. Revelation is consequently necessary 'to recover mankind out of their universally degenerate estate'.[2] This happens in a variety of ways. Reason is restored to something approaching its power in the time of man's innocency. The truths which it gropes after but cannot grasp are given their full distinctness and cogency. The intuitions of natural religion are confirmed. The morals and manners of the world are exposed to an influence strong enough to achieve their reformation. It is not the task of revelation to devise a new system of morality—almost every conceivable type of ethical theory had been propounded by the heathen philosophers of the classical age—but it makes good the defects and overcomes the weaknesses of every system. In particular it provides motives of precisely the kind in which natural religion is defective. 'In this', said Sykes, 'I conceive the great use and advantage of revelation consists; not in discovering any new moral duties, except as it shews new relations; not in making a more perfect rule of action; not in telling us anything which the rule of action to men as reasonable creatures was defective in, but in supplying free argument and new motives to do that which is known to be their duty. . . . If therefore revelation suggests to anyone more knowledge, and more motives for the practice of virtue than otherwise a man can have, in this case it becomes of singular use and service to mankind.'[3] Natural law constrains but does not encourage. Revelation holds out the assurance of pardon to those oppressed by their failures, and gives clear evidence of God's purpose to redeem the world.[4]

On one point, however, the mind of the age was uneasy. The

53

critics of Christianity made great play of the limited scope of revelation. It had been disclosed to so few people, in so remote a place, at such a distant time: did such want of universality really invalidate its claims to be the truth? But God never treats mankind with unvarying uniformity. He gives capacities to some which he withholds from others, yet the disparity of intellectual gifts has never been pressed as fit grounds for complaint. Therefore the plea for uniformity which the Deists advanced was absurd; the truths of natural religion were as unequally distributed as those of revelation, and if the charge held good in the latter case its force must be admitted in the former. If the Gospel was not proclaimed in Tartary or Peru it was doubtless because the necessary degree of preparation cannot be simultaneously achieved in all parts of the world. Even the much vaunted gifts of the Chinese, which so fascinated the men of the early eighteenth century, were defective precisely in the metaphysical understanding necessary to appropriate the Gospel. Those who demand a revelation universally disseminated will find that they have destroyed the case for natural religion and even for elementary moral obligation.[1]

The Latitudinarians believed that their age laid upon them a distinctive duty. Their task was not merely to defend revelation against its detractors, but to establish the foundations on which it rests. They returned repeatedly, therefore, to the 'evidences' which support belief, and they agreed that the proof of revelation is twofold. 'Miracles and prophecies are the two main pillars on which revelation is built. These show the immediate supernatural power and wisdom of God to be concerned in it. They are evidences of the truth of it which are infallible, and cannot fail to have effect.'[2] We have as many proofs of revelation as we have prophecies and since only God can know the things that are yet to come to pass, all true predictions must bear the stamp of his authority. 'This argument from prophecy is certainly a very strict and conclusive evidence of the truth of revelation; nor can it be subverted, unless it be shown either that the books were posterior to the times in which they are said to be wrote; or that the original books have been interpolated and corrupted.'[1] The purpose of prophecy is to give men an intimation of things as yet hidden in the counsels of God, and 'to exercise their faith by the expectation and belief of the things thus notified to them at a distance'. 'By prophecy', said Sherlock, 'I understand all the declarations which God has made concerning the future state of mankind in this world or in the next; consequently all the hopes and expectations which are grounded on God's promises and do not result from reason and natural knowledge, I refer to prophecy as their original.'[2] That there were prophecies is obvious. When Christ came, he found current among the Jewish people expectations concerning Messiah which were clearly the product of prophecy. The early Church did not therefore read back into the records hopes which they had not been designed to encourage. But were the prophecies really of the kind we often assume, and were they actually fulfilled? On this subject an immense amount of learned ingenuity was expended. The prophecies prove the messianic mission of Christ, and his ministry was their complete fulfilment. Passage by passage, verse by verse, the evidence was painstakingly examined.[3] But the argument was inconclusive at the time, and the progress of Biblical studies has left it only an antiquarian interest. Even the eighteenth century found it disappointing. When Warburton established a lectureship at Lincoln's Inn to expound the truths of prophecy, the appointees were soon embarrassed by the discovery that they had nothing new to say. To this unprofitable threshing of the straw there was one conspicuous exception. Sherlock's approach to the subject was fruitful as well as novel. He realised that the piecemeal discussion of isolated verses yields very meagre results. Only when the unity of the subject is appreciated can its true force be grasped. The thoughtful reader will then refuse to believe 'that a chain of prophecies reaching through several thousand years, delivered at different times, yet manifestly subservient to one and the same administration of providence, from beginning to end, is the effect of art and contrivance and religious fraud'.[1] Prophecies, as he pointed out, were not always understood by those who delivered them; they were not exact predictions, and sometimes it is impossible to assign to them a literal meaning.[2] Consequently prophecy does not prove the facts of the Gospel, though it may profoundly affect our estimate of their status.[3] Its evidential value is to establish the claims of Christ under the Gospel.[4] It is very easy, in dealing with this subject, to ask the wrong questions and so to get the wrong answers. The basic issue is simple: 'What end did the wisdom of God propose to serve by the ancient prophecies?'[5] The answer must be in keeping with God's purpose in all things, which is 'the promotion of virtue and religion, and the general peace and happiness of mankind'.[6] This provides a clue which Sherlock followed with considerable ingenuity, and the value of his enquiries is largely due to a basic conviction which few of his contemporaries had grasped: both the form and the content of prophecy are always relative to the religious condition of the people to whom it was delivered.[7]

Prophecy, of course, does not stand alone, and its evidential value is greatly increased by its intimate association with miracle. 'Prophecies also may and ought to be considered as the greatest miracles, being the immediate effects of divine omniscence, and objects of human understanding; as the miracles commonly so called are the works of divine power, and objects of human senses.'[8] A miracle is not rightly defined as an act of exceptional power: to arrest the sun is no more marvellous than to cause it to move, to give life is as wonderful as to restore it. 'The true definition of a miracle . . . is this: that it is a work effected in a manner unusual or different from the common and regular method of Providence, by the interposition either of God himself or of some intelligent agent superior to man, for the proof or evidence of some particular doctrine or in attestation to the authority of some particular person.'[9] The possibility of miracles is firmly grounded in God's control of the world he has created. He normally works through the laws of nature; but this does not prevent him from exercising his power with the freedom which is the mark of personal purpose.¹ At times he delegates this power to others, and miracles may be wrought by evil spirits as well as by good ones. The age was greatly exercised about false miracles. When did exceptional powers cease in the church? What is the significance of 'popish prodigies'? Conyers Middleton offered a solution, but it was considered more damaging than uncertainty could possibly be.² More adequate criteria were obviously needed. The Latitudinarians asserted that miracles were facts, and 'the evidence for the truth of them is of exactly the same nature with the evidence for all other facts'.³ We cannot prejudge what is natural and what is not, since we can only know certain regularities, and are in no position to say what might be possible under different conditions. Miracles do not invalidate the evidence of reason, and are not contrary to its principles.⁴ The test which can legitimately be applied to them is 'whether they are done to promote virtue and true religion'.⁵ So the legitimate ends of miracle need to be carefully distinguished from the false ones. There is no need to appeal to them for proof of the being of God, though they may be used to confirm his revelation of himself. They do not establish morality, whose laws are supplied by natural religion and are grasped by human understanding. They establish the authority of the person who performs them, and his authority, in turn, justifies us in accepting the doctrine which he proclaims.⁶

It is in their concern with moral obligations that the basic intention of the Latitudinarians appears. Much of their work may now seem doctrinaire, but its purpose was intensely practical. They believed that reason and revelation, prophecy and miracle were closely related to the important issues of the day. Everyone agreed that the age was confronted with an alarming collapse of ethical standards. The urgent question was how society could again be made subject to moral constraints. The Latitudinarians were contending for elementary virtue as much as for ultimate truth, and inevitably most of them turned, sooner or later, to the discussion of morality. 'Therefore it becomes us', said Samuel Clarke, 'to apply ourselves to our plain duty, and leave secret things to the Lord our God.'¹ There was general agreement that right and wrong could be distinguished by man's unaided reason. Conscience is a natural endowment and it operates even before the dawning of religious feeling. To neglect Christianity is not to escape moral responsibility. But religion is supremely relevant to moral concerns. Though man becomes aware of the law of nature before he is conscious of the will of God, the latter under-lies the former. The moral teaching of the New Testament con-sists of the elementary truths which reason can infer from natural law, but in their re-published form they are stripped of all super-stition and are invested with an authority which previously they could not claim. The ethics of nature have proved unequal to the pressures of man's fallen state; as matters stand, 'there cannot be any perfect morality expected where there is no belief in the first principles of religion'.² Wherever the Gospel is truly proclaimed we may note 'how it establishes upon immovable foundations universal benevolence, which is the cement of civil society, and makes it an indispensable duty for us to extend our love, duty and charity to all our fellow creatures; how it renews and heightens all the obligations and motives of natural religion and morality and even adds to these such as are stronger, such as divine wisdom only could contrive and divine power enforce with a sanction of rewards and punishments as lasting as our souls'.³

The eighteenth century had little faith in disinterested virtue. Temptations are strong; deterrents must be equally so. Where there is no 'expectation of future rewards and punishments, from any Invisible Being, there cannot . . . be any sufficient bond of morality between man and man'.⁴ The 'self-motive principle' is the only one by which most people can be persuaded to do what they should. The argument required judicious handling. The critics of Christianity—the very men whom the Latitudinarians accused of undermining all morality—claimed that the appeal to interest destroyed ethics: if you are good because it is to your advantage you are not good at all. The usual solution of this delicate problem was to show that God has designed man for true happiness, that this happiness is promoted by morality, and that morality is supported by religion. 'The end of virtue and religion', said Jackson, 'is to illustrate the perfections of God in the happiness of his rational creatures.' The next stage in the argument was set forth by Sykes: 'The great advantage of morality and of its true principle is that it leads men directly to their happiness; nor is it possible for them to attain their end, and be what they are capable of being, but by a steady and uniform pursuit of truth and right.' Clarke indicated the final step when, in discussing the major Christian doctrines, he declared that 'every one of them has a natural tendency and a direct and powerful influence, to reform men's lives and correct their manners. This is the great end and ultimate design of all true religion'.[1] The morality which the Latitudinarians favoured suggests that when good sense confronts human problems in realistic fashion it will use scriptural materials to construct an eminently practical way of life. The ethical teaching of the Latitudinarians was a sincere attempt to check the moral deterioration of the age. It was manifestly useless to harangue the world in obsolete religious language, and the doctrine of moral consequences tried to reach the ordinary man with terms and concepts which he could understand. Prudence alone should convince men that morality is the safest course to follow. The arguments were carefully marshalled and forcefully presented. When self-interest and divine imperative coincide, men will surely turn from their ways! But 'the more they demonstrated, the less people believed'. When justification by works failed to touch men's hearts, it was time to revert to the preaching of justification by faith, and the failure of the eighteenth century at this point was in part reponsible for the Evangelical reaction.[2]

If success be measured by widespread influence, the Latitudinarians could claim to have achieved it to an extraordinary degree. The echoes of their teaching were heard in many a country pulpit,

and all over England the grandeurs of Christianity were reduced
to the modest proportions of prudential ethics. 'The plainness
and simplicity of the Gospel' often degenerated into superficiality,
and the rationalised version of the faith had dangerous affinities
with legalism. It is surprising how many elements in Christianity
the Latitudinarians ignored. Because they consistently minimised
the power of evil, they felt little need to stress salvation. They had
no conception of the Church as a divine society, and consequently
laid little emphasis upon its worship and traditions. The sacraments played a modest and utilitarian role in their scheme, and
mysteries were an embarrassment which was best avoided. They
had little to say about the Incarnation and the Atonement, and
almost nothing about Christ as Mediator. These doctrines represented, of course, precisely the theological complexities which
seemed to the eighteenth century to have obscured the simple
essentials of the Gospel. It is pointless to abuse them for defects
which they considered virtues. And beyond question they had
the virtues of their defects. They noted with pardonable pride that
their works were marked by 'great liberality of sentiment, and
much rational interpretation, supported by sound learning and
good and useful criticism'.[1] Their sermons may strike the
impatient reader as abstract, if logical and reasonable, but they are
often more genuinely religious than he expects. Occasionally they
are soundly theological, and they are steeped in the Bible, even if
their use of it is sometimes perverse. In their relations with other
Christians they achieved a degree of tolerance which contrasts
sharply with the attitude of most of their predecessors and many
of their successors. 'Our inclination', said Archbishop Secker,
'is to live in friendship with all the Protestant Churches. We
assist and protect those on the continent of Europe as well as we
are able. We shew our regard to that of Scotland as often as we
have an opportunity, and we believe the members of it are sensible
that we do. To those who differ from us in this part of the kingdom, we neither attempt nor wish any injury. . . .'[2] Seldom was
the most deeply religious element in Latitudinarianism better

expressed than in one of Sherlock's letters to Philip Doddridge. 'Whatever points of difference there are between us', he said, 'yet I trust that we are united in a hearty zeal for spreading the knowledge of the Gospel. . . . I have lived long enough to know by experience the truth of what we are taught: that there is none other name by which we may be saved, but the name of Christ only. I have seen the true spirit and the comfortable hopes of religion lost in the abundance of speculation, and the vain pretences of setting up natural religion in opposition to revelation: and there will be little hope of a reformation till we are humble enough to be willing to know Christ and him crucified. In this necessary and fundamental point I am fully persuaded we do not disagree: and I earnestly beg of God to bless our united endeavour to make his ways known.'[1] As was natural with men who emphasised moral obligation, many of the Latitudinarians achieved a high measure of integrity in their intellectual life. Warburton is not always an attractive figure but it is impossible not to respect his intentions: 'I shall never willingly advance one falsehood, or conceal or disguise one truth.'[2]

It has been remarked that an age so intensely preoccupied with proving its creed had ceased to have a proper belief in it. This is a charge difficult to dismiss, but in fairness it must be added that the Latitudinarians were convinced that those who no longer respected their faith would soon cease to accept it. It seemed futile to deplore the mounting unbelief while taking no effective steps to combat it; the leaders of the age must be re-taught the faith, this time in terms they could appreciate. And in the process the Latitudinarians were performing a necessary service to the Church. They were preparing it for the changes which the intellectual environment of the new age demanded, and the value of their contribution must not be obscured by the limitations which they brought to their task.

CHAPTER III

THE AUTHORITY OF REASON
INDEPENDENT OF REVELATION

THROUGHOUT the latter part of the seventeenth century, reason had been steadily enlarging its domain. Mystery had increasingly been banished from belief, and what seemed to be the inherent scandal of Christianity had thus been carefully curtailed. In many quarters difficult doctrines were now discreetly ignored. Much had been conceded to the spirit of the new age; could not the lingering vestiges of superstition be swept away? Many felt that further changes were overdue; the Deistic controversy concerned the degree to which the Christian faith should be accommodated to the desires of a rationalistic age.

Few movements in English thought have claimed public attention so successfully or have engaged it for so long. For half a century, Deism kept English religious life in turmoil. 'How the press labours and readers are glutted!' cried John Balguy.[1] Deism appealed to an audience far wider than any which was normally reached by religious controversy. It was as eager to change the outlook of the ordinary reader as to modify the views of theological experts. The Deists wrote in the easy informal style made popular by the coffee houses, and they gave the impression that they were addressing a public alert to current intellectual issues. They transferred religious debate from the study to the drawing room. Peter Annet, one of the later Deists, tried to bring Deism within the reach of multitudes hitherto quite untouched by controversial divinity. A new standard of intelligibility was created; to be effective a pamphlet had to match the simplicity and directness which marked the Deists' writings. By eighteenth-century standards, Thomas Sherlock's *Tryal of the Witnesses of the Resurrection* was a best-seller; fourteen editions attest its popularity. It epitomised most of the virtues and defects of eighteenth-century controversial writing: it was clear, simple, rational and plausible. It purported to be the record of a mock trial staged by members of the Inns of Court; and it was as free from theological technicalities as you would expect the religious discussions of intelligent lawyers to be. It was not particularly original and it was not in the least profound. It was undeniably successful.

The challenge of Deism was too serious to be ignored. Not since the Reformation had religious debate been concerned with such fundamental problems. Seldom had the essential truths of Christianity been subjected to such ruthless scrutiny. 'This', wrote Dr William Harris, 'is the greatest controversy of the present age, and which ever was in the Christian world, where the whole revelation is placed at the bar, and after a long and laboured trial cast and condemned.'[1] Bishop Atterbury saw in Deism a threat as 'dreadful' as any which the faith was likely to encounter; truth was assaulted by 'the frequent and daring attempts of infidelity', virtue was exposed to 'the laughter and scorn of profane men'.[2] Atterbury never understated his case; in this instance men of sober judgment confessed that he did not overstate it.

The Deists, of course, protested that their sole purpose was to purify and strengthen Christianity. They merely wished to strip away the accretions of superstition and primitive misconception. They were restoring the faith to its pristine purity. Clearly they can be regarded as Christians only if Christianity is so drastically re-defined that it forfeits all its characteristic as an historic faith. Deism eludes precise definition. Its representatives never constituted a cohesive group. They did not establish anything approaching a school of thought. They represented a common outlook, but they made no attempt to discipline idiosyncrasy or to exclude individual caprice. Dr Samuel Clarke distinguished four types of Deists, but he added that there was 'no such thing as a consistent scheme of Deism'.[1] The Deists advocated a form of natural religion which they regarded as simple in itself and sufficient for every human need. They acknowledged a Supreme Being; they felt no need to define his nature with precision, since his will was embodied in the principles of morality and his laws were engraved on the hearts of men. They believed that the light of nature was sufficient for the solution of all religious and philosophical problems. Why should we complicate thought by appealing to supernatural considerations? Why should we confuse our simple duty by adding positive religious commands?

The Deists were a small group; they could claim to be a very representative one. They were closely related to the rationalism so prevalent in the early years of the eighteenth century. They insisted that they merely amplified the teachings of the foremost theologians of the age. Tindal's favourite stratagem was to advance his views under cover of quotations from Clarke, Sherlock, Tenison, or Wake. The Deists were effusive in their praise of Tillotson. To Collins he was 'the most pious and rational of all priests'; to Tindal he was 'the incomparable Archbishop Tillotson'.[2] And indeed the defenders of Christianity gave the Deists formidable tactical advantages. Bishop Gibson conceded that even revelation stands or falls by the verdict of reason; Tindal promptly retorted that a man who grants so much is radically inconsistent if he still insists on special revelation.[3] The typical churchman of the age declared that his faith was entirely rational. 'There is nothing here repugnant to reason', said a representative apologist; 'God's power, wisdom and goodness, the interest of which the Deists pretend to maintain, being far from receiving the least injury [from the Gospel], shine forth with all their splendour.'[4]

Like most of their contemporaries, the Deists were in conscious reaction against the preceding age. Controversies which had led to persecution and theological debates which had erupted into violence had discredited all claims to exclusive possession of the truth. The real enemies of religion had been the fanatics, not the much-maligned philosophers.[1] Moderate churchmen blamed the Puritans; dogma, said Bishop Sprat, had been discredited by 'the spiritual vices' of over-confident Calvinists.[2] The Deists extended the argument to cover all who appealed to ancient standards. The conviction had been gaining ground that a man ought to take his religion moderately; what could be wiser than to substitute reason and nature for dogmas and creeds? Authority was clearly the issue at stake. The unseemly and inconclusive wrangles about the meaning of Scripture had discredited the Bible as a court of appeal. The vagaries of the sects had taught reasonable men to dismiss as a mark of fanaticism even the most casual reference to the Holy Spirit. The eclipse of royal authority had shown that the king himself was subject to law, and the overthrow of the theory of Divine Right had shattered ancient concepts of authority. Natural religion was disposed to brush aside the whole problem in all its familiar forms; it was indifferent to the authority of the Church or of the Bible or of traditional doctrines of any kind. Here, also, Deism pushed the argument to its extreme conclusion: it was determined to emancipate human reason from any kind of external control. Private judgment was insisting on its rights. Churchmen claimed that an honest mind could not resist the manifest truth of the Gospel;[3] the Deists insisted that for the first time men were really free to decide for themselves.

Because Deism reflected an outlook which recurs in many ages, its lineage was both ancient and varied. For practical purposes, Lord Herbert of Cherbury may be considered its English pioneer. He was an aristocrat, a diplomat, and a man of the world; he was an appropriate forerunner of a movement which was lay rather than clerical and amateur rather than professional. He enunciated five principles which his successors amplified but did not seriously modify. He taught that God exists; that it is our duty to worship him; that the practice of virtue is the true way of honouring him; that men should repent of their sins; and that there will be rewards and punishments after death. Here we have the essentials of Deism. Human reason, unaided by revelation, can grasp the fundamental truths of religion; and human happiness is promoted when these truths are intimately related to the practical duties of life. Since Deism was a temper rather than a creed, its growth was often fostered by men who had little sympathy with its distinctive teachings. Hobbes challenged authorities which were regarded as sacrosanct, and freed religious speculation from the restraints by which it had been bound. The Cambridge Platonists, weary of controversies which were embittered but indecisive and interminable, encouraged the hope that human reason could recognise and appropriate divine truth. They refused to divorce the rational from the spiritual. They admitted no boundaries between theology and philosophy, or between natural and revealed religion. The reason which they exalted was very different in quality from the pedestrian rationalism which satisfied the eighteenth century, but they taught their age to trust the mind of man. Moreover, the new science encouraged a new outlook. An orderly and harmonious universe, ruled by law, provided impressive support for natural religion. The mounting authority of Newtonian physics inspired the hope that all branches of knowledge could be reduced to a few, simple, uniform laws which any educated man could understand and every reasonable person would accept. More decisive still was the influence of John Locke. With vociferous and embarrassing enthusiasm, the Deists insisted that they derived all their principles from him. Locke indignantly repudiated the inferences which they drew from his position. Everybody, of course, appealed to Locke. He certainly differed from the Deists on many crucial points, but he created the atmosphere in which Deism could flourish and established the presuppositions to which its leaders invariably appealed.

The inherent character of the controversy makes it difficult to indicate its course. Late in the seventeenth century, Charles Blount, a young man of good family who took his own life, amplified Herbert's basic position, and showed that natural religion could be used to attack Christianity, not merely to supplement it. Defenders of the faith began to sense a serious danger. When Stillingfleet argued against Deism he treated it as a general spirit of imprecise religious speculation. When Charles Leslie wrote his *Short and Easy Way With the Deists* he took account of many of the arguments which Blount's successors merely amplified. His method is really 'short and easy' only when it is superfluous; the fact that it was necessary showed that confidence had already been shaken. The active stage of the debate opened with John Toland's *Christianity Not Mysterious* (1696). Toland, an Irishman of facile gifts and flexible ideas, passed through most stages of thought from Romanism to pantheism. His most celebrated work owed its fame less to its intrinsic merits than to its remarkable ability to crystallise views already in the ascendant. Toland claimed that he was merely popularising Locke's position, though in interpreting 'reason' as equivalent to what is 'not mysterious' he certainly distorted Locke's meaning. By juggling with words, Toland tried to prove that Christianity had never countenanced anything that the human mind could not completely grasp. Reason, he claimed, was competent to judge anything that revelation was capable of disclosing: the jurisdiction of the one was co-extensive with the scope of the other. His book marked a crucial development in the debate because it clearly reversed the relative authority hitherto assigned to reason and revelation.

The next important stage in the controversy was initiated by Collins' *A Discourse of Free Thinking* (1713). Anthony Collins was a cultivated country gentleman; he was intelligent and widely read, but his social standing was better than his scholarship. He reiterated and amplified reason's right to pronounce on the contents of revelation, but his conspicuous advance on Toland lay in his claim that the human mind need accept no restrictions on its freedom in pursuing moral and religious speculation. Deism appealed to the reason of the ordinary man; Collins saw that it could do so effectively only if each person were free to follow the truth wherever it led him. Eleven years later another work by Collins, *A Discourse of the Grounds and Reasons of the Christian Religion*, inaugurated a further stage in the debate. Collins turned from the question of the relative authority of reason and revelation in order to challenge the foundations on which it was generally assumed that revelation rested. Could prophecy and miracle be trusted? They had generally been regarded as the external buttresses of the truth; they authenticated the claims of the Christian faith. They had been considered above criticism; now they were exposed to vigorous attack. Collins had raised important issues, and the response of the champions of orthodoxy showed that they were quite aware of the seriousness of the assault on their position. Thomas Sherlock, then dean of Chichester and later bishop of London, Edward Chandler, bishop of Lichfield and Coventry, Dr Sykes, Dr Bullock, Dr Whiston, Samuel Chandler and John Leland all rushed into the fray. In reply to his critics, Collins published *The Scheme of Literal Prophecy Considered* (1727). He had opened a field of debate which was to be explored in considerably greater detail before the controversy ended. Discussion had originally been concerned with the nature of religious truth and the way in which it is communicated; now the question of the external evidences of Christianity increasingly monopolised attention.

The gradual decline of Deism had already begun. Thomas Woolston, an erratic and unbalanced fellow of Sidney Sussex College—'of whom charity must hope', said Dr Pearce, 'that his malignity was inflamed by madness'[1]—developed the attack on miracles in a strain so extreme and so abusive that he ran foul of the law in an age not unduly prone to persecution. Thomas Gordon poured forth a stream of pamphlets which embellished the anticlericalism so popular with all the Deists. Thomas Chubb began to issue the popular tracts which carried to the common people the claims of a purely reasonable faith. Dr Thomas Morgan, while contributing little that was new, displayed in full measure the Deist flair for reaching an extensive audience. But before the marks of decline had become apparent, Tindal's *Christianity as Old as the Creation* (1730) effectively epitomised the Deist position as it had hitherto been developed. Tindal had previously participated in a number of controversies, and he had learned that restraint is often more forceful than violence, and that personal abuse forfeits more than it gains. With a sobriety often tinged with sarcasm, he set forth as a unified system the scattered arguments which his predecessors had advanced. Tindal was not a creative thinker, but by judicious arrangement he tried to present Deism as a coherent theory. No other book so faithfully reflected both the strength and the weakness of the Deist position. Its defects—its lack of historical insight, its blindness to the power of evil, its tone of supercilious superiority, its consistent silence about Jesus Christ—form part of its value; a better book would have offered a distorted reflection of Deism as a whole. Few works attracted so much attention; none provoked so many replies. Its crucial position in the controversy warrants a brief summary of its argument.

The nature of God, said Tindal, never changes; and from this he drew the inference that God must always have treated all men in precisely the same way. In particular, he must always have made uniformly accessible to all the knowledge both to recognise and to discharge their duty. Conscience, he assumed, has always been the same, and from the outset, therefore, men have been able to foresee the consequences of their behaviour and act in such a way as to deserve the happiness which they were entitled to enjoy. Like conscience, reason has played its proper role ever since the beginnings of human life. This is according to God's will, and 'the reason of things or the relation they have to each other teaches us our duty in all cases whatsoever'.[1] Here we have the foundation of natural religion: reason illuminates our life, shows us our duty, and instructs us in its performance. By judicious quotation from prominent theologians, Tindal suggested that in essentials his position was indistinguishable from that of the leading spokesmen of the established church. They, too, seemed to

69

imply that natural religion was superior to any alternative form of truth. Tindal merely pressed his point further than others: revelation must be superfluous, since it can neither add to nor detract from what natural religion provides. Both in faith and morals, truth must commend itself to man's reason; if it cannot be demonstrated, it cannot be true. Christianity will be restored to its purity when our reason eliminates from it all that is unworthy of having 'God for its author'. The relative claims of natural and revealed religion can thus be simply stated: 'what reason shows to be worthy of having God for its author must belong to natural religion, and whatever reason tells us is unworthy of having God for its author can never belong to the true revealed religion'.[1]

The wide diffusion of Deistical views is reflected in the attitude of three men whose relation to Deism itself is slightly equivocal. The Earl of Shaftesbury stood somewhat apart from the general course of the debate. He was more interested in ethics than in metaphysics, and he was only incidentally concerned with the issues which absorbed the attention of the Deists. Apparently he was a man of genuinely religious temperament; his works everywhere reflect his belief in a wise, just and merciful God, but his sense of the absurd tempted him to treat in a bantering spirit many subjects which his orthodox contemporaries regarded as topics unsuitable for mirth. His influence (particularly in ethics) is clearly seen in Hutcheson and Butler, but it was not restricted to scholars and philosophers. Gibbon reports that Shaftesbury was one of the favourite authors of his aunt (an estimable but not a learned woman), and John Leland regarded him as one of the most pernicious, because one of the most popular, writers of the early eighteenth century.[2]

Bolingbroke had less influence on the Deistic controversy than might have been anticipated. After the death of Queen Anne, he was, of course, in political eclipse, but he was a man of acknowledged brilliance, with a genuine though superficial interest in philosophy. His sympathies were never in doubt; if he had pressed his views with greater courage he might have achieved considerable influence on the intellectual life of his age. But he held back the publication of most of his works; when they appeared, after his death, the issues with which they were concerned had lost all relevance. Warburton and Leland, unaware of their failure to capture public interest, published ponderous refutations. The most caustic assessment of the situation was provided by Dr Johnson: 'Sir, he was a scoundrel and a coward; a scoundrel for charging a blunderbuss against religion and morality; a coward because he had not resolution to fire it himself, but left half-a-crown to a beggarly Scotchman to draw the trigger after his death.'[1]

Pope's position was even more ambiguous. Many of his couplets give succinct and memorable expression to views which are unadulterated Deism. But Pope was largely indebted to others for the material he used. In his *Essay on Man*, there are numerous lines which are simply a versified form of statements which appear in one of Shaftesbury's works, *The Moralists*. Pope may have borrowed the material directly from Shaftesbury; perhaps he got it from Bolingbroke, who was the poet's mentor and undertook to provide him with a philosophical foundation for his work. Pope was naturally flattered. The glamour of Bolingbroke's reputation, the facility with which he represented cosmopolitan culture, his assurance in handling the simplified philosophical abstractions of the period made him appear the ideal guide, and Pope paid extravagant tribute to the master whose wisdom he versified. But the exact nature of the dependence was questioned at the time, and has been debated ever since.[2] When the *Essay* appeared, Pope (who was a loyal Roman Catholic) was distressed to find his poem denounced as a handbook of Deism. He was proportionately relieved when William Warburton, a rising critic, demonstrated its essential orthodoxy. Pope may well have been surprised to learn that the *Essay* had 'a precision, force, and closeness of connection rarely to be met with in the most formal treatises of philosophy'.[3] Warburton had not initially

71

regarded the poem with such enthusiasm, but he considered it adroit strategy to claim Pope for Christianity.[1] The *Essay* abounds in striking couplets, but in essential structure it is weak. 'Never', said Johnson, 'was penury of knowledge and vulgarity of sentiment so happily disguised.'[2] The poem is divided into four epistles. In the first—the most famous and the most ambitious —Pope undertook to vindicate God's ways by interpreting his universe. He laid bare 'the great chain of being' which binds all creation in one, and in which everything occupies its appointed place. Order and symmetry point to a wise purpose which ordains all things for beneficent ends. 'Nature and Nature's God' teach us wisdom and inculcate a due obedience. We find God everywhere:

He fills, he bounds, connects and equals all.

He has no favourites; this natural religion embraces all, and (though Pope did not see this) such a theodicy makes all revelation superfluous.[3] He did not realise that the natural consequence of the rationalism of the age was pantheism.

All are but parts of one stupendous whole,
Whose body Nature is, and God the soul.

Pope is important partly because he was not original. He responded to the current climate of opinion; he gave the widest possible currency to the prevailing school of thought.

The Deistic controversy was confused. It was often unedifying as well. The issues about which it was concerned were philosophical rather than religious in character, but the implications were usually theological, and the debate united the bitterness usually generated between rival schools of thought and between competing interpretations of faith. The eighteenth century had not entirely outgrown the controversial methods of the past; too many authors were still 'disposed to squabble and fight [their] way through every syllable of a quotation'.[4] Nor did the Deists' tactics make their writings pleasant reading. It is a fair expedient to embarrass your opponents by magnifying their confusion; Collins, with urbane good humour, did it constantly and with considerable effect.¹ It is legitimate to exploit issues which others have already raised. Locke had no sooner demonstrated the reasonableness of Christianity than Toland exaggerated his findings; when high churchmen and low churchmen fell out about the rights of church and state, the Deists turned the conflict to their own advantage; as soon as Whiston raised the question of prophecy, Collins and Tindal deflected the issue into a major attack on the foundations of revelation.² Such opportunism might be irritating but it was not reprehensible.

Unfortunately the Deists stooped to much more questionable methods. The priests, they said, had descended to fraud; apparently they saw no reason why they should be more scrupulous. Yet they were loud in their protestations of superior virtue. They deprecated bitterness—till they fell into it themselves.³ They demanded that their case be heard with all possible gravity, yet ridicule was their favourite weapon of attack. Tindal scarcely troubled to veil the sneer with which he implied that Christianity was much the same as—certainly no better than—the other superstitions which had darkened men's minds.⁴ When Bishop Gibson protested that 'there's no subject, how grave and sublime soever, but may be turned into jest and ridicule',⁵ Tindal retorted that only things inherently absurd can be made to appear so by means of words: Gibson's attitude implied that, given the Deists' approach, everything in religion can be exposed to ridicule—and 'perhaps', said Tindal, 'it may be so with relation to this writer's religion'.⁶ Shaftesbury had already made the point that things above ridicule are untouched by its shafts, but this did not meet the objection of those who disliked the spirit in which serious and sacred subjects were treated. Whiston, whose Arianism had cost him his chair at Cambridge, claimed some of the liberties due to emancipation, but he found the bantering tone of Collins' *Discourse of Free Thinking* intolerable. He had no sympathy with an attempt to make great themes seem 'contemptible and uncertain' by treating them with amused contempt. 'No man has a right to trifle or be knowingly impertinent.' Serious debate was the great need of the hour; this superficial attitude could only yield negative results. Nothing could be achieved if important subjects were approached in this 'vain, loose, trifling and ludicrous manner'.[1] Whiston conceded that ridicule might sway the unthinking masses, but to many it seemed merely a pose designed to imply that those who adopted it were 'the only wits'.[2]

Even more exasperating was the tendency of the Deists to argue by innuendo. They consistently implied more than they were willing to state. Shaftesbury had remarked that to resort to irony was a contemptible expedient: 'it is a mean, impotent and dull sort of wit which leaves sensible people in a doubt and at a loss to understand what one's true mind is'.[3] But Shaftesbury himself did not practise what he preached, and his successors gave greater heed to his example than to his precepts. With mock seriousness Tindal and Collins quietly removed with one hand what they had apparently conceded with the other. In exasperation Clarke declared that 'such men as these are not to be argued with, till they can be persuaded to use *arguments* instead of *drollery*. For *banter* is not capable of being answered by reason.'[4] It was one thing to debate by indirection; it was another to create a belief that the claims of fundamental sincerity were being ignored. An unpleasant atmosphere of duplicity and pretence was early created and was preserved throughout the controversy. Bentley, who brought his critical acumen to bear on Collins' *Discourse of Free Thinking*, attacked the mock reverence with which Collins treated sacred things: 'a fulsome repetition or a blasphemous irony'. Bentley dealt indirectly (though none the less effectively) with Collins' central plea, but he attacked with pulverising severity the details of his argument. He mercilessly exposed the tissue of careless references, inexact quotations, inaccurate translations, misconceptions, and distortions which paraded as classical learning. He showed that Collins had deliberately suppressed evidence, twisted the context of his quotations and treated his material with a carelessness which was either ignorant or unprincipled. Whether Collins was incompetent or malicious, he was certainly guilty of equivocation. Bentley demolished Collins' pretensions to be regarded as a writer of honesty or competence: what happened, then, to the claim that the Deists were the free thinkers of the new age? 'O dullness, if this was done by chance! O knavery, if it was done by design!'[1]

A controversy which encouraged insincerity was not likely to be marked by a serious or resolute quest for the truth. John Balguy claimed that Tindal's arguments were 'often specious and sometimes subtle, but seldom sound': he constantly appealed to vague generalities (e.g., 'the sufficiency of the *light of reason*') but he never bothered to define the crucial terms.[2] Yet combined with incurable superficiality was invincible complacency. Woolston boasted that he had 'cut out such a piece of work for our Boylean Lecturers as shall hold them tug so long as the ministry of the letter and a hireling priesthood shall last'.[3] Woolston might be dismissed as an unbalanced crank, but Tindal was exposed to no such charge, and the words with which he ended his major work suggest that he cannot be accused of excessive modesty.

The bitterness of the controversy is reflected in the kind of charges to which the contestants sometimes stooped. The Deists freely interspersed their more serious arguments with fierce denunciations of priestcraft. Bolingbroke claimed that 'in natural religion the clergy are unnecessary, in revealed they are dangerous'.[4] To Blount 'the covetous, crafty sacerdotal order' was exclusively concerned with 'shearing the sheep'.[5] 'The mischiefs that priests, as priests, perpetrate affect the whole community', said Tindal. Consider the condition to which they have reduced Christendom: 'a perpetual scene of persecution, sedition, tumults, murders, wars, massacres; and, I may add, of pious frauds, religious treachery, and holy forgeries, as well as dispensing with oaths, and all moral duties, for the good of the church'. The great ends of religion have been made subservient to their gain, and 'all, from the meanest person on earth, to the most High God in heaven, are to be employed in this vile drudgery of executing the arbitrary commands of priests'.[1] This is one of the constant and staple ingredients in the Deists' attack on religion. It is sarcastic in Collins, suave in Tindal, hysterically abusive in Woolston,[2] but constant in all of them. In Pope's eyes, anticlerical venom was their distinguishing mark: 'Toland and Tindal, prompt at priests to jeer.'[3] The clergy retaliated in kind. The vaunted plea for free thinking was, they insisted, merely a thin disguise for free living. Whiston spoke darkly of 'plainly vicious and profligate persons that cannot bear the restraints of religion nor its severe threatenings'.[4] Clarke claimed that 'certain vicious and profane men ... only seek, under the pretence and cover of infidelity, to excuse the vices and debaucheries which they are so enslaved to'.[5]

The argument was usually conducted on a more serious and responsible plane. Both sides admitted that the issue of freedom was central to the debate. In their better moments, the Deists advanced a worthy plea for liberty of thought. Free enquiry, they said, has always been the only safeguard against ignorance and superstition; it is still the only way man's inherent dignity can be preserved and the truth finally achieved. So long as men's minds are curbed there can be no progress in religion or ethics. 'To be informed consists in being made to think justly and truly of things: but how should men think justly who do not think freely?' 'By free thinking, then, I mean, the use of the understanding in endeavouring to find out the meaning of any proposition whatsoever, in considering the nature of the evidence for and against it, and in judging of it according to the seeming force or weakness of the argument.'[6] Free enquiry is the only foundation of reasonable belief; it is the only way of defeating error and superstitition, of banishing witchcraft and the fear of demon possession. 'A spirit of enquiry ... is the foundation of all true sense, learning, virtue, religion, as aversion to enquiry is the foundation of ignorance, error, vice and enthusiasm.'[7] This was an argument which (in theory at least) few churchmen were prepared to deny. The authority of Locke had invested toleration with such prestige that persecution had been stripped of the last shreds of respectability. But occasionally a churchman like Bishop Gibson, nettled at the impertinence of the Deists, felt that the civil authorities might reasonably be asked to discountenance error.[1] This was a lapse from tolerance which so shrewd a tactician as Tindal knew how to exploit to the full; the real danger to religion, he insisted, was posed by those who revived the spirit of persecution, not by those who deviated slightly from rigid orthodoxy.[2] But sarcasm and innuendo can do as much injury to the cause of truth as repression, and Dr Chandler, who as a nonconformist was sensitive to the slightest encroachment on toleration, claimed that the Deists' methods harmed the cause of liberty more seriously than their advocacy could possibly promote it.[3] Richard Bentley pointed out that freedom presupposes responsibility, and the Deists usually overlooked this simple fact. They claimed liberty of thought for themselves, but actually everyone else did so too—always within the framework of the postulates which they happened to lay down.[4] The contest was not between those who upheld freedom and those who denied it; it was between men who interpreted its implications in different ways.

All except the most superficial pamphleteers recognised the gravity of the issues which the Deists raised. Nothing less than the authority of the Christian faith was at stake. It would be folly to pretend that the case argued by the adversaries of Christianity was not a searching challenge; 'nor is it of any use', added Sykes, 'to conceal a strength which an adversary knows, and makes his boast in; nor can any cause suffer, that is to be tried by truth, when an objection is set in its full light'.[5] Wisdom demanded that the Deists' strength be acknowledged; it presupposed that their weaknesses should be resolutely exposed. They had made capital out of the perplexities which were latent in the Christian faith, but did not difficulties of equal magnitude lurk in their own position? Their problems were different from those of the Christians; they were not less grave. The Deists had used every resource of ingenuity to expose the weaknesses and inconsistencies of the early Christians; but on their hypothesis could they explain how a company of blundering simpletons had transformed the ancient world?[1] It was recognised, however, that the Deist controversy was as much a crisis within Christianity as an attack upon it from without. Was the church more than a custodian of respectability? Had it a task beyond that of encouraging morality in the lower classes? Mandeville's *Fable of the Bees* had, in effect, denied the relevance of Christian virtue to eighteenth-century life. But if Christianity was no more than a bastion of middle-class respectability it deserved to succumb to the attack of the Deists. Defence presupposed the exposition of truth as the Christians understood it, but it also demanded counter-attack. This in turn would be ineffective unless based on a just appraisal of the elements of strength in the antagonists' position. What, then, were the chief ingredients in the Deists' case?

They asserted, with vehement insistence, that traditional authority was no foundation for the faith of rational men. Belief must justify itself at the bar of reason. In this respect the position of the Deists was extreme but not unique. Everyone conceded the importance of reason; even the most orthodox divines fortified the authority of revelation by an appeal to reason, but Deists were particularly emphatic in enforcing reason's claims. Blount, one of their pioneers, had insisted that reason is supreme: it provides us with the fundamental articles of religion and all who live according to the rules of reason are really Christians. 'What proceeds from common reason we know to be true, but what proceeds from faith we only believe.'[2] It was Locke who inaugurated the new era. As Bolingbroke remarked, Locke 'rendered all he advanced intelligible'.[3] Both Toland and Tindal frankly admitted their indebtedness to Locke; they recapitulated his theory of knowledge and applied it to Christianity. For most eighteenth-century writers, reason is distinguished from logic. It is less sharply defined (since it is not governed by rules); it is more extensively diffused (since man's intuitive insights enable everyone to grasp its implications). Its dictates, like those of logic, were considered certain, infallible, and universal. 'By reason', said Collins, 'I understand that faculty of the mind whereby it perceives the truth, falsehood, probability or improbability of propositions.'[1]

The exercise of reason is the distinctive glory of man. 'Reason is the law and rule of his actions', said Tindal; no mathematical truth is clearer than the conviction that man is essentially a rational agent.[2] If reason and religion are the distinguishing marks of man, they cannot contradict each other at any point.[3] 'Reason then must be its own guide', and it follows that if man's religion is related in any significant way to his nature, that religion must be rational.[4] Reason is the only means which God has given us by which to tell whether there be a God; therefore 'nothing can be requisite to discover true Christianity and to preserve it in its native purity, free from all superstition, but, after strict scrutiny, to admit nothing to belong to it, except what our reason tells us is worthy of having God for its author'.[5] If Christianity is true it must be reasonable, and 'whosoever live by reason are Christians'.[6]

This intimate relation between reason and religion powerfully affected the content of faith. The Deists claimed that anything which could not bear the test of logical scrutiny must be discarded. It is as criminal to reflect on the sufficiency of reason as to challenge the content of belief. 'Are not the dictates of reason the dictates of God himself? Or what can more show the perfection of the law of reason than that God can't dispense with his creatures, or with himself for not observing it?'[7] Tindal volunteered 'six short propositions by which reason demonstrates not only the being and unity of God but the most substantial points of religion, on which the rest depend'.[8] There could be no place for paradox. The inscrutable must be rigidly excluded. Robert South had admitted 'certain things, were they not to be adored as mysteries, ought to be exploded as absurdities'; Tindal claimed that they should be exploded without more ado. This attitude presupposed, of course, that truth is always simple, clear, and immediately intelligible. Religious terms in which there lurked any suggestion of mystery were instantly ruled out of court. Language should not provide shelter for anything incomprehensible. A word like *infinity* 'should stand for an idea which we can as well comprehend as the number *three* or the colour *red*'.[1]

The primacy of reason implied the unquestioned authority of natural religion. No one, indeed, denied the importance of this pattern of belief, but one of the chief subjects of debate was the type of primacy which it could claim. The radicals wished to extend its province; the conservatives tried to restrict it. No one questioned its significance. To the eighteenth-century mind, nature's evidence provided a defence of religion no less important than that afforded by reason's arguments. With varying degrees of enthusiasm, Wollaston and Jenkin and Conybeare all conceded the authority of natural religion. The distinguishing feature of Deism was its elevation to a pre-eminent position of something which everyone else assigned to a subordinate place. What was generally accepted was seldom explicitly defined. Blount regarded the laws of nature as 'God's universal Magna Carta, enacted by the all-wise and Supreme Being from the beginning of the world. . . . We certainly know', he added, that they 'are the eternal decrees and volitions of God.'[2] Tindal, mixing his metaphors in his enthusiasm, declared that 'the light of nature' is 'the voice of God himself'; in a more sober mood he merely described the law of nature as perfect, eternal and unchangeable.[3] Deism is intelligible only in the light of this devotion to natural law. Its religious convictions were the result of the application to this particular field of the principle of natural uniformity. The Deists believed in a God who was the first cause of this ingeniously contrived universe. Nature, they argued, is perfect; so is the religion which is based on it. Tindal exhausted the resources of his vocabulary in praising the attractions of natural religion. Its importance is as great as its inherent beauty. 'True religion can't but be plain, simple and natural, as designed for all mankind, adapted to every capacity, and suited to every condition and circumstance of life.'¹ Any additions to nature would merely detract from its excellence; similarly any attempts to supplement natural religion would be either unnecessary or pernicious. From the very beginning God has provided men with a law to serve as a rule for their actions. This was a part of the original revelation with which he furnished mankind. Since God is perfect, his first and most important gift must also be perfect. This is the religion of nature, which is perfectly adapted to the intelligence with which God has endowed man. So Tindal triumphantly posed the dilemma which he considered insoluble: Christianity must be identical with the religion given at the creation; in so far as it differs from it, it represents a deviation from the perfect pattern promulgated at the very outset. The Gospel itself is simply a re-publication of this clear and simple religion of nature. It may help to strip away the accretions of superstition which have disguised the simple outlines of the faith which God himself designed for men, but it can make no changes nor can it add anything new.² The Deists showed surprising hesitancy about defining with any exactitude this perfect religion which is so readily available to mankind. 'The religion of nature', Tindal assures us, 'consists in observing those things which our reason, by considering the nature of God and man, and the relation we stand in to him and to one another, demonstrates to be our duty'.³ A belief in God, and the practice of those duties which are the inferences we draw from that belief—this is the heart of the matter. The important thing is not what we accept but what we do.⁴ The moral law clearly outweighs all credal systems; and since the conduct dictated by nature and reason has always been perfect, Tindal saw no relation between men's beliefs and their actions. He was sure that the light of nature would emancipate mankind from bigotry, fanaticism and superstition, and in this he expected that all men of sense would concur at once.⁵ This natural religion, compounded of a reasonable faith and manifest duties, had certain specific objectives in view. 'It can't be denied that the end for which

God had implanted this religion in human nature was to make men happy here and hereafter.'¹

The Deists exalted reason and nature; by implication, therefore, they challenged the validity of revelation. Sherlock, in a moment of exasperation, claimed that Deism 'is to believe in a God and to deny all revealed religion',² but this is clearly an exaggeration. The Gospel was not strictly necessary but it might play a useful though subsidiary role. In so far as it corroborated what natural religion taught, its assistance could even be welcomed. The Deists had no doubt that nature and reason were more dependable sources of truth; revelation was both later and less reliable. Jesus taught pure morals and encouraged simple worship of God ('the word of the Lord in his mouth was truth'³) and in so far as he made religion plain, easy, and readily intelligible to all men he could be regarded with respect. It was assumed, of course, that the purpose of revelation was to communicate ideas—'to give to men, especially the common people, just conceptions and right notions of the nature and perfections of God'.⁴ In this respect, revelation was considered as definitely inferior to natural religion. It could neither add to nor detract from what reason provides.⁵ At best it 'could only be a republication or restoration of that religion which is founded on the eternal reason of things'.⁶ So we again reach the dilemma to which Tindal constantly returned: either revelation merely confirms what reason and nature provide (in which case it is superfluous) or it contradicts it (in which case it is pernicious).⁷ Revelation suggested that God worked in irresponsible ways, through violations of his own natural laws; it implied that he had revealed himself primarily to a remote and barbarous tribe, in a very insignificant place and at a very remote time. His chosen method was unabashed favouritism (with nothing to commend his choice). He had deliberately left mankind in at least partial darkness for four thousand years, and even then had done nothing to make the light generally available. Those who believe in revelation accept an irrational theory based on gross favouritism, 'and neglecting what God speaks plainly to the whole world take up what they suppose he had communicated to a few'.[1] And consider the results which follow: a religion based on revelation inspires fears, doubts and scruples, and leaves the divine commands in uncertainty and confusion.[2]

The record of revelation was to be found in the Bible, but when churchmen cited Scripture to prove the reliability of revelation, the Deists demurred. Most of them conceded to the Bible a limited authority. For Toland it was a useful source of information.[3] Collins admitted that it came from God, but he regarded it as one of God's lesser gifts.[4] Whiston claimed that the Deists acknowledged the authority of the Bible, but merely in order to discredit it the more completely.[5] They subordinated the Bible to the witness of reason and the authority of natural religion, and when these views were criticised their attitude to Scripture stiffened. They all agree that the Bible had no clear claim to authority; it must always be interpreted by reason. This is necessary, but very difficult. The material is unreliable. We have only 'the copy of a copy', and, since variant readings abound, errors have manifestly crept in.[6] The New Testament conflicts with the Old: both are full of inconsistencies and absurdities. The sacred writings are the work of primitive and ignorant men; much of their teaching (e.g., on riches) must be repudiated in the light of modern standards. In their more arrogant moments, the Deists insisted that the Gospels were a worthless tissue of forgeries.[7] Woolston found the literal meaning of Scripture so indefensible that he claimed that only a consistently allegorical interpretation could save the Bible from contempt. But to Collins this offered no escape from an acute dilemma: if we accept the Bible as it is, we must interpret it allegorically—a notoriously arbitrary and irrational method; if we admit that in its present condition it is wholly corrupt, we must embark upon a highly speculative restoration of the text.[8] The Deists were trying to evolve a critical approach to the Bible, but they lacked the necessary tools—historical understanding and textual skill. They

83

insisted on treating an ancient literature as a flat and uniform surface and they applied to it the tests which the eighteenth-century outlook suggested. Both Tindal and Collins quoted the great French critic, R. Simon, but they saw only the destructive potentialities latent in his theories.[1] Conyers Middleton, who occupied an ambiguous position on the frontiers between Deism and the Church, groped his way towards a more constructive critical view. He saw that the Christian apologists placed themselves in an untenable position when they tried to defend the historical accuracy of every statement in the Bible; to accept the infallibility of every writer in everything he says puts an intolerable strain on credulity.[2] His *Free Inquiry* took the revolutionary step of setting the Scriptures in the context of secular history and examining them in the light of human experience. But the Deists could see no intermediary ground between a blind acceptance of the Bible and an increasingly strident rejection of it. Criticism took the form of open attacks, delivered in the name of common sense, on the moral probity of Biblical heroes. Moses, Abraham, and David were guilty of faults which (it was assumed) no eighteenth-century gentleman would commit. 'The holier men in the Old Testament are represented, the more cruel they seem to be, as well as more addicted to cursing.'[3] Paul was a scoundrel and a fanatic; Jesus Christ himself was not above reproach. As the century progressed and the controversy floundered in inconclusiveness, the attacks on the Bible became more unrestrained. 'I doubt not', said Annet, 'but undeniably to prove... that the Christian traditions destroy their own authority.'[4]

If the Bible was a record of revelation, prophecy and miracle were its twin supports. To these the defenders of orthodoxy made their appeal; against them, therefore, the Deists directed their attack. Few denied the fact of prophecy; all (except Woolston) challenged its evidential value. Collins urged with particular incisiveness the general Deist position, and Warburton regarded his *Grounds and Reasons* as the most plausible assault ever mounted against Christianity. Collins' strategy was first to prove that the fulfilment of prophecy is the chief guarantee of the truth of the Christian religion, and then to expose the weakness of the appeal to prophecy. Christianity, he said, is founded on Judaism; the New Testament rests upon the Old. Both the apostles and the evangelists appeal to prophecy and find in its fulfilment the strongest argument for accepting the Gospel. But if these grounds of belief should prove delusive, then Christianity would stand exposed as an elaborate cheat. So Collins undertook to show that none of the Old Testament prophecies to which apologists so confidently appealed had been fulfilled in an exact or literal sense. When challenged by his critics Collins merely restated his case in more uncompromising form: the Jews had never really expected a Messiah, and strictly speaking there were no prophecies which could be fulfilled.[1]

The attack on miracle rested on the pristine authority and the inviolable sanctity of natural law. Even the biblical writers had left men 'to learn from the light of Nature or right Reason (which alone is able to reach it) that the power of God and the power of Nature are one and the same, and that all her laws are his eternal decrees'.[2] God cannot contravene the natural order. He would not if he could. 'I take the liberty to conclude *de novo*', said Blount, 'that a miracle against nature or above nature is a mere absurdity.'[3] Ignorance and the circumscribed outlook of primitive people account for most miracle stories. So the Deists first challenged, then denied, the evidential value of miracles. They insinuated that the criticisms which they levelled against the claims of that sham magician, Apollonius of Tyana, applied with equal cogency to the mighty acts recorded in Scripture.[4] They pressed to its extreme limits the naturalistic approach suggested by Spinoza. It was Thomas Woolston who stated in its most vehement form the Deistic case against miracles. At the outset he advanced his views with some degree of caution. 'The literary history of many of the miracles of Jesus, as recorded by the evangelists, does imply absurdities, improbabilities and incredibilities.' As he proceeded he threw aside all restraint. 'If Jesus' miracles, literally taken, will not abide the test of sense and reason, they must be rejected, and Jesus' authority with them.' He considered the story of the healing of the paralytic such a tissue of absurdities 'that a man of the most easy faith, if he at all thinks, can't digest' it. He curtly dismissed the raising of Lazarus as 'a fraud'. His *Sixth Discourse* is devoted entirely to a consideration of the Resurrection, and he swept it aside as 'the most barefaced imposture ever put upon the world'. It was a gross deception, deliberately contrived but ineptly executed.[1] Once Woolston had shown the way, the other Deists followed. Morgan and Chubb also attacked the Resurrection. Annet, who began by claiming that circumstantial evidence could never make so improbable an event seem credible, finally marshalled all his efforts to discredit the entire story.[2] The criticism of the foundations of revelation had become an uncompromising attack on Christianity itself.

The eighteenth century was rationalistic in temper, but its interests were practical rather than theoretical. Though the Deistic controversy sometimes got entangled in abstract debate, it was primarily concerned with man—with human nature and human conduct. The Deists were singularly unaware of the darker mysteries of human experience. They held an optimistic view of man's basic nature. If error and even wickedness seemed rife, this was not due to a defect in man's constitution. Evil could be explained by bad example, by the prevalence of superstition, and above all by the sinister influence of priestcraft. To believe in original sin is immoral and absurd. The necessary change in human life can easily be effected. Education will provide the key; teach the young to associate virtue with happiness and vice with misery and the problem will be solved.[3] Let man, who is a rational being, behave in a manner suitable to his nature, and the turbulence which disrupts society will be completely curbed. Man will then behave as he should.

With the Deists right conduct was a paramount concern. It is a curious paradox that on the one hand they were accused of purveying mere morality, and on the other they were attacked for subverting ethical standards. Eighteenth-century religion was convinced that the relation between belief and conduct was close. Wollaston, who hovered near the frontiers of Deism, claimed that religion is 'nothing else but an obligation to do what ought not to be omitted, and to forbear what ought not to be done'.[1] The Deists pressed this view to its logical conclusion. Samuel Clarke considered that their distinguishing marks were the acknowledgment of a divine providence and an insistence upon discharging all the duties of morality.[2] A legalistic age regarded obedience to the divine laws as the primary element in religion. The foundation of ethics was man's native perception of the difference between right and wrong, and the justification of morality was its power to conserve social values. It inspires conduct which accords with the dictates of reason.[3] The Deists did not deny that religion and ethics are closely related. 'Morality', said Tindal, is 'acting according to the reason of things considered in themselves', religion is 'acting according to the same reason of things considered as the will of God'.[4] But the religion which the Deists so confidently equated with ethics was, of course, natural religion. 'The morality of Holy Scripture is not to be precisely and distinctly understood without an antecedent knowledge of ethics or the Law of Nature.'[5] Revelation sometimes confirms morality. In its native state Christianity was pure ethics, and Jesus was a teacher repeating ancient moral precepts. 'By Christianity', said Morgan, 'I mean that complete system of moral truth and righteousness, justice and charity, which, as the best transcript of the religion of nature, was preached to the world by Christ and the apostles.'[6] But the craftiness of priests had perverted the simple Gospel into a system of supernatural mysteries. There must be a return to the simplicities of natural ethics. 'They, and they alone, have a just regard for morality who consider it as in its own nature most excellent; and mix nothing with it to depreciate it. . . .'[7] The demands of this simple and natural ethic are plain and palatable. We are commanded to promote the common happiness, and this can be achieved by doing what is for our own good. 'Whosoever so regulates his natural appetites as will conduce most to the exercise of his reason, the health of his body, and the pleasures of his senses taken and considered together (since herein his happiness consists) may be certain he can never offend his Maker.'[1]

Right conduct, said the Deists, is more important than correct belief,[2] and they might reasonably have been expected to submit their theories to this test. Yet Tindal insisted that the truth of a system must not be judged by the lives of its adherents,[3] and he made this seemingly inconsistent claim in order to counter the attacks of his opponents. Bishop Gibson warned the people of the diocese of London 'not to regard what is said by men, who, in the general course of their lives, have been vicious and irregular'. He went further and claimed that the Deists had devised an accommodating system of ethics because it did not interfere with their daily lives. 'No wonder they take such pains to reason themselves into infidelity, without which their minds can't be easy in the enjoyment of their vices.' And they try to make their vices appear 'the less infamous by being more fashionable'.[4] The accusation was frequently repeated. Few of the prominent Deists were men of dissolute behaviour, but unquestionably they gave comfort and confidence to many who were. The age witnessed a distinct decline in moral standards, and the collapse was most pronounced in those circles which were most susceptible to Deist influence. This was certainly not the intention of most of the leading Deists. They believed 'there's nothing can atone for want of strictest sincerity, impartial justice, and universal benevolence; and that they are obliged to govern their activity by that eternal law by which God governs his own actions'.[5]

During the first half of the eighteenth century, Deism kept English thought in a furore of excitement. By the end of the century the issues so hotly debated had lost their urgency and seemed both irrelevant and remote. 'Who, born within the last forty years', demanded Burke in 1790, 'has read one work of

Collins, and Toland, and Tindal, and Chubb, and Morgan, and that whole race who called themselves Free thinkers? Who now reads Bolingbroke? Who ever read him through? Ask the booksellers of London what is become of all these lights of the world. In a few years their few successors will go to the family vault of "all the Capulets".'¹ Certain elements of real strength explain the initial success of the Deists; many serious weaknesses account for their complete eclipse. Their greatest virtue was their readiness to examine old problems in a new light. They were prepared to think for themselves, and to search for answers that would be relevant to their own day. In so doing, they were determined to accept only those beliefs which could claim to rest on a foundation sufficient for their support. In the eighteenth century that meant that reason must justify faith, and adequate evidence must warrant belief. As long as the authority of reason was unchallenged, Deism was the working creed of many honest men who were persuaded that nature and reason provided all the truth that men could reasonably ask.

Deism was a self-consciously enlightened and emancipated position. Its adherents were peculiarly exposed to the temptation of complacency. Those who are self-satisfied easily become prosaic. The Deists were always reasonable but often dull. Because they believed that they had found sure grounds on which belief can rest they often fell into the sin of intellectual arrogance. There lurks about their writings an unpleasant air of conscious superiority; with a supercilious condescension they disposed of miracle and prophecy—and, indeed, of the Bible itself. But their self-satisfaction rested on two wholly unwarranted assumptions; they claimed that since nature's laws are clear and unalterable, man's deductions from them must be equally so; and they believed that the exercise of reason can dispel all the mysteries and uncertainties of life. It was at the latter point that Hume's criticism proved so damaging. Man is not a rational creature in the sense that the Deists imagined, and a natural state of enlightenment does not exist. Moreover the Deists were devoid of any sense of historical perspective. They could measure other centuries only by the standards which their own age provided, and their judgments were sometimes flippant, sometimes foolish. They could not understand the Bible, nor use it intelligently in their own work. Their naïve confidence in the superiority of their own times could not conceive that the standards of an earlier period might have been different without ceasing to be valid.[1]

Their weaknesses are sufficiently apparent in the intellectual sphere; they are more serious in the area of religious thought and practice. Their view of God was benign; their estimate of man was optimistic. Evil was an unpleasant enigma; since they could not even estimate its power they preferred to ignore its presence. They were strangely unaware of the dark complexities of man's life or of elements of its agony and bitterness. So superficial an understanding of human experience could neither support religious life nor quicken religious sensibilities. Collins, for example, had no feeling for the religious traditions which he was so eager to destroy, and no awareness that the counterpart of criticism should be some kind of constructive endeavour. Perhaps their gravest weakness was their blindness to the significance of Jesus Christ. They were insensitive to his spiritual appeal and unaware of his transforming influence in human history. They ignored the basic dilemma which their position posed. They insisted that all men can discover the truth so easily—by reason and the light of nature—that revelation is entirely superfluous. But, why, in that case, have so few people appropriated what is so obvious, so accessible, and so desirable? The Deists claimed that a priestly conspiracy was responsible, but the explanation was not convincing. It was Atterbury who, early in the controversy, pointed to one of the serious weaknesses of Deistic thought. It did not really represent a tenable intermediary position between orthodoxy and atheism. Those who rejected so much could hardly retain the bare essentials of the Christian faith, and, having gone so far, they would find that the logical outcome of their arguments would be stark unbelief.[2]

The Authority of Reason Independent of Revelation

The inconclusive character of the Deistic controversy was due to a failure of resources. Each side lacked the means of answering the kind of questions which the other was able to ask. The debate ended in an indecisive impasse, but it had far-reaching results. Deism was always a creed for emancipated minds; it increased the prevailing scepticism, although most of its advocates conceded that Christianity was at least socially useful: it had a salutary influence on the masses. But by increasing indifference among the ruling classes, Deism made it impossible for the Church of England to cope with the needs of the new industrial proletariat. By its effect both on the rich and on the poor, it paved the way for the evangelical revival. Its influence in England rapidly waned, but in France its vogue increased and spread. At many points Voltaire merely disseminated ideas which he borrowed from the Deists. Even in England, its indirect results were both extensive and important. The prevailing patterns of thought were subtly altered. Both sides had relied heavily on reason; but their initial assumptions proved increasingly untenable. The authority of reason was seen to be vulnerable in a way its first proponents had never dreamed. The direction of theological studies was also altered. The relevance of history appeared in a new light, though as yet few had any understanding of its proper uses. Deism, which proved a failure as a constructive force, provided a strong impetus to the critical study of the Scriptures, though in this respect its results were more conspicuous in Germany than in England. Deism also appreciably relaxed the hold which the Church had tried to maintain on the minds of men. In a variety of ways, the methods and conclusions of orthodox apologists were modified. Gibson told his clergy that the best way to counter Deism was to make their religion impervious to attack; and they could do this by teaching, preaching and study. The needs of a new day demanded a new measure of informed intelligence. 'In an age of controversy and enquiry', wrote Dr William Harris, 'when the reason and curiosity of men are so much awakened and exercised, and the foundation of all revealed religion questioned and opposed, it certainly concerns every man to examine the grounds of his religion, and to be a Christian upon principle and not merely by education or wordly interest.'[1] This alert and responsible attitude contributed to the development of a new theological approach. The modern age dates from the eighteenth century. Both method and manner change. Theology becomes less dogmatic in tone, less scholastic in structure, and more spiritual in quality. The change did not take place at once. Rationalism was discredited; it was far from dead. Indeed, even after it had prompted a reaction, Deism lurked in many of the unconscious assumptions which survived to colour the modern mind. Its philosophic authority may have been shaken by Butler and Hume, but it still shapes the unexamined presuppositions which govern men's outlook, and those who make no allowance for its contribution are at a loss to understand the modern mind.

CHAPTER IV

THE RETORT TO REASON—
LAW, BERKELEY, BUTLER

The leaders of early eighteenth-century thought did not question the authority of reason; their controversies concerned its suffici-ency. Everyone conceded the range and power of human intelli-gence. On this point the orthodox and the heretics were agreed; both conceived themselves loyal disciples of John Locke. With increasing confidence the Deists claimed that reason is our only means of discovering what God requires of us. In all religious duties its light is a guide so full, so certain and so sufficient that revelation can add to it nothing that we need to know. And this, they insisted, follows inevitably from the nature of God himself; he gives us the means of attaining the truth, and he extends this privilege equally to all men. Revelation is therefore redundant; the Church is superfluous and its doctrines are the last relics of a system of superstition. The Deists were challenged at every point, but the controversy was largely concerned with matters which left the fundamental issues untouched. On both sides basic questions were ignored because it was assumed that what was obvious could not provoke disagreement. It is the distinguishing merit of William Law, George Berkeley and Joseph Butler that they refused to be distracted by secondary problems. They compelled a complacent age to re-examine its favourite assump-tions.

Law's *The Case of Reason* was a reply to Tindal's *Christianity as Old as the Creation*. Law had already proved his capacity in a variety of fields. *A Serious Call to Devout and Holy Life* had placed him in the select company of those capable of composing a religious classic. His *Letters to the Bishop of Bangor* had established his reputation as a particularly cogent controversialist. He had shown that he could isolate the fundamental issue in a debate, and could refuse to be deflected to minor matters. In his *Remarks upon the Fable of the Bees* he had attacked Mandeville's paradox that 'private vices' are 'public benefits'.[1] He now brought to bear on Tindal the same incisive powers of analysis, the same remorseless exposure of careless and haphazard thought. Law began with an accurate summary of Tindal's position. He pointedly ignored 'the railing accusations and scurrilous language which this author pours out, at all adventures, upon the Christian clergy . . . my intention being only to appeal to the reason of the reader, and to add nothing to it, but the safe, unerring light of divine revelation'.[2]

Tindal had claimed that man's nature is such that he can concede divine authority only to doctrines which his own reason can deduce from the nature of things. Now Tindal had also remarked that 'spiritual pride is the worst kind of pride', and Law had little difficulty in proving that undue reliance on human reason is the most vicious form of pride. The other expressions of man's arrogance are inconsiderable 'when compared with a self-confiding reason, which it cannot fully comprehend; or to submit to any directions from God but such as its own wisdom can prescribe'.[3] This is the sin which makes us akin to fallen spirits; and since it exposes the fundamental problems of man's life it compels us to examine man's nature with scrupulous care. 'This enquiry into the state and condition of man' is 'plainly the true point of this controversy'. There is nothing in human nature which makes revelation either impossible or unnecessary. Man's life is not free from mysteries simply because it is divorced from dependence upon God. The great problems of the moral and spiritual world do not become clearer when we rely upon reason alone; they simply become insoluble.[4] It is thus apparent that Tindal's argument proves the reverse of what he supposed. He had claimed that the sole rule of God's actions must be 'the nature, reason and relations of things and persons', and consequently everything would always be clear and rational. But if God acts 'constantly as the perfections of his own nature made it fit and reasonable for him to act, then there is an utter impossibility of our comprehending the reasonableness and fitness of many of his actions'. God, after all, is God, and we cannot fathom the full mystery of his being. But many others things which Tindal assumed to be obvious are also far from simple. 'No revealed mysteries can more exceed the comprehension of man than the state of human life itself.'¹ We cannot define the relation of soul and body; we cannot describe the origin of life; we cannot explain the problem of evil. These things intimately concern our moral life, and natural religion can supply us with no answers. We accept them by an act of implicit faith, and the man who trusts to reason does the same. Tindal, in fact, has used against revelation a line of argument which is equally destructive of natural religion. Law can enter a plea for reverent agnosticism; Tindal, with his confidence in the sufficiency of reason, dare not do so. And it is precisely because of the 'incomprehensible relation between God and his creatures' that revelation becomes at once inevitable and intelligible. In no other way can we discover things which it is urgently important for us to know.²

The powers of reason are obviously far more circumscribed than we have been led to believe. The further you explore the great realities of moral experience the more obvious these limitations appear. Reason can tell you nothing about the effect of sin on the soul; it cannot break its power; it cannot restore the sinner to fellowship with God. 'And he who rejects the atonement of sins made by the Son of God as needless because he cannot prove it to be necessary is as extravagant as he that should deny that God created him by his only Son because he did not remember it.'³ But, as Law pointed out, you can make an equally cogent case against the sufficiency of reason by considering areas to which Tindal readily appealed. It is unwarranted to assume that our own experience of wisdom and goodness can really tell us much about the same qualities as they exist in God. Tindal, in fact, consistently reversed the due precedence of things. He did not realise that other causes do not determine the will of God: 'we have not found the will of God till we have found a will that has no mover or director or cause of its perfection.'¹ The abstract qualities which Tindal treats as self-sufficient have no existence save as they co-exist with God.

Tindal had fallen into the error of confusing identity and analogy. There is reason in both God and man, as there is also power, but the form they take in man gives us no warrant for prejudging the range they may possess in God. Consequently we cannot judge the sufficiency of the divine purpose; our reason can determine neither the need for revelation nor its nature. We can only accept God's declaration that here we have a disclosure of his mind and will. Yet even here we must observe that there is nothing 'half so mysterious in the Christian revelation, considered in itself, as there is in that invisible providence which all must hold that believe in God'.² If the inherent reasonableness of revelation is not sufficient to authenticate it, what evidence can we ever have that in a particular instance we are confronted with a manifestation of God's will? The answer is simple; Law accepted without question the testimony of prophecy and miracle. But to go beyond the sufficiency of human reason is not to deny it its due and proper place. Law carefully maintained a balanced position, halfway between credulity and intellectual arrogance. The controversy concerned the right use of reason—'not whether reason is to be followed, but when it is best followed? not whether it is to be our guide, but how it may be our safest guide? . . . For Christians pretend to no guide, but under the guidance of their reason; not to assert anything, but because it can't be reasonably denied. They oppose unbelievers, not because they reason, but because they reason ill. They receive revelation, not to suppress the power, but to improve the light of their reason; not to take away their right of judging for themselves, but to secure them from false judgments; and whatever is required to be believed or practised by revelation, is only so far required, as there is reason for it; or because it is more reasonable than the contrary.'[1]

The argument for the sufficiency of reason is ultimately to be settled not by appeal to theory but by reference to experience. And here the weight of fact and the testimony of history both refute Tindal's exaggerated claims. Nor is it easy to be patient with the claim that man's natural capacity was sufficient to afford him full understanding of religious truth, had not priestcraft intervened. With equal logic one might insist that man was capable of perfect health till the medical profession arose. 'For as a perfect state of health . . . seems to be out of all danger from physicians, so had mankind been ever conscious to themselves of a sufficient natural knowledge of what is true or false in religion; . . . what room had there been for frauds or impostures in religion?'[2] Tindal simultaneously defended the complete sufficiency of reason and admitted that no one has ever been wholly guided by it. The way in which reason actually operates must be examined with far greater care. It is unrealistic to treat the mind as a sovereign and separate faculty which dispassionately judges the issues of life. It is plainly affected by 'the mutability of our tempers, the disorders of our passions, the corruptions of our hearts'. It reflects 'all the contradictions and absurdities that are to be found in human life and human opinions'.[3] The distinctions which we commonly draw may be useful but are nevertheless artificial. Human life is a unity; it must be seen as such: '. . . all the disorders of our human nature are precisely the disorders of human reason'.[4] To keep reason and morality in completely separate compartments makes nonsense of our personal life. 'All virtue is nothing else but reason acting in a certain manner, and all vice is nothing else but reason acting in a certain contrary manner. All the difference is in the actions, and none at all in the agents.'[5]

As to the cogency of Law's controversial writing there can be no doubt. He showed that Tindal's view of reason is abstract and doctrinaire, confused in itself and out of touch with the realities of man's ordinary life. So far from being transparently clear, Tindal's treatment was ill-digested and ill-defined. Law also exposed the ways the Deists' complacency had betrayed them into glib but petty assumptions about the nature of our understanding of God. It has been suggested that Law's attack on reason was too successful and that he demolished the foundations of his own case as well.[1] He showed, indeed, that natural religion is subject to precisely the same criticisms as revealed; so far from providing a sure basis for belief, it leads inevitably to atheism. There is consequently no escape from the need for revelation. After the fashion of his day, Law found the vindication of revelation in miracle and prophecy, and he accepted their authority with a somewhat undiscriminating confidence. But he firmly grasped the unity of man's nature, the mystery of man's life, and the magnitude of the categories with which faith must deal. Here lies the true power of his work; over against the easy superficialities of Deism we have the confident affirmations of a man who was deeply aware both of the wonder of life and of the majesty of God.

In one sense George Berkeley rose above the controversies of his age; in another, he was intimately involved in them. He can be studied as a philosopher, standing in the great tradition; he learned much from Descartes and Locke, he transmitted much to Hume and Kant. But his aims and interests are intelligible only in the light of contemporary trends of thought. His dependence upon Locke was intimate, and his principal philosophical doctrines were suggested by problems to which his predecessor either gave confused and unsatisfactory answers or which he left entirely unsolved. Berkeley was convinced that he had cleared up the confusion which lurked in Locke's system; he believed that he had done so by enunciating a new philosophical principle of beautiful clarity and simplicity. At length he had found a means of delivering men from erudite complexities and restoring them to an outlook ruled by sanity and common sense. Yet few philosophers have been so persistently misunderstood. The ordinary man has usually dismissed Berkeley as a deviser of perverse fantasies—indeed, as the very caricature of a philosopher.

This widespread misconception does not alter the fact that Berkeley's purpose was intensely practical. He was deeply disturbed by the forces which apparently governed English intellectual life. He was alarmed at the latitude claimed by the pundits of the coffee-houses: 'in these and the like fashionable places of resort, it is the custom for polite persons to speak freely of all subjects, religious, moral or political'.[1] He viewed with dismay the materialistic implications which he detected in the new science. The self-assured superficiality of much of the prevailing unbelief shocked him. The metaphysics which generally held the field seemed to him a perverse darkening of judgment, in large measure responsible for the decay of faith. Berkeley was not a controversalist in the narrow sense of the word, but all his works were designed to meet existing needs, and some (like *Alciphron*) were avowed essays in religious and moral apologetics. It is neither necessary nor feasible to expound Berkeley's philosophical position in detail, but it is important to note how his chief convictions were related to the intellectual problems of the age.

While still an undergraduate at Trinity College, Dublin, Berkeley enunciated what he considered a new and revolutionary principle. As he remarked in the note-book to which he committed his observations, the meaning of 'existence' had received very unsatisfactory treatment, yet it was crucial to any philosophical system. ''Tis on the discovering of the nature and meaning and import of Existence that I chiefly insist. This puts a wide difference betwixt the sceptics, etc. and me. This I think wholly new.'[2] Initially Berkeley stated his discovery in a very condensed form. 'Existence', he said, 'is *percipi* or *percipere* (or *velle, i.e. agere*)': to exist is either to be perceived or to perceive. The same truth can be expressed in an alternative form: it is 'impossible' that 'anything besides what thinks or is thought should exist'. He believed that he had stumbled on a vital truth; it had, for some inexplicable reason, eluded all previous philosophers. He marvelled that he himself had not discovered it earlier. This was the illuminating insight which would render obsolete many of the problems with which philosophers had traditionally been concerned. It would no longer be enough to ask what we know and how we know it. It would be his task to enunciate the fundamental truth about existence and to elaborate its implications. Essentially this truth convinced him that if existence correponds to his new understanding of it, such existence can be attributed to God (the infinite mind), to other minds, and to ideas. But it can be attributed to nothing else.

Berkeley knew that revolutionary ideas are often unpalatable to the public, so he cleared the ground before exposing the full implications of his new principle. His first published work expounded a new theory of vision. Optics was currently a popular subject. Newton's researches had made the intelligent public aware of the problems inherent in it, and Berkeley offered some valuable contributions to a subject which combined scientific and philosophical aspects. He discussed the way in which we estimate size and distance, and the relation between sight and the sense of touch. What is the correlation between the information which we derive through our eyes and the information which comes to us through our hands? We have learned how to weave into a body of unified knowledge the material provided by the different senses, and we assume that it must all be congruous. But must it? Berkeley was acutely aware of the epistemological problems posed by vision, and at this point he made an interesting suggestion. 'Upon the whole', he wrote, 'I think we may fairly conclude that the proper objects of vision constitute an universal language of the Author of nature, whereby we are instructed how to regulate our actions, in order to attain those things that are necessary to the preservation and wellbeing of our bodies, as also to avoid whatever may be hurtful and destructive of them.'[1] This concept of a 'divine visual language' is related to Berkeley's belief that the perfect correlation between the evidence provided by our various senses is a direct consequence of God's goodness to us. His providential care is the only guarantee that discrepancies in the information collected by our different senses will not arise.

This 'universal language', provided by God, is the guarantee of rationality and consistency in human thought. But there are also other kinds of language, and among ourselves the medium of speech is the means by which we communicate meaning one to another. Language is potentially a marvellous instrument, but if carelessly used it can be the source of endless confusion. We perplex ourselves with problems for which we ourselves are responsible. We wrongly conclude that we face difficulties which outstrip our comprehension. 'Perhaps', said Berkeley, 'we may be too partial to ourselves in placing the fault entirely in our faculties, and not rather in the wrong use we make of them. . . . Upon the whole, I am inclined to think that the greater part, if not all, of those difficulties which have hitherto amused philosophers, and blocked up the way to knowledge, are entirely owing to ourselves. That we have first raised a dust, and then complain, we cannot see.'[1] The first step before us, therefore, is to clear up the confusion which we ourselves have created and in the lamentable results of which we have so meekly acquiesced. But if this is to be done, we must note exactly what language is capable of doing. Locke had suggested that words communicate knowledge, and that a speaker has gained his end if he is understood. Berkeley dismissed this as a very imperfect account of the matter. We ask questions in order to elicit information; we give commands in order to be obeyed. A lecturer may be content if his words convey information, but a politician hopes that they will arouse emotion, create a new attitude, or encourage active support. But the greater the subtlety of which speech is capable, the more serious are the consequences of its misuse. Berkeley admitted that words 'are of excellent use'; but, he added, 'at the same time it must be owned that most parts of knowledge have been strangely perplexed and darkened by the abuse of words, and general ways of speech wherein they are delivered'.[1] At one stage, Berkeley even advocated the abandonment of language, but he dropped this suggestion because it was manifestly impracticable and extreme. It served to underline his contention that words must be used only when they clearly convey meaning. In particular, they must be kept within the context of sense experience.

As we must always remember, Berkeley regarded his fundamental doctrine as a marvellous simplification of basic intellectual problems. He considered it an appeal to immediate experience, and he believed that all philosophical arguments must be brought to the same bar: they must be tested by experience. They must be related to what, on reflection, we find that we really perceive. At this point, his fundamental presuppositions coalesce with his objections to inexact language, and explain his vehement attack on the doctrine of abstract ideas. In this particular concept he detected the source of the confusion responsible for most philosophical difficulties. It is impossible to make much progress in interpreting Berkeley's system without taking account of his criticism of abstract ideas.

Berkeley's treatment of this subject resolves itself into a sustained attack on Locke's position. This is the more remarkable since Berkeley was powerfully influenced by Locke, and in particular was indebted to him for his understanding of 'ideas'. 'It is evident', said Berkeley, 'to anyone who takes a survey of the objects of human knowledge that they are either ideas actually imprinted in the senses, or else such as are perceived by attending to the passions and operations of the mind, or lastly ideas formed, by the help of memory or imagination, either compounding, dividing, or barely representing those originally perceived in the aforesaid ways.'[2] This is clearly an amplification of Locke's view that ideas are the products of sensation or of reflection on sensation. Granted this interpretation, it clearly follows that the things we think about can be analysed into combinations of ideas; these simple ideas are given by the senses, and there can be no objects of thought other than such simple ideas and what the mind makes of them. Berkeley felt that he was being loyal to Locke's fundamental thesis; he also believed that in his doctrine of abstract ideas Locke had been inconsistent with his own basic position. At this point, of course, Locke had notoriously fallen into ambiguities from which no amount of subsequent exegesis has extricated him. Whether Berkeley treated Locke fairly is a complex technical question; that Locke gave him ample pretext is a simple matter of fact.

Berkeley denied that we can frame abstract ideas. In describing the process of abstraction, Locke suggested that it is an 'appearance' in the mind, which, though it differs from any one of the ideas out of which it has been framed, nevertheless resembles a simple idea. Berkeley insisted that the process which Locke described is impossible. You cannot really think of man-in-general. 'The idea of man that I frame to myself must be either of a white, or a black, or a tawny, a straight, or a crooked, a tall, or a low, or a middle-sized man. I cannot by any effort of thought conceive the abstract idea above described.'[1] Locke had cited triangularity as an abstract idea, but can we really entertain 'the general idea of a triangle, which is *neither oblique, nor rectangle, equilateral, equicrural, nor scalenon, but all and none of these at once?*'[2] A moment's introspection is enough to expose so palpable an absurdity: 'what more easy than for anyone to look a little into his own thoughts, and there try whether he has or can attain to have' the kind of ideas which Berkeley has attacked. A little self-examination will convince us, he said, that our minds contain images (which he identified with ideas), and even composite images are particular, not abstract. We cannot have universal ideas of qualities which are not directly associated with what perception affords us. We cannot have the concept of motion without the correlative idea of a body, moving with a certain velocity in a given direction.[3]

Berkeley, however, admitted that generalisation is an indispensable process; without it human knowledge is impossible. He found the key to the matter in the way in which ideas are used, not in the way in which they are framed. 'An idea, which considered in itself is particular, becomes general by being made to represent or stand for all other particular ideas of the same.'[1] It is perhaps more important, for our purposes, to notice the cause of Berkeley's preoccupation with this problem rather than the details of his solution of it. He believed that the popular notion of abstract ideas, reinforced by Locke's careless acquiescence in it, had done incalculable harm. 'The plainest things in the world, those we are most intimately acquainted with, and perfectly know, when they are considered in an abstract way, appear strangely difficult and incomprehensible.'[2] This is the source of the metaphysical confusion which he had so strongly opposed from the first. In his *Philosophical Commentaries* there is a significant entry: 'Mem: to be eternally banishing Metaphysics etc. and recalling men to common sense.' Bad philosophy was responsible for the stupid pride of arrogant rationalism; in combination, the cause and the effect encouraged the atheism and vice which he so deeply deplored.

Berkeley believed that by his theory of the material world he was also striking a mortal blow at unbelief. His idealism was a vital part of his protest against the godless rationalism which was rampant on every hand. It had generally, but wrongly, been assumed that material things exist in their own right. 'It is, indeed, an opinion strangely prevailing amongst men that houses, mountains, rivers, and in a word all sensible objects, have an existence, natural or real, distinct from their being perceived by the understanding.'[3] This error is due, Berkley thought, to the persistent tendency to distinguish between the existence of an object of sense and its perception by the mind. But this cannot be done. Berkeley's point is, of course, related both to his new principle and to his conception of ideas. What we call 'things' are only collections of ideas, and ideas exist only as they are perceived. 'Their *esse* is *percipi*, nor is it possible they should have any existence, out of the minds or thinking things which perceive them.'¹ Material things are simply objects of the mind, and it is a serious error to imagine that they can exist in any other way. Above all, Berkeley was determined to sweep away the misconception that there is a kind of material substratum by which they are supported. It is also evident that the 'ideas, sensations, or the things which we perceive . . . are visibly inactive, there is nothing of power or agency included in them'. But from their nature—their orderly sequence combined with their infinite variety—we conclude that they must be subject to some controlling cause. A cause is active, and hence not another idea; therefore it must be a substance, which means (in Berkeley's terminology) that it must be a spirit—'an incorporeal active substance or spirit'.² Some ideas may have their cause in finite minds, but it is self-evident that many ideas belong to a different category. They are caused by things which are there for me to see, whenever I choose to look at them. They are therefore not 'creatures of my will'. Consequently there must be 'some other will or spirit that produces them', and we are forced to the inescapable conclusion that God is their only source. The order of the existence of ideas is determined by divine agency, and this is what is meant by the 'laws of nature'.

Thus the general character of Berkeley's view of the world is determined by his interpretation of the nature of ideas. It presupposes minds or spirits as the percipient agents who are responsible for the existence of things. Man's spirit has a limited power of causing ideas; consequently the varied character of the universe about us can only be explained by its origin in the mind of God, and its continued existence by the support afforded it by his spirit. All this seemed to Berkeley to be transparently clear. 'Some truths are so near and obvious to the mind, that a man need only open his eyes to see them.'³ He believed that a few minutes' reflection would satisfy any unprejudiced observer that this is obviously the correct explanation of the world. The general reaction, however, was to dismiss Berkeley's views as elaborate nonsense. What sensible man would believe that the horse is in the stable only because he sees it there, or that my desk owes its existence to the fact that I am looking at it? But Berkeley did not advocate so crude a doctrine. He was not denying the existence of real things, but placing them in a context in which alone they can be intelligently interpreted. It is true 'that all the choir of heaven and furniture of earth, in a word all those bodies which compose the mighty frame of the earth, have not any subsistence without a mind, that their *being* (*esse*) is to be perceived or known; that consequently so long as they are not actually perceived by me, or do not exist in my mind or that of any other *created spirit*, they must either have no existence at all, *or else subsist in the mind of some eternal spirit*'.[1] The world is the perpetual manifestation of the spiritual presence of God. From this doctrine it also follows that continuous communication is possible between the Divine spirit and the human spirit, and that the medium through which it takes place is sensible experience.

Berkeley's position is a powerful protest against the suggestion, implicit in so much of early eighteenth-century discussion, that God can only be known as the conclusion of an intricate argument. It is true that Berkeley sometimes used a form of the teleological argument, but he principally relied on a view of God which interpreted him as active power or efficient cause. On the strength of this he sketched the outlines of a theological idealism which is parallel to his philosophical idealism, but he did not develop in detail its full implications.

This was because Berkeley felt immediately involved in the practical religious issues which were uppermost in his day. He was shocked by the doctrinaire rationalism of the Deists, and he believed that in his new principle he had found a retort to their claims as convincing as it was obvious. As we have noticed, he felt that this principle and its implications were so self-evident 'that a man need only open his eyes' in order to see them. His position, he insisted, was perfectly congruous with the common-sense outlook of the ordinary man. But the ordinary man, both then and since, has treated Berkeley's system either as sheer nonsense or as a particularly perverse display of philosophical subtlety. Since Berkeley's philosophical treatises failed to convince the sceptical, he felt obliged to apply their consequences more specifically to contemporary needs. In his *Dialogues between Hylas and Philonous* he gave a slightly more popular exposition of his views, while in *Alciphron* he addressed himself directly to the moral and religious controversies of the day. He examined with some seriousness a theory to which Mandeville's *Fable of the Bees* had given wide currency—that private vices redound to the public advantage. Mandeville complained that he had been misunderstood and misinterpreted, but if Berkeley treated a sally of wit as a solid piece of argument, he did no more than thousands of others had done. Many of his contemporaries were ready enough to appeal to Mandeville's fable in justification of their licentious conduct. As a spokesman for this position complacently remarked, Mandeville's thesis had 'been published and met with due applause in this most wise and happy age of free-thinking, free-speaking and free-acting'.[1] If Berkeley's refutation seems a little heavy-handed, he could plead that he was attacking the interpretation which the public had attached to the book. It was fashionable in certain quarters to believe that 'our philosophers' had 'demonstrated that [order and virtue] have no foundation in nature',[2] and Berkeley was determined to demolish this specious plea. He also attacked Shaftesbury's position. As concerns ethical teaching, the two men had a good deal in common, but Berkeley felt that Shaftesbury's 'moral sense' was ill-defined, and he thought that Shaftesbury had not adequately distinguished morality from aesthetics. Moreover, Berkeley disliked the diffused pantheism which he detected in Shaftesbury's work, and he resented the flippancy with which Shaftesbury treated serious subjects.

Berkeley's opposition was most pointedly directed against the Deists. In a general way he included Mandeville and Shaftesbury in their number—Mandeville because he advocated the overthrow of traditional morality, Shaftesbury because he himself invited possibly unfair but perfectly natural confusion between his views and those of the Deists. But Berkeley dealt more explicitly with the much more radical scepticism represented by Anthony Collins. In such works as *A Discourse of Free Thinking*, Berkeley sensed the negative qualities which made Deism a destructive influence. He also detected a fundamental lack of seriousness which accorded ill with the Deists' professed zeal in the free search for truth. He believed that his basic philosophical position, however elusive it might seem to the casual reader, was particularly relevant to the issues which the current controversy had raised. He felt that the irreligious rationalism of the Deists was buttressed by an implicit appeal to the reality of matter. If he could break the tyranny of materialism, he would shatter the foundations of unbelief. All Berkeley's work was consequently an indirect retort to the rationalism of the Deists, but in *Alciphron* he explicitly criticised their position from the standpoint of his spiritual interpretation of reality.

He was not content, however, to demolish the pretensions of his opponents. There is a positive case for revealed religion as well as for natural religion. In the first four dialogues of *Alciphron*, Berkeley contended that natural religion can be supported by very powerful arguments. In the three final sections of the work he showed that his basic principles could be invoked to defend the doctrines of traditional Christianity. The general trend of his argument reveals the position which commended itself to an acute apologist in the eighteenth century. Berkeley believed that the arguments for the existence of God on which many of his contemporaries relied were little better than atheism. Belief, after all, is more than an exercise in logic. Yet Berkeley allowed full scope to reason and insisted that natural religion should occupy its proper and legitimate place. 'God', he said, 'is the common father of lights: and all knowledge really such, whether natural or revealed, is derived from the same source of light and truth. . . . But this much is generally acknowledged—that there is a natural religion, which may be discovered and proved by the light of reason, to those who are capable of such proofs.'[1] But it points beyond itself, and finds its completion in a wider whole: 'the real belief of natural religion will lead man to approve of revealed'.[1] But Berkeley was satisfied that both a general pattern of belief and a particular system of dogma must rest on an acceptable interpretation of the world and our life in it. His reconciliation of natural and revealed religion differed radically from the popular exercises in Procrustean surgery, in which inconvenient elements were lopped off if they could not be adjusted to a pattern arbitrarily determined in advance.

Berkeley opened his defence of revealed religion by stressing the utility of Christian faith and worship. The truth of revelation is reinforced by 'its tendency to do good, which seems the north star to conduct our judgment in moral matters, and in all things of a practical nature; moral or practical truths being ever connected with universal benefit'.[2] The devotees of the antique virtues can find nothing in the annals of Greece and Rome that cannot be equalled in the records of the Church. 'The Christian religion, considered as a fountain of light and joy and peace; as a source of faith and hope and charity . . . must needs be a principle of happiness and virtue.'[3] It has purified manners and lifted standards of conduct. It has fostered learning and encouraged the arts of civilisation. Berkeley conceded that the structure of the Christian society has provoked the ridicule of its critics. Tithes and church lands have been denounced as abuses; an undue reliance on repression has been detected in the church's defence of its truth; its servants have often been maliciously attacked. But 'the evils accidently occasioned by religion, bear [no] proportion either to the good effects it hath really produced or the evils it hath prevented'.[4]

The test of revelation, however, is not utility but truth, and Berkeley devoted his sixth dialogue to a discussion of the testimonies which support the Christian faith. He did not pretend that the evidences are stronger than they are. Tradition has its values but also its defects. The Scriptures are certainly not free from difficulties, but obscurity is not always a fatal weakness.

Inspiration may be mysterious; this does not make it false. If the form and manner of revelation prompt criticisms, its substance and matter provide satisfactory answers. The content of revelation is not inherently unreasonable; indeed, the real victims of prejudice are often infidels who imagine that it is enough 'to say, things are contrary to common sense, to make us think they are so'.[1] Many of the objections to revelation spring from the fact that by nature we cannot fully know 'the divine economy', and we are reluctant to receive help in the only way open to us. We insist that the wisdom of God should accord with our expectations, and that he should work in ways that we are ready to accept. Prophecies may seem doubtful and obscure, but Berkeley believed that there are convincing answers to the cavils of the critics. Miracles may perplex us, but we often misconstrue their meaning. But above all, Berkeley insisted that we must approach revelation with realistic expectations. We cannot have exact demonstration or scientific proof; 'probable arguments are a sufficient ground of faith'.[2] Faith is really the response which revelation presupposes, and 'provided that in the main and upon the whole men are persuaded, thus saving faith may consist with some degrees of obscurity, scruple, and error'.[3]

Berkeley was satisfied that if we avail ourselves of 'the moral evidence and probable arguments within our reach' we shall find that the traditional faith—'requiring submission in points above our knowledge and for the rest recommending doctrines the most agreeable to our interest and our reason'[4]—provides us with sufficient grounds of confidence. But though Berkeley had thus reached a point at which he might appropriately have stopped, he concluded his work with a specific application of his views on faith and knowledge to the problems of revealed religion. He discussed abstract general ideas and demonstrated, in this context also, their utter impossibility. He considered language in relation to belief, and indicated the proper ends of speech, reason, science and faith. He applied his theory to the great theological terms— to Grace, Original Sin, the Incarnation and the Trinity. The conclusion to which Berkeley moved is that the real need of a cynical age is not less thought on serious questions but better education about them. When the mind, divorced from emotion and actions, plays with abstract issues, the result is general scepticism.[1] But when the life of the enquirer is united and harmonised in seeking the truth and doing it, he will achieve enough insight to meet his needs. He will 'take a comprehensive view of the whole, consider it in all its parts and relations, trace it to its original, examine its principles, effects and tendencies, its proofs internal and external. He will distinguish between the clear points and the obscure, the certain and uncertain, the essential and the circumstantial, between what is genuine and what foreign. He will consider the different sorts of proof that belong to different things —where evidence is to be expected, where probability may suffice, and where it is reasonable to suppose there should be doubts and scruples. He will proportion his pains and exactness to the importance of the enquiry and check that disposition of his mind to conclude all those notions groundless prejudices, with which it was imbued before it knew the reason of them. He will silence his passions and listen to truth. He will endeavour to untie knots as well as tie them, and dwell rather on the light parts than the obscure. He will balance the forces of his understanding with the difficulty of the subject, and, to render his judgment impartial, hear evidence on all sides, and, so far as he is led by authority, choose to follow that of the honest and wisest of men. Now, it is my sincere opinion the Christian religion may well stand the test of such an enquiry.'[2]

Many of the works which magnified the claims of reason or which tried to modify them scarcely survived the controversy which brought them forth. Bishop Berkeley has a permanent place in the history of thought because of his contribution to philosophy. For a somewhat different reason Bishop Butler won for himself a secure position. He was not an original thinker; he did not even fashion a comprehensive philosophy of religion.

But in dealing with the problems of his day he discussed so many issues of perennial interest that he remains one of the most important figures in the intellectual history of his age.

The Analogy of Religion, Natural and Revealed, to the Constitution and Course of Nature did more to silence the Deists than any single work which the long controversy evoked. Yet Butler seldom mentioned either his opponents or their writings. He refused to be lured into debate with particular authors; he resisted the temptation, to which most of his contemporaries succumbed, of wrangling his way, clause by clause, through the text of an opponent's book. He was concerned with fundamental issues, not with their representatives. But Deism determined the problems with which Butler dealt. It is impossible, therefore, to appreciate his work apart from the threat to religion and morality which he detected in Deism. This fact did not limit his scope in dealing with major issues, nor has it circumscribed the subsequent effect of his work.

The *Analogy* owed its influence partly to its mood and atmosphere, partly to its content and quality. It epitomised a whole generation of hitherto indecisive argument. It did not raise new issues nor break fresh ground. Its merit lay in its comprehensive scope. It gathered up the stray ends as well as the central issues of the protracted debate. Moreover, it was admirably arranged. Butler stated his purpose and clearly defined the limitations to which he submitted. He provided a detailed outline, and adhered to it with scrupulous care. At the end he recapitulated what he had said and summarised the conclusions to which he had come. Every element in his case had been carefully examined and duly assessed. He refused to accept any argument which could not stand in its own right; only when a point had satisfied his stringent demands was it assigned to its particular place in his pattern. His caution, he admitted, might seem excessive, 'but to me nothing appears so, which at all comes towards determining a question of such importance . . .'.[1]

A significant feature of the *Analogy* is the accuracy with which it reflects a certain type of mind. Butler never tried to score a point by glossing over a difficulty. He never claimed for his views a cogency greater than he felt they possessed. When he had pursued a train of thought to its conclusion he did not exaggerate the results he had achieved. 'In some few instances', he said of his argument, 'it may amount to a real practical proof; in others not so.'¹ He did not imply that the evidence he had marshalled was stronger than it actually was. He carefully pointed out instances where apparently it did not apply. 'And', he admitted, 'there may be several other exceptions. Observations of this kind cannot be supposed to hold minutely and in every case. It is enough that they hold in general.'² 'Upon the whole' represents the degree of cogency he could attach to one of his most important points.³ He sometimes suggested 'high probability'; he never claimed absolute certainty. He did not pretend that he had easy answers for the enigmas of experience. He did not know why high endeavour often produces negligible results, any more than he could explain the appalling wastefulness of nature. 'The whole end and the whole occasion of mankind's being placed in such a state as the present is not pretended to be accounted for.'⁴ This kind of guarded exposition stands in striking contrast with the Deists' blithe assurance that they possessed the whole truth. But we are here confronted with something more than the innate modesty of a sober mind. Butler kept in proper balance an awareness of man's restricted powers and a keen perception of the wonder and mystery of life. Some people, he remarked, contend that 'veracity and justice [in God] would be nothing but benevolence governed by wisdom'. Butler hesitated to agree. 'Now surely', he said, 'this ought not to be asserted, unless it can be proved; for we should speak with cautious reverence upon such a subject.'⁵ *The Analogy* also reflects the diffidence of a singularly judicious person. Butler knew the laws of evidence, and he kept strictly within them. He realised that what matters in a work of this kind is not the attractiveness of the parts but the cumulative effect of the whole. The reader, said

Butler, 'will observe several things, which will appear to him of very little, if he can think things to be of little importance, which are of any real weight at all, upon such a subject as religion. However, the proper force of the following treatise lies in the whole general analogy considered together.'¹ So he never moved forward without fully consolidating his most recent advance and preparing carefully for the next. It is to this that his argument owes its air of authority and finality.

Butler's achievement has often been misjudged because his purpose has been misconceived. Yet few writers stated their aims so unequivocally as Butler. He did not intend to offer a complete philosophy of religion, or even a reasoned argument for the existence of God. He wrote his book in a certain situation, to meet a specific need, and its character was determined by this fact. 'It is not the purpose of this chapter, nor of this treatise, properly to prove God's perfect moral government over the world, or the truth of religion.'² Since his purpose was primarily defensive, he did not debate what his opponents were prepared to admit. They conceded the existence of God, so Butler could buttress his argument by interjecting the comment, 'an Author of Nature being supposed'.³ He could advance more rapidly when he could assume that 'no one who does not deny all final causes, will deny' his presuppositions.⁴ Butler took advantage of the things which his opponents did not dispute and used them to prove the things which they were unwilling to accept. The *Analogy* was addressed to those who conceded order and regularity in nature but were sceptical about the claims of Christianity. The easiest retort to the Deists might have been a simple denial of the charges they levelled against revealed religion. Butler's reply is much more subtle, and can be summarised as follows: 'If a man says, "I am invincibly persuaded of the truth of proposition A, but I cannot receive proposition B because objections a, b, c are opposed to it; if these were removed my objections would cease"; then, if you can show that a, b, c equally apply to proposition A, his reception of which, he says, is based on invincible evidence, you really do compel such a man to believe not only that B *may* be true, but that it *is* true, unless he be willing to abandon proposition A as well as B.'¹ The Deists invoked the testimony of nature to support their triumphantly assured view of the simple religion of nature. Butler pointed out that if they appealed to nature, they would have to accept its evidence in whole, not in part, and that the results would be a good deal less simple than the certainties to which they had usually laid claim. Actually, as Butler pointed out, we have to be content in daily life with assumptions which are not demonstrable. 'Probable evidence', he said, 'in its very nature, affords but an imperfect kind of information; . . . but to us probability is the very guide of life.'²

The method on which Butler relied is a constant use of analogy. He did not make excessive claims on its behalf: 'it is enough to the present purpose to observe that this general way of arguing is evidently natural, just and conclusive'.³ He did not suggest that it was original. He cited Origen, but much closer to him in time were Archbishop King, Bishop Browne and Bishop Berkeley, and they had all, in various ways, employed this method. Butler, however, applied it with a consistency and with a degree of insight far greater than any of his predecessors. 'If', he said, 'there be an analogy or likeness between that system of things and dispensation of Providence which revelation informs us of, and that system of things and dispensation of Providence, which experience together with reason informs us of, i.e. the known course of nature; this is a presumption, that they have both the same author and cause.'⁴ Butler explained his view of analogy with some care, and then indicated how he intended to apply it. 'The design of the following thesis will be to show, that the several parts principally objected against in this moral and Christian dispensation, including its scheme, its publication, and the proof which God has afforded us of its truth; that the principal parts principally objected against in this whole dispensation are analogous to what is experienced in the course and constitution of Nature, or Providence; that the chief objections themselves which are alleged against the former are no other than what may be alleged with like justness against the latter, where they are found in fact to be inconclusive; and that this answer from analogy is in general unanswerable, and undoubtedly of weight on the side of religion, notwithstanding the objections which may seem to lie against it, and the real ground there may be for difference of opinion, as to the particular degree of weight which is to be laid upon it.'[1]

This rather lengthy quotation, with its careful reservations and its modest claims, provides a good example of Butler's involved style and a full statement of his purpose. It is difficult to summarise the argument of the *Analogy*, because of its condensed character; in a sense it is unjust even to try, because the strength of the work lies in the organic completeness with which the parts are worked into an integrated whole. Nevertheless the attempt must be made if Butler's contribution is to be properly assessed. He began, of course, with the postulate that there is order in the universe and that the world makes sense. Deny this, and reasonable discussion ends. In any case, the Deists were emphatic in asserting precisely this kind of rationality. Butler, therefore, proceeded to spell out its implications. Order points to final causes; these in turn involve God's rule of the universe. And this divine sovereignty is in no way incompatible with human immortality. We know very little about any future life; but if we begin with what nature teaches us about life in this world, Butler was satisfied that we would find evidence for a life hereafter which would serve our essential purposes 'in like manner as a demonstrative proof would'.[2] We know that our present life is subject to what we can only describe as a system of moral justice. Virtue and vice entail their appropriate and inevitable results. Integrity is rewarded, deception is punished. This is rooted in the natural order; it points forward and will find its appropriate consummation in eternal and righteous judgment. 'And thus the whole analogy of Nature, the whole present course of things, most fully shows that there is nothing incredible in the general

116

doctrine of religion, that God will reward and punish men for their actions hereafter.'[1] Moreover, order in the universe implies not only intelligence on the part of its author, but control over what he has made; and when applied to intelligent creatures this means moral government. This moral government is exercised by means of trial and testing. But the examination of our present life clearly indicates that 'our happiness and misery are trusted to our conduct, and made to depend upon it'.[2] It is therefore reasonable to assume that what we now experience is a state of probation, and that it is 'intended for our moral discipline and improvement'. Nature itself imposes a kind of training similar to that which in childhood prepares us for maturity; it is only reasonable to assume that the former process, like the latter, presupposes a suitable completion in an appropriate state of further development.[3] Nor can even the theory of necessity really touch the affirmations of religious faith. Even if it 'were speculatively true, yet, with regard to practice it is as if it were false so far as our experience reaches'.[4] Butler was at some pains to prove that the theory cannot stand; for his evidence he relied principally on the way our life is ordered in this world, and he reached the confident conclusion that 'the analogy of nature shews us, that the opinion of necessity, considered as practical, is false'.[5]

Butler did not claim that his analogical method resolves every doubt. It might give 'a strong credibility to the general doctrine of religion',[6] but it did not silence all objections. He frankly admitted that these still persist, that they are many, and that they are serious. But the same applies to the constitution and the government of the natural world. Many things are wholly beyond our understanding, yet they are not adduced as arguments against the wise ordering of nature. Of course, 'it is not perhaps easy, even for the most reasonable men, always to bear in mind the degree of our ignorance, and make due allowance for it', but it is strange that they should be most prone to forget it when discussing religion.[7] But since we so imperfectly understand the world with which we are immediately familiar, it is no argument against religion to admit that it embraces many mysteries. 'For, upon supposition that God exercises a moral government over the world, analogy does most strongly lead us to conclude, that this moral government must be a scheme or constitution beyond our comprehension.'[1]

Thus far Butler has been concerned with natural religion. It is true that many of his contemporaries must have been taken aback by his proof that neither nature, nor the belief founded upon it, was as free from problems as they had assumed. Butler's argument was intended to show that, given the obscurities which we find in nature, we may reasonably expect to find similar perplexities in religion—in natural as well as in revealed religion. But it was against the latter that contemporary criticism had been principally directed, and to its defence Butler devoted the second part of his work. He conceded that under ideal conditions, Christianity would be superfluous. But iniquity and vice have so far obscured man's native understanding that natural religion is insufficient. Thus Christianity is 'a re-publication, and external institution, of natural or essential religion, adapted to the present circumstances of mankind, and intended to promote natural piety and virtue'.[2] More specifically, it provides essential information which can be obtained in no other way. It had been assumed that miracles provided an irrefutable proof of this system of religious truth and precept as disclosed by revelation, but Butler's contemporaries had challenged the supporting evidence as cogently as the doctrine itself. But we are wholly mistaken, said Butler, in assuming that only miracles are mysterious. We deceive ourselves when we pretend that we understand natural law and so are offended by any infringement of it. The arguments advanced against miracles are inconclusive, and if we examine nature we discover that there are strong and sufficient reasons for accepting them as facts. Since we are incapable of understanding many things within the reach of our unaided powers, it would be unreasonable to look for a revelation which would be free of difficulties. In this respect natural and revealed religion are on the

118

same footing. They are concerned with different questions, but they have the same qualities. It would be presumptuous to expect revealed religion to inaugurate a wholly new method as well as to supplement acknowledged defects. What Christianity provides is 'a dispensation of Providence, which is a scheme or system of things; carried on by the mediation of a divine person, the Messiah, in order to the recovery of the world; yet not revealed to all men, nor proved with the strongest possible evidence to all those to whom it is revealed; but only to such a part of mankind, and with such particular evidences as the wisdom of God thought fit'.[1] Butler concluded with a careful examination of the relevance of the analogy he had used. He was quite aware that some would challenge the applicability of evidence drawn from nature to questions inspired by revelation. He faced the possible objections candidly and one by one; and was satisfied that his system remained unshaken. 'The whole then of religion is throughout credible; nor is there, I think, anything relating to the revealed dispensation of things more different from the experienced constitution and course of nature, than some parts of the constitution of nature are from other parts of it.'[2]

In the course of this extended argument Butler had occasion to deal at some length with a number of problems with which his contemporaries were particularly concerned. He was firmly rooted in the thought of his age, yet at one point after another his approach was subtly different from that which prevailed around him. Every eighteenth-century writer was preoccupied with nature. The dramatic advances of science had laid bare a marvellous system of universal law, and the urge was irresistibly strong to impose on other areas of thought a parallel symmetry. Butler admitted that 'the natural government of the world is carried on by general laws'.[3] He detected in them a reflection of the wisdom and creative power of God. He believed that they found their counterpart in the moral realm, and that here, too, cause produces effect, and the whole is so organised that happiness is the consequence of virtue. The facts of nature, so far from threatening the principles of religion, powerfully confirm their truth, since 'the scheme of Christianity is by no means entirely unlike the scheme of nature'.[1] Nor does this provide merely recondite information. 'The course of nature . . . furnishes us with a real practical proof of the obligations of religion.'[2] But this is only one aspect of a complex truth. As we have already seen, nature abounds in anomalies and perplexities. Though 'we know indeed several of the general laws of matter . . . we know in a manner nothing, by what laws, storms and tempests, earthquakes, famine, pestilence become the instruments of destruction to mankind'.[3] We really know very little about natural law, and almost nothing of its aims and purposes. The evidences of order compel us to believe that we are dealing with 'a scheme or system; not a fixed but a progressive one'. 'But we are greatly ignorant how far things are considered by the Author of Nature under the single notion of means and ends.'[4] Therefore it behoves us, in a mood of chastened humility, frankly to acknowledge the insufficiency of 'the light of nature'.[5]

Butler was drawn into the Deistic controversy by the exaggerated claims which had been advanced on behalf of reason. How serious and how misleading such a distortion could be, Butler made clear to his readers,[6] but he was careful to allow reason its due place and its full rights. 'I express myself with caution', he said, 'lest I should be mistaken to vilify reason; which is indeed the only faculty we have wherewith to judge concerning any thing, even revelation itself.'[7] In language reminiscent of the Cambridge Platonists, he spoke of 'the faculty of reason, which is *the candle of the Lord within us*'.[8] Those who denied it the right to assess revelation misunderstood both the divine gift and the proper human response. 'Reason can, and it ought, to judge, not only of the meaning, but also of the morality and the evidence of revelation.'[9] But Butler carefully delimited the scope of what he had so generously conceded. We must allow for misconceptions begotten of pride: 'we are in no wise judges of many things, of which we are apt to think ourselves very competent ones'.[10]

There are many truths 'which reason does not at all shew us'.[1]
It provides no complete system of knowledge; and in questions
of fact it yields at best probable conclusions. The insufficiency of
reason is due, in Butler's opinion, to the place it holds in the
economy of man's nature. 'Reason alone', as he pointed out in
one of his sermons, 'whatever anyone may wish, is not in reality
a sufficient motive of virtue in such a creature as man; but this
reason, joined with those affections which God has impressed
upon his heart: and when these are allowed scope to exercise
themselves, but under strict government and direction of reason;
then it is we act suitably to our nature and to the circumstances
God has placed us in.'[2] Reason is but one of man's endowments,
and it must not usurp the prerogatives of other faculties. Reason's
scope is further restricted by the fact that in many areas its
authority is co-ordinate with that of experience. If we are to
understand the 'laws of God'—if, that is, natural religion is to be
intelligible to us—we must rely at least as much on what our
daily life teaches us as on what our minds can tell us. In the last
analysis the precedence must be assigned to experience, for 'God
instructs us by experience (for it is not reason but experience
which instructs us)'.[3]

It is clear that in his attitude to reason Butler attached far greater
weight to practical considerations than to theoretical ones. He
had little use for abstract arguments. 'Speculative reason', he
pointed out, 'may be neglected, prejudiced and deceived.'[4]
He insisted on examining things as they are; for this salutary
discipline it is no substitute to speculate about things as they may
be. 'Everything is what it is, and not another thing.' 'The constitution of nature is what it is.' 'Things are what they are, and
the consequences of them are what they will be.' It is folly to
claim 'to act upon reason in opposition to practical principles . . .
and to pretend to apply our reason to subjects, with regard to
which our own short views and even our experience, will shew
us it cannot be depended upon; . . . this is vanity, conceit, and unreasonableness'.[5] At few points does Butler's impatience with

abstract rationalism appear so clearly as in his discussion of the lack of uniformity in the distribution of religious understanding. The Deists had attacked Christianity because the revelation had not been given equally to all men, in all places and at all times. This argument may seem specious, said Butler, but it is very doctrinaire. In no other area would it be accepted as even plausible. Diversity, not uniformity, is the rule of life. 'A system or constitution in its notion implies variety, and so complicated an one as this world, very great variety.'¹

Man's knowledge is very imperfect; obviously he stands in need of help. It is precisely for this reason that he has been supplied with revelation. 'In this darkness, or this light of nature, call it which you please, revelation comes in.'² Actually, the fact that further knowledge has been vouchsafed is the clearest proof that 'the light of nature' is insufficient. Butler, of course, was convinced that revelation is entirely congruous with natural religion; 'there is a great resemblance between the light of nature and of revelation'³ and if any meaning is imputed to Scripture which conflicts with natural religion 'we may most certainly conclude such seeming meaning not to be the real one'.⁴ The relation between the two types of religious knowledge is therefore close, and their testimony, though different in detail, is congruous in aim. Thus Christianity is 'a re-publication and external institution of natural or essential religion'; it provides 'an account of a dispensation of things not discoverable by reason, in consequence of which several distinct precepts are enjoined us'. But 'though natural religion is the foundation and principal part of Christianity, it is not in any sense the whole of it'.⁵ Inevitably there are elements in revelation which cannot readily be reduced to categories transparently intelligible to man's finite understanding. Otherwise there would have been no need for revelation at all. But the mysteries which it harbours do not really distinguish it from natural religion or from nature itself. Since we find perplexities all about us, need we wonder that revealed religion has its share of them? On much of this Butler's position was not perceptibly different from that of many of his contemporaries. Other writers had also insisted that revelation is useful in interpreting natural religion, and that it is necessary to explain the scheme of the universe. His originality lay in his contention that by definition revelation consists of a scheme in which a large number of interrelated parts are knit together. It is indefensible to isolate one of these parts from the rest and to criticise it without reference to all the others.

Butler devoted a good deal of attention to revelation and its meaning, yet it is here that his defects appear most prominently. He appealed to revelation, yet he left unresolved precisely the kind of problem which revelation might be expected to solve. He proved with some cogency that nature suffers from the same defects as revealed religion, but a critic might reasonably complain that the argument should prove more than this; he might claim that revelation ought to clarify the points which nature leaves confused. Butler sometimes implied that revelation does accomplish this, but he left the implications vague. The trouble lay partly in the approach he employed. He proved that the objections to revelation apply in equal measure to natural religion. He realised that this did not constitute positive proof, but he was satisfied with the fact that few of his contemporaries were disposed to dispute the validity of natural religion. Consequently he could afford to ignore the sceptical implications of his argument. Perhaps more serious is the fact that Butler nowhere sufficiently indicated that religious belief is an act of faith, not the conclusion of an argument.

But Butler's merits far outweigh his defects. It is difficult to resist the impact of his deliberate and measured advance. The critic can cavil at specific segments of his case and yet be profoundly impressed with the massive weight of his argument as a whole. Butler had the conspicuous merit of dealing with an important subject in a way more convincing and more satisfying than anything his predecessors had achieved. By any standard the *Analogy* is one of the most important books of the century—

indeed, it remains one of the major works in its field. According to Professor Broad, it is 'perhaps the ablest and fairest argument for theism that exists'.[1] By approaching the problems of his day from the standpoint of empirical rather than of abstract reason, Butler dealt a telling blow to the rationalism which had been so dominant in the early part of the eighteenth century. The overthrow of the Age of Reason can be attributed to Hume's scepticism and to Wesley's appeal from an abstract theory to a living faith, but in preparing the way for these momentous changes Butler played a conspicuous and important role.

CHAPTER V

SCEPTICISM AND ITS CHALLENGE TO AUTHORITY

ONE Sunday morning in July, 1776, James Boswell called on David Hume in Edinburgh. Hume remarked that 'he was just approaching to his end', but he discussed a variety of subjects 'with a tranquillity of mind and a clearness of head which few men possess at any time'. Hume, it was apparent, had no interest in personal survival and no belief in any religious system. 'I left him', records Boswell, 'with impressions which disturbed me for some time.'[1] In his reaction to Hume, Boswell was typical of his generation. Hume challenged the favourite assumptions and the cherished beliefs of his age; in this respect he was an unsettling influence. But his genial temper and his serene outlook made it impossible to dismiss him as a crank. He typified much that was best in the eighteenth century, yet more than any other man he undermined the foundation on which it convictions rested. It had been generally assumed that certainty would reach its apex as reason unfolded the character of knowledge. Hume showed that the nature of reason had been seriously misconstrued: in spite of its confidence, it could lead only to the bleakest scepticism. The rules of conduct, it appeared, were related to principles very different from those by which they had usually been supported. An age which had ventured to challenge revelation had assumed that natural religion was impregnable; Hume reduced it to a tenuous shadow of its former self.

Hume was clearly and consciously indebted to his predecessors. Locke had shown that all our ideas are related to experience. Berkeley had developed, after his own fashion, the empiricism which he had derived from Locke. Berkeley had attacked the distinction between ideas and things; Hume pressed further this process of analysis and repudiated the distinction between ideas and the mind. His drastic restatement of Locke's position showed that, far from leading to the confident rationalism on behalf of which continental thinkers invoked Locke's authority, his essential principles end in scepticism. Hume did not claim that his own method or approach was original. The subtitle of his *Treatise of Human Nature* describes the work as 'an attempt to introduce the experimental method of reasoning into moral subjects'. Here also Locke had shown the way. Moreover, he had seen that the science of mind might point to an inclusive system of thought; in his *Essay Concerning Human Understanding* he had implied that the problems of psychology are essentially the same as those of a theory of knowledge. Hume pressed the matter considerably further. He brought to his task a consistency greater than Locke's and he conceived the problem in a much more comprehensive fashion. He believed that all the sciences—even those which seem but slightly concerned with human nature—have a 'dependence on the knowledge of man'. Everything that is worth examining brings us back at length to this fundamental question. 'In pretending therefore to explain the principles of human nature, we in effect propose a complete system of the sciences, built on a foundation almost entirely new, and the only one on which they can stand with any security.' Beyond experience we cannot hope to go. Observation alone can provide us with our materials, and the general method which has already proved so useful in the study of the universe must now be applied to the study of man. We cannot discover 'ultimate original qualities of human nature'; it is presumptuous to try. There is no sphere of endeavour in which we 'can go beyond experience, or establish any principles which are not founded on that authority'.[1]

In the first few pages of his first major work, Hume has thus indicated his method of approaching philosophical questions. His presuppositions had important implications. Hume claimed that when human knowledge is systematised, it will be seen to possess certain general features, and these common qualities can be attributed to something in human nature. He was convinced that our way of acquiring information leaves its stamp on all we know and sets strict limits to our knowledge. Since we know only what we experience, it follows that metaphysical knowledge is entirely beyond our reach. A great deal of what has passed for philosophy stands revealed as idle speculation; it was inspired by 'rash arrogance', it issued only in 'lofty pretensions' and 'superstitious credulity'.[1] In Hume's treatment of the problem, psychology displaces philosophy. He believed that when we understand how we respond to the world about us, we can both interpret the nature of our knowledge and define its limits.

At the very outset, therefore, Hume has challenged one of the favourite assumptions of his age. It was generally believed that by the exercise of reason man could obtain satisfying answers to ultimate questions. The knowledge thus gained would profoundly affect human life; it would vindicate our freedom, govern our moral conduct, confirm our religious intuitions, and illuminate our final destiny. But Hume was convinced that the importance of reason had been gravely exaggerated. We do not possess the kind of freedom we imagine. Our rational faculties cannot control the passions, and consequently cannot ensure that we will achieve the good life. Reason, said Hume, can neither inspire actions nor prevent them, and is quite incapable of checking impulse or appetite. 'Thus it appears that the principle which opposes our passion cannot be the same with reason, and is only called so in an improper sense. . . . Reason is, and ought only to be the slave of the passions, and can never pretend to any other office than to serve and obey them.'[2] On few subjects, indeed, did Hume write with greater emphasis than on the limited powers of human reason. It can 'reduce the principles, productive of natural phenomena, to a greater simplicity'; it can even 'resolve the many particular effects into a few general causes'. Further than this it cannot go: 'as to the causes of these general causes, we should in vain attempt their discovery, nor shall we ever be able to satisfy ourselves by any popular explication of them'.[1] This was an uncompromising challenge to the cherished tenets of the eighteenth century. 'The most perfect philosophy of the natural kind only staves off our ignorance a little longer: as perhaps the most perfect philosophy of the moral and metaphysical kind serves only to discover larger portions of it. Thus the observation of human blindness and weakness is the result of all philosophy, and meets us at every turn, in spite of our endeavours to elude or avoid it.'[2]

Hume insisted that we are in no position to assume anything concerning eternal truth. Experience is our only source of knowledge; it provides nothing that we can legitimately describe as ultimate reasons, nor can imagination supply the defect. What Hume actually did was to limit the powers of reason by circumscribing the scope of imagination. We can imagine what we can experience, and we can experience only what we can perceive. Perception, therefore, was one of the key concepts in Hume's system of thought. It provided him with his point of departure. In the opening words of Book I of his *Treatise*, he tells us that 'all the perceptions of the human mind resolve themselves into two distinct kinds, which I shall call IMPRESSIONS and IDEAS'.[3] They differ only in the degree of vivacity which they possess. 'The less forcible and lively are commonly denominated *thoughts* or *ideas*. . . . By impressions . . . I mean all our more lively perceptions, when we hear, or see, or feel, or love, or hate, or desire, or will.'[4] We begin, then, with the immediate data of experience and our reflections on them. Our ideas are derived from impressions, but they have a sequence and a pattern of their own. Simple ideas are combined into complex ones. Thus we fashion such concepts as relations, modes, and substances. If we look for their effective cause, we find it in 'the association of ideas'. But why are some ideas linked together, while others are not? The answer is provided by the way in which association operates. Hume believed that he could here detect three principles of connection at work: resemblances, contiguity in space and time, and cause and effect.[1]

This approach worked havoc with many concepts which the Age of Reason had taken on trust. Time and space, belief, the self, necessity and freedom all assumed a very different guise. Hume's infallible test for exposing the meaninglessness of many a philosophic term was to 'enquire from what impression is that supposed idea derived?'[2] He realised that it was easier to demolish than to reconstruct, and he did not minimise the difficulty of his task. He had described human nature and its simpler operations; on this basis, could he explain knowledge and morality? Association governs what Hume called imagination; in knowledge ideas are linked by different relations. Here he believed that his predecessors and even his contemporaries had been content with answers which had no meaning. It had been widely assumed that the prestige which science had acquired was due to the mathematical method which it employed. But Hume did not believe that absolute knowledge was within man's grasp. Even mathematics is suspect, and scientific knowledge itself must be interpreted in a new way. In his *Treatise* Hume examined what he called 'philosophical relations' and proved that they are of more than one kind. With great subtlety he showed that geometry is a less exact science than either arithmetic or algebra, and he placed his finger on the weakness which he detected even in mathematical knowledge. But when he reduced his material to briefer compass and more popular form (in his first *Enquiry*) he was content with 'relations of ideas' and 'matters of fact'. The former yield formal propositions, the latter empirical hypotheses. In each category it is possible to apply stringent tests which will expose the vain pretensions of much that passes for knowledge. 'When we run over our libraries, persuaded of these principles, what havoc must we make? If we take in our hand any volume; of divinity or school metaphysics, for instance; let us ask, *Does it contain any abstract reasoning concerning quantity or number?* No. *Does it contain any experimental reasoning concerning matter of fact and existence?* No. Commit it then to the flames: for it contains nothing but sophistry and illusion.'[1] Mathematics (with reservations) and natural science (in some sense) can be salvaged from the havoc he has wrought, but each with definite limitations. The authority of science, in particular, depends on a proper grasp of the nature of causation.

Hume obviously gave very serious thought to the problem of cause and effect. To many of his contemporaries few beliefs could compete in certainty with the conviction that everything must have a cause. But the idea is not derived from any inherent quality in objects, since reflection proves that we cannot identify anything which serves as the common and causative factor. 'The idea then of causation must be derived from some *relation* among objects',[2] and as an initial step Hume examined contiguity and temporal priority. A cause must have some effective connection with its effect, and it must precede it in point of time. Though useful, these suggestions are insufficient: 'an object may be contiguous or prior to another, without being considered as its cause. There is also *necessary connection* to be taken into consideration; and that relation is of much greater importance than any of the other two above mentioned.'[3] But here again the crucial words required further scrutiny, and Hume found that he had to examine why we conclude that causation is a necessary connection, and especially why particular causes must have specific results. At this point we are guilty of a great deal of loose thinking. 'If we reason *a priori*', said Hume, 'anything may appear able to produce anything. The falling of a pebble may, for aught we know, extinguish the sun or the wish of a man control the planets in their orbits.'[4] Actually it is not intuitively certain that everything must have a cause, and certainly it cannot be demonstrated that this is so. Philosophers like Locke and Clarke had produced ingenious arguments, but their reasoning collapses under scrutiny. Since proof is impossible, Hume concluded that our belief in causation is an inference which we draw from the pattern of our daily life. 'It is therefore by *experience* only that

we can infer the existence of one object from another.'¹ When
one phenomenon regularly follows another, we jump to the conclusion that they are causally related, 'and without further
ceremony we call the one *cause* and the other *effect*'. As far as most
people are concerned, a belief in causation is merely an inference
drawn from customary conjunction. In our own minds habit has
established an association between two objects; we assume that
there is a corresponding objective link between them, but we are
wrong. This '*supposition that the future resembles the past* is not
founded on arguments of any kind, but is derived entirely from
habit, by which we are determined to expect for the future the
same train of objects to which we have been accustomed'.²
'All inferences from experience, therefore, are the effects of
custom, not of reasoning.'³ Hume conceded that as a working
'maxim' philosophers and scientists assume that 'the connection
between all causes and effects' is necessary,⁴ but this is simply the
product of habit. Given Hume's basic principles about impressions and ideas, this conclusion can hardly be disputed. Causal
connection is a misinterpretation of certain psychological facts,
and natural science has built its elaborate structure on a simple
misconception.

Hume, of course, was not content to infer that the future cannot
be deduced from the past. The theories which he criticised presupposed that correct belief is a matter of choice; Hume strongly
disagreed. We associate fire and heat, not because rational
inference persuades us to do so, but because experience leaves us no
alternative. 'Belief', he said, 'is the necessary result of placing the
mind in such circumstances. It is an operation of the soul, when
we are so situated, as unavoidable as to feel the passion of love,
when we receive benefits; or hatred, when we meet with injuries. All these operations are a species of natural instincts, which
no reasoning or process of thought and understanding is able
either to produce or to prevent.'⁵

Here, again, Hume has destroyed a favourite assumption of the
Age of Reason. Certain questions, he insisted, do not admit of

logical or metaphysical answers. We can describe how beliefs arise. We can explain why we hold certain convictions. In applying his principles, Hume dismissed first the independent existence of bodies, then the reality of the self. 'For my part', he wrote, 'when I enter most intimately into what I call *myself*, I always stumble on some particular impression or other, of heat or cold, light or shade, love or hatred, pain or pleasure. I never can catch *myself* without a perception, and never can observe anything but the perception.'[1] Thus, though Hume started with a constructive purpose, he ended with a sceptical result. So far from creating that 'complete system of the sciences' which he anticipated, he had dissolved the fabric of knowledge.[2] Yet he admitted that total scepticism is impossible: 'nature, by an absolute and uncontrollable necessity has determined us to judge as well as to breathe and feel'.[3] We always 'retain a degree of belief, which is sufficient for our purpose either in philosophy or common life'.[4] Indeed, the effort to grasp the subtlety of sceptical arguments diminishes their power; fortunately nature itself breaks their force and 'keeps them from having any considerable influence on the understanding'.[5] 'The chief and most confounding objection' to a thorough-going scepticism is that 'no durable good can ever result from it. . . . All discourse, all action would immediately cease; and all men remain in a total lethargy, till the necessities of nature, unsatisfied, put an end to their miserable existence'.[6] Hume refused to be dogmatic about his doubts, but he believed that a '*mitigated* scepticism or academical philosophy' would inculcate a proper caution and would restrict 'our enquiries to such subjects as are best adapted to the narrow capacity of human understanding'.[7] Though scepticism dissolves the confidence of reason, necessity compels us to use our mental faculties. We cannot reject all abstract reasoning—'we have no choice but between a false reason and none at all'.[8] Nature provides the appropriate remedy, and scepticism is most perfectly revealed in blind submission to our senses and our understanding. The only justification of scepticism is our inclination towards it; and the most agreeable guide in daily life is a philosophy whose errors are merely ridiculous, and whose excesses do not warp our lives.¹

With great boldness Hume has challenged the position hitherto assigned to reason. No less striking is the place he gave to feeling, and his ethical theory provides the clearest example of both tendencies. Moral distinctions, he claimed, cannot be derived from reason. 'Morals excite passions, and produce or prevent actions. Reason of itself is utterly impotent in this particular. The rules of morality, therefore, are not conclusions of our reason.'² A moral sense is responsible for moral distinctions, and the springs of good and evil are to be sought in a natural quality or disposition of human nature. We distinguish virtue from vice by the particular pleasures or pains which each occasions. 'To have the sense of virtue is nothing but to *feel* a satisfaction of a particular kind from the contemplation of a character.'³ There are, of course, two kinds of virtue; the natural ones, like benevolence, tend to produce pleasures directly and immediately, but the artificial virtues, exemplified by justice, mediate satisfaction through the social system which they sustain. This is hedonism of a kind, but not hedonism in the customary sense. The pleasure associated with virtue is excited only by the character and sentiments of a person, and only when these are considered without special regard to our individual advantage. The sense of right and wrong must not be confused with the sense of interest. Thus moral approbation implies sympathy; through sympathy 'the same man is always virtuous or vicious . . . to others who is so to himself', and he can even condemn a quality which is advantageous to himself if it proves displeasing to others.⁴ Morality, moreover, presupposes appropriate motives. 'Virtuous actions', said Hume, 'derive their merit from virtuous motives and are considered as signs of those motives.'⁵ Nor can ethics ignore our passions, since 'all morality depends on the ordinary course of our passions and actions'.⁶

Hume developed his ethical system within limits which were

carefully defined. He accepted a naturalistic interpretation of human existence. Even our rational capacities, he held, do not indicate a destiny which in any way transcends our present life.[1] Similarly moral distinctions are relevant only to man's immediate situation; in themselves they have no permanent significance. There are no eternal laws of justice, since justice depends on utility. Hume has based his morality on a careful study of empirical data. His theory is hedonistic, but not in the conventional sense. Nor is it centred in personal satisfactions in an egotistic way. It allows an important place to utility, but it is not essentially a form of utilitarianism. Hume has attempted to show that morals are pre-rational and find their origin in the emotions. It might appear that he has produced in ethics a relativity as pronounced as his scepticism in philosophy. Actually his theory is a subtle and ingenious attempt to refute the sceptical interpretation of morals.[2]

The early years of the eighteenth century had witnessed a sustained attempt to define the nature of religion in predominantly rationalistic terms. Even though belief might be confirmed by other considerations, it was founded on reason. Here, too, Hume called in question the favourite assumptions of his age. 'As every enquiry which regards religion is of the utmost importance, there are two questions in particular, which challenge our attention, to wit, that concerning its foundation in reason and that concerning its origin in human nature.'[3] Hume has here repeated, with even sharper emphasis, a distinction he had already introduced into the study of morals. On one side he set man's rational powers, on the other, his passions and emotions. He admitted that there are rational grounds for the 'primary principles of genuine theism', but he insisted that men do not really believe in God because arguments have satisfied their minds. Polytheism, not theism, was the original form of faith, and it was inspired by men's 'hopes and fears', not by their 'speculative curiosity'. 'They are guided to that notion, not by reason, of which they are in great measure incapable, but by the adulation and fears of the most vulgar superstition.'¹ But though Hume had found a new approach to an important subject, he pursued it with an inflexibility which accurately reflected the temper of his age.

Hume's attitude to religion was as enigmatic as it was original. He had reacted strongly against the rigid Calvinism in which he had been reared; for the darker doctrines of that creed his hatred was unbounded. In one of his letters he described his search, first for confirmation of his faith, then for an alternative foundation on which to base his outlook on life. As he searched for arguments to support his belief he found that doubts were creeping in, to be dissipated but to return in greater force.² As its permanent legacy his background left him with a dread of superstition only matched by his contempt for 'enthusiasm'. 'Popular religions', he declared, 'are really, in the conception of their more vulgar votaries, a species of daemonism.'³ Hence arises the contrast between the theory of religion and its practice. 'What a noble privilege is it of human reason to attain to the knowledge of the supreme Being; and from the visible works of nature, be enabled to infer so sublime a principle as its supreme Creator. But turn the reverse of the medal. . . . Examine the religious principles which have, in fact, prevailed in the world. You will scarcely be persuaded that they are anything but sick men's dreams.'⁴ The pernicious effect of conventional forms of religion is due to their intrinsically artificial character. The ceremonial worship of ancient paganism had a certain attraction for Hume. By contrast the exclusive claims of theism seemed to him dangerous as well as arrogant. When unity of faith entails uniformity of worship the consequence is persecution, 'that sacred zeal, the most furious and implacable of all human passions'.⁵ When the exaltation of God seems to imply the abasement of man we are left to infer that only 'the monkish virtues of mortification, penance, humility, and passive obedience are acceptable to him'.⁶ In Christianity, in particular, reason has been diverted from its proper function; it has been made the auxiliary of faith, and draws from dogmas their *logical* conclusions. But dogma is not really subject to reason and the attempt to make it so usually issues in the charge of heresy. From this unnatural union of reason and superstition 'modern religion' arose; to this we can attribute its 'fanatical', 'intolerant', 'grotesque' 'scholasticism'.[1] No less serious are the moral consequences of religion. It deflects our attention from the genuine duties of daily life by multiplying frivolous types of merit. It promotes insincerity and thus vitiates all virtue. 'Men dare not avow, even to their own hearts, the doubts which they entertain on such subjects. They make a merit of implicit faith, and disguise to themselves their real infidelity, by the strongest asseverations and most positive bigotry.'[2] Both in private relationships and in public affairs religion has always proved a pernicious and disruptive force. History is too largely the sad story of how priests, encroaching on areas where they do not belong, have established a baneful 'ascendant over mankind'. Ideally religion should be a salutary force in society, but we must consider it as it is.[3] Experience teaches that the person who parades his piety cannot be trusted. 'And when we have to do with a man who makes a great profession of religion and devotion, has this any other effect upon several, who pass for prudent, than to put them on their guard, lest they be cheated and deceived by him?'[4]

Much of this invective can be ascribed to Hume's antipathy to the perversions of true religion. His writings abound in statements which presuppose the validity of religious belief, if indeed they do not inculcate it. In the *Natural History of Religion* Hume claimed that the structure of the natural world so clearly suggests an intelligent creator that no rational enquirer can question 'the primary principles of genuine theism and religion'.[5] 'What truth', exclaims one of the characters in his *Dialogues*, 'so obvious, so certain, as the *being* of a God, which the most ignorant ages have acknowledged, for which the most refined geniuses have striven to produce new proofs and arguments? What truth so important as this, which is the ground of all our hopes, the surest foundation of morality, the finest support of society, and the only principle which ought never to be a moment absent from our thoughts and meditations?'¹ 'The divine Being', said Philo (also a character in the *Dialogues*), 'discovers himself to reason, in the inexplicable contrivance and artifice of nature'; 'a purpose, an intention, a design strikes everywhere the most careless, the most stupid thinker'.²

But the tenor of Hume's writings leaves the nature and extent of these 'primary principles' in considerable doubt. His later revisions of the *Dialogues* are unquestionably more radical in their scepticism than the initial draft. Possibly Hume himself realised that only verbal similarities linked his position with anything that could pass for religious belief. At all events he maintained a politic reserve. The eighteenth century permitted a wide latitude of debate provided certain decent conventions were observed. Implicit in atheism the age detected a dogmatism which was not less reprehensible than superstition merely because it happened to be negative in character. And infidelity was certainly bad form. Hume sometimes chafed at these discreet restraints. He believed that an emancipated society would tolerate an emancipated outlook. 'I see not what bad consequences can follow, in the present age, from the character of an infidel; especially if a man's character be in other respects irreproachable.'³ But on the whole he conformed to the rules of religious discussion. He often gave verbal assent to belief in God, though he left little of its traditional significance untouched. He maintained that to subject religion to the test of reason is the surest way to weaken its authority; he described its claims as resting wholly on revelation, whose customary supports he was at some pains to undermine. His favourite expedient was to revert to the use of dialogue. In his *Enquiry Concerning Human Understanding*, only section XI ('Of a particular Providence and of a future State') is not direct and analytical in form. The most striking example of his method is provided by his *Dialogues Concerning Natural Religion*. With great skill Hume passed the argument from one speaker to the next. The presumed sceptic apparently defends the eternal mystery of God, while the supposed theist introduces arguments which effectually nullify the case for belief. The censorious were thus confounded. Hume introduced with great ingenuity his editorial comments, and at the end could put forth unchallenged his radical conclusions.[1] The method was deliberately adopted, and Hume appreciated the skill with which he applied it. 'On revising [the *Dialogues*]', he wrote to Adam Smith, 'I find nothing can be more cautiously and artfully written.'[2]

Though Hume's exact position is difficult to define, there is no question as to his influence on theology. The general trend of his thought shook the certainties on which men had learned to rely. In certain writings he concentrated on specific problems. Few of his works attracted so much contemporary attention as his essay 'Of Miracles'.[3] His argument begins with the assumption that the 'laws of nature' are established by uniform experience; he concludes that 'miracles' are a violation of these laws, and that the evidence which corroborates a miracle is always inferior to the 'testimony of the senses' which confirms the laws of nature. Curiously enough this argument occurred to Hume when he was writing his *Treatise*, yet it is inconsistent with the fundamental assumptions of that work. Hume had there argued that all events are 'loose and separate'; the analysis by which he proved his position would destroy the meaning which he subsequently assigned both to the laws of nature and to the miracles which infringe them. Though Hume believed that he had developed a 'decisive' argument, its force really lay in the circumstantial evidence with which he supported it. He pointed out that belief in miracles is most prevalent among backward peoples. Miracles themselves minister to surprise and wonder, and when these emotions are fortified by religion they lead to excesses of all kinds. He suggested that miracles are usually impostures. They originate in 'a system of religion', and this is 'full proof of a cheat, and sufficient with all men of sense not only to make them reject the fact, but even reject it without further examination'.[4] The purpose of an appeal to miracles, Hume claimed, is to confirm the particular faith which they purportedly prove; but in religion, what is different is contrary, and the miracles of each religion destroy the credibility of the miracles of all the rest. Hume believed that the evidence which he had marshalled against miracles was overwhelming; in each instance, therefore, the relevant question was not whether a particular miracle had really happened, but why people believed that it had. But throughout this section there is an unavowed assumption which is more significant than the arguments actually adduced: Hume can see no grounds in reason or experience for believing in the kind of God to whom alone the miracles of Scripture could appropriately be ascribed.

Though Hume's attitude to religion is elusive, it embraces a good deal more than vague statements of formal belief and attacks on the excesses of superstition. He speaks of religion as 'nothing but a species of philosophy', and thereby indicates that it can never carry us beyond 'the usual course of experience'. 'No new fact', he said, 'can ever be inferred from the religious hypothesis; no event foreseen or foretold; no reward or punishment expected or dreaded, beyond what is already known by practice and observation.'[1] The consequences of such a view appear in the *Dialogues Concerning Natural Religion*. With scintillating brilliance Hume examined the conventional arguments for the existence of God. He assigned to Demea, the weakest participant in the debate, the view that *a priori* reasoning can establish belief in God, and gave it no quarter. The fundamental issue, as Hume saw it, turns on the argument from design, and he naturally dealt with it in the form in which it was current among his contemporaries. It did not contend that the natural order fulfils an end of absolute and intrinsic worth and so points beyond itself to God. It claimed that there is an analogy between the handiwork of God and the objects which man produces. From the consideration of ourselves and our relation to our handiwork, we can frame an adequate conception of God as a creating and ordering intelligence. In this form, the argument is patently insufficient. We cannot validly infer the nature of the whole from an examination of the parts. In any case, why start with so feeble a principle as the reason of creatures on this particular planet? 'What peculiar privilege has this little agitation of the brain we call thought?'[1] Our experience is too limited to bear the weight which the argument imposes upon it. 'A very small part of this great system, during a very short time, is very imperfectly discovered to us. And do we thence pronounce decisively concerning the origin of the whole?'[2]

In any case, is it true that God's wisdom is manifestly revealed in creation? Hume used as illustration a house so designed that every feature magnifies the discomfort of its occupants. When the whole plan is basically defective it is futile to debate the desirability of improvements in minor details. If we begin with the idea of God we might reconcile the world with it; if we begin with the world we would never reach a belief in God.[3] Nor is scrutiny of the nature of animal life more reassuring. A casual glance may suggest a 'prodigious variety and fecundity'. But closer inspection shatters all easy illusions. Life, wholly devoted to internecine strife, entails misery upon the participants and awakens revulsion in the spectator. 'The whole presents nothing but the idea of a blind nature, impregnated by a great vivifying principle, and pouring forth from her lap, without discernment or parental care, her maimed and abortive children.'[4] Hume agreed that it is possible to argue from man's rational power to an intelligence which is responsible for life and order in the universe, but he hedged about his concession with qualifications. Our knowledge of God exhausts itself in 'one simple, though somewhat ambiguous, at least undefined proposition, *that the cause or causes of order in the universe probably bear some remote analogy to human intelligence*'.[5] Hume immediately added that any inference we may draw concerning intelligence cannot be extended any farther than this. In particular, it 'cannot be transferred . . . to the other moral qualities of the mind'. To this point he recurred repeatedly and with great emphasis. First causes, he claimed, 'have neither goodness nor malice'. The 'original source of all things is entirely indifferent' to all moral considerations; it 'has no more regard to good above ill than to heat above cold, or to drought above moisture, or to light above heavy'. Rectitude and benevolence may be the marks of deity, but we have no right to infer that they resemble the same qualities as they appear in man.[1] Hume thus admitted God's existence as an intellectual proposition, but by reinterpreting this to carry a meaning quite different from that usually attributed to 'God' he withdrew far more than he apparently conceded. He further concluded that religion, thus re-defined, 'affords no inference that affects human life or can be the source of any action or forbearance'.[2] A correct form of belief may save us from superstition and fanaticism; beyond that it cannot go.

The negative character of Hume's views thus becomes clear. He continued to use the vocabulary of belief, but he did so in a sense incompatible with its normal meaning. He denied the reality of miracles; he excluded special revelation; he denied the value of religious duties in this life and the possibility of personal fulfilment in the next; and he left no room for a God who has moral attributes or who can recognise them in us. Religion had become the repudiation of superstition, whether in belief or in practice. Hume's strength as a critic of theological views lay in his detachment; his position as a neutral observer was also his greatest weakness. He restricted his argument to matters which could be discussed on purely intellectual grounds. His gifts fitted him for analysis, and he declined to be drawn into areas where his limitations would have proved a serious handicap.

Hume did not delude himself about the nature and extent of his influence. Shortly before his death he confessed to Adam Smith that he would be hard pressed to devise a plea which would wring from Charon, the boatman of the dead, the concession of a little extra time on earth. 'But I might still urge, "Have a little patience, good Charon; I have been endeavouring to open the eyes of the public. If I live a few years longer, I may have the satisfaction of seeing the downfall of some of the prevailing systems of superstition".' But he was well aware that on such grounds Charon could offer no reprieve.¹ Yet his personal reputation stood high. The breath of calumny had never touched him; 'though I wantonly exposed myself to the rage of both civil and religious factions, they seemed to be disarmed in my behalf of their wonted fury'.² His scepticism had doubtless created enemies, yet Adam Smith boldly declared that 'Upon the whole I have always considered him, both in his lifetime and since his death, as approaching as nearly to the idea of a perfectly wise and virtuous man, as perhaps the nature of human frailty will permit.'³

Though Hume was feared and distrusted in some quarters, the philosophical importance of his work was not fully appreciated by his contemporaries. This was not due to abstruseness of style; no English philosopher has written with comparable lucidity and grace. Possibly the fault lay in a certain reluctance on the part of the public to grapple with theories which were assumed to harbour subversive implications. It can hardly be attributed to the defects of Hume's system: these, though genuine enough, are subtle and elusive. Here Hume was his own most searching critic. He had no desire to disguise his errors; only his 'real unaffected ignorance' prevented him from confessing them more freely than he did.⁴ He recognised the weak points in his empiricism and diagnosed them more searchingly than any of his critics. He admitted that by reducing cognition to single perceptions, while providing no intellectual faculty for recording or modifying their results, he had destroyed real knowledge. 'In short', he wrote in the remarkably candid Appendix to his *Treatise*, 'there are two principles which I cannot render consistent, nor is it in my power to renounce either of them; viz. *that all our distinct perceptions are distinct existences, and that the mind never perceives any real connection among distinct existences.* . . . For my part, I must plead the privilege of a sceptic, and confess that

this difficulty is too hard for my understanding.'¹ Hume saw
that if conscious experience is restricted to isolated states, no
progress can be made in explaining human knowledge. The only
hope of further development must lie in a drastic reinterpretation
of experience. Kant saw this with equal clarity; he also grasped
the nature of the changes which the inherent difficulties of the
empirical theory demanded. Hence Kant's critical philosophy
provides the true sequel to Hume. In a more limited sense Hume
bequeathed his heritage to the English Utilitarians. John Stuart
Mill reproduced much of Hume with little change and with no
appreciable development. For his own day Hume's significance lay
in his defence of nature against reason. His great contribution was
to break up the old ground and prepare for new developments.²

In many quarters the initial response to Hume's works was to
dismiss their author as an atheist. John Hey, the first Hulsean
professor of divinity at Cambridge, dealt with Hume both
courteously and critically, but he largely restricted himself to an
examination of the essay, 'Of Miracles'. Much more serious in
scope and in character was the reply of the Scottish School of
Common Sense. This group of Aberdonian philosophers maintained respectful, even cordial relations with Hume. They
submitted to him their criticisms of his views and carried on a
correspondence which is a model of intelligent good will.³ The
earliest contribution to the controversy was George Campbell's
Dissertation on Miracles. Philosophy, Campbell claimed, rests on a
foundation very different from that of history. The latter is
based on testimony, and Campbell insisted that testimony is
able to yield complete certainty.

The most important member of the School was Thomas
Reid, and his *Inquiry into the Human Mind on the Principles of
Common Sense* was the most notable single statement of the
position common to the group. Reid conceded the validity of
Hume's arguments; he attacked his premises. The source of the
trouble can be traced back to Descartes; from him Locke derived

his theory of ideas, and Berkeley and Hume carried it to its logical conclusion. Reid raised the basic question whether there are sufficient grounds for believing that 'the objects of my knowledge are ideas in my own mind'. The English empiricists had produced no evidence to support their view; they had simply assumed it. They believed that the immediate object of knowledge is something in the mind called ideas; with this initial premise they could not prove that anything exists outside the mind, or even that the mind itself exists. Reid's solution was simple: he denied the existence of ideas. Sensation, he claimed, cannot be divorced from perception, and what we perceive is the external reality. We do not start with separate realities, 'mind' and 'sensation', and then try to bridge the gulf between them. 'One of the related things suggests to us both the correlate and the relation.' 'Every operation of the senses', he claimed, '. . . implies judgment or belief, as well as simple apprehension; . . . and this judgment or belief is not got by comparing ideas, it is included in the very nature of the perception.'¹ Fundamental judgments of this kind are an original gift of nature: 'they make up what is *called the common sense of mankind*; and what is manifestly contrary to any of those first principles is what we call *absurd*'.²

Unfortunately Reid did not define his key terms with adequate precision, and he was inconsistent in his use of some of his basic concepts. Even 'common sense', it is apparent, could bear more meanings than one, and his doctrine of immediate perception was far from clear. He and his associates were too apt to adopt principles without submitting them to critical scrutiny. Because they never developed a comprehensive theory of knowledge, their reply to Hume was necessarily partial and imperfect. They were fully justified, however, in contending that Hume's impressions and ideas, isolated as they are from each other, do not correspond to what is real in experience. It is illegitimate to fragment our life as Hume has done. The elements of experience cannot be completely separated from their context, and they 'imply a reference to mind and to objective order'.

With Hume scepticism was a cogent critique of the power of reason; with Gibbon it was merely a general habit of mind. The historian was not interested in philosophical theory. He was concerned to 'render to posterity a just and perfect delineation of all that may be praised, of all that may be excused, and of all that may be censured'. When he declined to debate his position with Joseph Priestley, he justified his refusal by defining more precisely the exact scope of his enterprise: 'without interposing his own sentiments he had delivered a simple narrative of authentic facts'.[1] But though Gibbon did not pose as a preceptor of his age, he occupied an important place in its intellectual history. He reflected its outlook with extraordinary accuracy; he influenced it as well. In reporting the success of his first volume, he noted with pardonable pride that it lay on every drawing-room table and in every boudoir. The dismay which he spread among the pious was certainly intensified by the popularity which he had won. Young people, said an anxious evangelical, must be protected against 'the scoffs with which the Christian religion . . . is treated; when such cynical infidelity was abroad, parents should take special pains to direct the thoughts of their children to the truth'.[2] This kind of concern was wide-spread; it was a reluctant tribute to Gibbon's influence.

Gibbon's attitude to his material was detached but not impartial. His vivid sense of the grandeur of imperial Rome and of the pathos of its long decline made him a partisan of the ancient ways. He made no secret of his sympathies. 'The primitive church,' he wrote, 'which I have treated with some freedom, was itself at that time an innovation, and *I* was attached to the old pagan establishment.'[3] In his celebrated account of the genesis of his *History*, there is a subtle but unmistakable contrast between the dignity which has vanished from the earth and the uncouth superstition which has usurped its place. 'It was on the fifteenth of October, in the gloom of the evening, as I sat musing on the Capitol, while the bare-foot friars were chanting their litanies in the temple of Jupiter, that I conceived the first thought of my history.'[1] Even superstition seemed less repulsive in its pagan than in its Christian guise. In outlook he was a classical humanist; this determined his attitude to the clergy (whose vices 'are far less dangerous than their virtues') and to theology (which 'may perhaps be superseded by the full light of religion and reason').[2] Gibbon had no doubt that the fall of the empire was inseparably connected with 'the propagation of Christianity'.[3] In apologising for the attention which he had devoted to synods, to councils and to 'spiritual wars', he explained that he had no alternative, 'so deeply did they affect the decline and fall of the empire'.[4] Gibbon's antipathy to Christianity is so obvious that it has often been assumed that he regarded the new faith as the chief, indeed the only, cause of the collapse of Rome. But Gibbon was too cautious and too exact to level an indictment against a whole religion. In describing an age when the Church was still a despised minority, Gibbon noted the relaxation of discipline, the decay of martial spirit, the failure of military ardour which were already exposing the empire to disaster, and which he attributed to the growth of luxury. He described a society which could not help but fall.[5] He candidly admitted that though Christianity fostered fanaticism and intolerance, it also taught the barbarians justice and mercy.[6] When he assessed the causes of the fall of the empire in the west,[7] he began with a sociological fact: 'the decline of Rome was the natural and inevitable effect of immoderate greatness'. In the course of this carefully balanced survey he finally came to the effect on the stability of governments in this world of a faith which offers rewards in the next. The Church, he believed, diverted men and money from necessary duties in the state to useless duties in the cloister. It inculcated doctrines of patience and pusillanimity which sapped the fighting spirit of the army, even while it fostered the religious strife which destroyed the unity of the empire. But Gibbon immediately pointed to the obverse side of the medal. The vices which brought about the fall of Rome would have flourished under a different guise even if Christianity had not appeared, and the Church did much to create new standards and to foster new virtues. So Gibbon finally recorded his judicious and objective verdict: 'if the decline of the Roman empire was hastened by the conversion of Constantine, his victorious religion broke the violence of the fall and mollified the ferocious temper of the conquerors'. This is hardly the militant hostility which was popularly attributed to Gibbon.

The consternation which the *History* caused on its first appearance found its immediate pretext in two famous chapters. Doubtless a diffused resentment, inspired by a diffused scorn, fixed on chapters fifteen and sixteen because this material seemed to provide specific points on which the critic could seize. But, again, it was the underlying spirit which was really responsible for the offence he gave. Actually Gibbon advanced with considerable caution. He proposed to conduct 'a candid but rational enquiry into the progress and establishment of Christianity'.[1] While focusing attention on five secondary causes, he admitted that the victory of the new faith 'was owing to the convincing evidence of the doctrine itself, and the ruling providence of its great Author'. But having conceded this fact, he henceforth ignored it. He treated secondary causes as though they were primary.[2] More serious still, he consistently treated unworldly events in the tone and spirit of this world.[3] The subtle and insinuating temper of the age of reason dwarfed the scale both of virtue and of vice. The stories of early persecutions, he suggested, had been greatly exaggerated. Very few Christians had actually been martyred; their sufferings had been unduly magnified—and so Gibbon ended by disparaging the real martyrs as well as the fictitious ones. The imperial government is depicted as so rational in its approach, and so humane in its attitude, that the reader recalls with a shock that those who suffered actually *died*. The scale of everything is reduced. By careful revision and condensation Gibbon had considerably compressed these chapters; in doing so, he had also blurred the essential outlines of his material. At many points an insidious obscurity hides his real intention. He hints obliquely, he does not argue. A qualifying clause, artfully inserted, revokes a concession which he has seemingly made. A neatly balanced antithesis often leaves the reader where Gibbon intended him to be—on the horns of a dilemma.

The chapters which gave the greatest offence afford perhaps the most striking demonstration of Gibbon's powers of historical exposition. They also brought the development of the Church firmly within the province of scientific study. Gibbon's attitude often sears the spirit of reverence. He certainly intended it to burn away the false and sanctimonious piety which had often enveloped the discussion of sacred things. But the gain in scientific accuracy was achieved at a serious cost in insight and understanding. His lack of comprehension robbed him of the power to give either suitable form or satisfactory content to the chapters which dealt with the Christian era. At no point did his theological presuppositions exact so heavy a penalty as in his delineation of the Byzantine empire. In a thousand years of rich and varied history, he saw only a 'tedious and uniform tale of weakness and misery'. He failed to see that the eastern empire, while transmitting the classical heritage, was fashioning a new and sumptuous civilisation; to him its subjects were people who 'assume[d] and dishonour[ed] the names both of Greeks and Romans', who presented 'a dead uniformity of abject vices which are neither softened by the weaknesses of humanity nor animated by the vigour of memorable crimes'.[1] Here, oddly enough, it was his scepticism which betrayed him. It was too selective in its operation. It was always alert when the virtues of monks were mentioned; it was so quiescent that it accepted without scrutiny a blanket verdict on the vices of Byzantine civilisation.[2] He concentrated on the fortunes of classical culture; he forgot that new cultures were rising to replace the old. His perceptions were blunted by 'the cultural absolutism' to which he succumbed.[3] His restricted sympathies are a serious blemish on his work. His objectivity enabled him to survey with cool detachment many things which had occasioned heated controversy. Even his irony is the mark of one who refuses to be implicated. He stands aside, without commitment. He describes the fluctuations of the contest, but he declines to be entangled in the strife. This is a genuine gain; it is also a serious loss. He did not enter into the hearts of his characters. He could interpret their thoughts; he could not appreciate their emotions or their convictions. But religious issues when seen from outside are scarcely understood at all. This explains the erudite misunderstanding which marks his work. It makes his account of the growth of Christianity gravely defective; it also aggravates the impression, which he undoubtedly created, of an inveterate hostility towards it.

Gibbon's attitude toward religion is not quite so simple as is sometimes suggested. On occasion he could speak of its value with some warmth. 'Whatever you may have been told of my opinions,' he wrote to Hester Gibbon, 'I can assure you with truth that I consider religion as the best guide of youth and the best support of old age; that I firmly believe that there is less real happiness in the business and pleasures of the world than in the life, which you have chosen, of devotion and retirement.'¹ This is clearly less than sincere; a man may not be entirely candid in writing to a pious aunt whom he has offended but from whom he still hopes for a legacy. At times he could refer, with a touch of wistfulness, to convictions he no longer held.² In a conventional way he believed in the existence of God; he could have repeated the first clause of the Creed, though he could probably have gone no further. His outlook was the modified Deism which was the working faith of many intelligent men in the eighteenth century.³ He had little understanding of religious experience and no patience with creeds, confessions, or forms of worship. As a legacy from his youthful conversion to Roman Catholicism and from the protracted debates with Pastor Pavilliard which led to his reconversion he retained a lively interest and a surprising skill in the niceties of theological discussion. This was natural in one who regarded religion as primarily an intellectual phenomenon, a problem which reason ought to solve. He could respond to certain facets of paganism; after all, the ancient faith was a matter of custom and outward form, not of conviction or belief. Though not conventionally religious, Gibbon was by no means indifferent to moral standards. He admired the classical virtues: justice, fortitude, reason and restraint.[1] It was high praise of an emperor to say that 'his application was indefatigable, his temper cool, his understanding vigorous and decisive; and in his practice he observed that rare and salutary moderation, which pursues each virtue, at an equal distance between the opposite vices'.[2]

On certain points his views were sharp and unmistakable. He regarded with grave suspicion any religion which appealed to sacred books or relied on prescribed forms. He believed that a historian had no right 'to dissemble the difficulty of adopting such a theory as may reconcile the interest of religion with that of reason'.[3] His most intense antipathy was reserved for superstition, especially in its clerical, and above all in its monastic, forms. 'His mind', he writes of the emperor Leo the 'Philosopher', 'was tinged with the most puerile superstition; the influence of the clergy and the errors of the people were consecrated by his laws.'[4] In describing the beginnings of the Churches of the West he noted that 'we must supply the silence of antiquity by those legends which avarice or superstition long afterwards dictated to the monks in the lazy gloom of their convents'.[5] But this alone does not explain the peculiar virulence which pervades Gibbon's work. He himself claimed that after his reconversion 'I suspended my religious enquiries, acquiescing with implicit belief in the tenets and mysteries which are adopted by the general consent of Catholics and Protestants'.[6] But he wrote like a man nursing an ancient grievance. Porson, the great classical scholar, justified Gibbon's right to attack Christianity, but deplored his method. 'He often makes, when he cannot readily find, an occasion to insult our religion; which he hates so cordially, that he might seem to revenge some personal injury.'[7] Nor is there any easy explanation for another quality which gave immediate offence. Sainte-Beuve found the right phrase when he spoke of 'une obscenité érudite et froide'.¹ To Porson 'a rage for indecency' pervaded 'the whole work, but especially the last volumes. . . . If the history were anonymous, I should guess that these disgraceful obscenities were written by some debauchee, who having from age, or accident, or excess, survived the practice of lust, still indulged himself in the luxury of speculation.'²

Hume had awaited the publication of the *History* with interest. 'I was a little curious', he wrote to Gibbon, 'to see how you would extricate yourself from the subject of your last two chapters. I think you have observed a very prudent temperament but it was impossible to treat the subject so as not to give grounds of suspicion against you, and you may expect that a clamour will arise.'³ Hume's prediction was speedily fulfilled. The clergy, Gibbon reported, 'seem (I know not why) to shew their teeth'. They regarded the two notorious chapters as a satire on Christianity, 'all the more dangerous because disguised by a veil of moderation and impartiality'. But the replies, when they began to appear, were of a quality which carried little weight. It is true that Dr Watson, of Cambridge, was 'uncommonly genteel' in manner. His 'mode of thinking', Gibbon added, 'bears a liberal and a philosophic cast; his thoughts are expressed with spirit, and that spirit is always tempered by politeness and moderation'. Gibbon respected a courteous opponent, and was content to leave the issue where it stood.⁴ Of Dr Chelsum of Christ Church, he remarked, with that two-edged irony which he handled so deftly, that his performance would win him 'more glory in the next world than in this'. Mr Davis of Balliol 'presumed to attack not the faith but the good faith of the historian', and Gibbon replied with his pulverising *Vindication*. He concentrated his most crushing retort into a classic comment: 'a victory over such antagonists was a sufficient humiliation'.⁵ His critics committed a serious tactical blunder: they attacked him on his most invulnerable side—his accuracy. They uncovered an occasional misprint and a few slips of the pen, but little of serious account. Porson's tribute was the more impressive because of the sarcasm with which he edged it. 'An impartial judge, I think, must allow that Mr Gibbon's History is one of the ablest performances of its kind that has ever appeared. His industry is indefatigable; his accuracy is scrupulous; his reading, which indeed is sometimes ostentatiously displayed, is immense; his attention always awake; his memory retentive; his style emphatic and expressive; his periods harmonious. His reflections are often just and profound; he pleads eloquently for the rights of mankind and the duty of toleration; nor does his humanity ever slumber, unless when women are ravished or the Christians persecuted.'[1] Gibbon was a very difficult opponent. While the exactness of his learning deflected criticism, his sustained sarcasm made his attitude peculiarly exasperating. He was at once too strong to be attacked and too elusive to be refuted. 'Who', asked Paley, 'can refute a sneer?'[2]

Gibbon's attack on Christianity was more offensive in manner than incisive in content. There was little sustained argument but much innuendo. His urbanity thinly disguised his contempt. His favourite instrument was irony. Pascal taught him, he said, 'to manage the weapon of grave and temperate irony, even on subjects of ecclesiastical solemnity'.[3] The cool detachment of his sceptical mind makes the claims of the Church, the pattern of its life, the forms of its worship all seem slightly absurd. Synods were established because they were 'so well suited to private ambition and public interest'; the clergy are 'a celebrated order of men which has furnished the most important, though not always the most edifying, subjects for modern history'. In the case of Cyril of Alexandria 'the title of *saint* is a mark that his opinions and his party have finally prevailed'.[4] Even more insidious is the sarcasm which glides through his footnotes. There is a sterilising quality in Gibbon's irony; enthusiasm, loyalty, devotion, reverence are cauterised by his acid comments. Gibbon's famous account of worship in the ancient world is an excellent example of this method. His neatly balanced judgment leaves the impression that all religions were absurd; but he is talking about worship not faith, and he ends by admitting the social benefits it produces. 'The various modes of worship which prevailed in the Roman world were considered by the people as equally true; by the philosopher as equally false; by the magistrates as equally useful. And thus toleration produced not only mutual indulgence, but even religious concord.'¹

Gibbon unquestionably influenced his age; he is even more important because of the faithfulness with which he reflected its outlook. His pages mirror the eighteenth century more accurately than they do the long period which saw the emergence of a civilisation which he regarded with distaste. His self-satisfaction, bordering on complacency, was characteristic of his times. 'I must applaud the felicity of my fate', he wrote, 'which has cast my birth in an age of science and philosophy, in a free and civilised country, in a family of honourable rank, and decently endowed with the gifts of fortune.'² He believed that a scepticism similar to his own was widely prevalent. The clergy might object to Conyers Middleton's views on miracles, but the public at large made no complaint. 'In modern times, a latent, and even involuntary scepticism adheres to the most pious dispositions. Their admission of supernatural truths is much less an active consent than a cold and passive acquiescence. Accustomed long since to observe and to respect the invariable order of Nature, our reason, or at least our imagination is not sufficiently prepared to sustain the visible action of the Deity.'³ When his *History* aroused a storm of protest, he confessed that he had not believed 'that the majority of English readers were so fondly attached even to the name and shadow of Christianity', yet he consoled himself with the reflection that in an enlightened age the 'devotion of the vulgar' lags behind the emancipation of the wise.⁴ Even his literary style reflects the standards of his age. Balance and form, propriety and decorum are more important than conviction. Gibbon was an exponent of pomp and order. He is grave and solemn with the dignity inseparable from ceremonial occasions.

He is at home among Roman patricians in the senate; he has no understanding of Christian slaves at worship in the church. His *History* is concerned with things which can be described in the grand manner. His style is always in full regalia. 'In endeavouring to avoid vulgar terms he too frequently dignifies trifles, and clothes common thoughts in a splendid dress that would be rich enough for the noblest ideas. . . . Sometimes in his attempts at elegance, he loses sight of English, and sometimes of sense.'[1] The faults of the man are the defects of the age. Gibbon's irony is a part of the surface finish of a sophisticated period. But though his work is often superficial it has its characteristic convictions and so its distinctive dignity. In the freedom of the mind he found 'the source of every generous and rational sentiment', and he was determined that this liberty should not be undermined by 'habits of credulity and submission'.[2]

CHAPTER VI

THE AUTHORITY OF A REVITALISED FAITH

By the middle of the eighteenth century, English thinkers had expounded in detail most of the views with which the age is usually associated. The Deists had exalted the authority of reason in its most uncompromising form. The Latitudinarians had carefully balanced its claims against a decorous reinterpretation of revelation. Berkeley and Butler had shown that a fundamentally religious position can be supported by massive argument; they had also proved that the views of men of genius cannot always be easily assimilated or widely accepted. Many of the most popular systems of thought were showing signs of atrophy, and reaction was obviously under way. Hume had already pointed out that the province of reason is much more restricted than his contemporaries had imagined. Hartley had begun to relate the insights of the new science to the interpretation of man's nature. But in the extent of its immediate influence the Wesleyan revival was probably more important than the contributions of either Hartley or Hume.

The success of John Wesley's mission was partly due to the message he preached; it was due in even larger measure to the way in which that message satisfied the needs of the people whom it reached. Wesley's appearance on the English scene coincided with a growing conviction that mere argument about religion is basically futile. He reached, of course, multitudes who had been quite untouched by current theological debates—indeed by religious influence of any kind. But it is easy to misconceive or to exaggerate the nature of the reaction he initiated. It is assumed that because he appealed to the verdict of religious consciousness he exalted experience and depreciated thought. This charge was current in his own day. The Bishop of London accused the Methodists of 'making inward, secret and sudden impulses the guides of their actions, resolutions and designs'.¹ To Bishop Warburton, Wesley seemed a particularly dangerous enthusiast, 'because in parts and learning he is far superior to the rest, and formed of the best stuff that nature ever put into a fanatic to make a successful head and leader of a sect'.² Sir Leslie Stephen claimed that Wesley appeals to the heart from the intellect. This is a facile over-simplification, but even Methodists have sometimes been content to regard their founder chiefly as a man whose 'heart was strangely warmed' and whose head, by inference, remained untouched.

Though Wesley appealed to emotion and assigned an important place to experience, he was in many respects a typical child of his century. Even the sobriety of his prose—its directness, its simplicity, its vigour—belongs to the age of reason. He could describe the most extraordinary religious phenomena in the most matter-of-fact language. He shared many of the antipathies of his age; he had nothing but contempt for 'those enthusiasts who suppose the dreams of their own imagination to be revelations from God'.³ He cherished the values by which his contemporaries set the greatest store, even though he interpreted them in his own way. 'What do you apprehend to be more valuable than good sense, good nature, and good manners? All these are contained, and that in the highest degree, in what I mean by Christianity. Good sense (so called) is but a poor dim shadow of what Christians call faith.'⁴ His dislike of '*speculative* latitudinarianism' did not lessen the value he placed on clear and definite convictions. He had no patience with pious people who considered themselves religious simply 'because' (as he told them) 'you are of muddy understanding, because your mind is all in a mist; because you have no settled, consistent principles, but are for jumbling all opinions together'.⁵

A man who thus esteemed intellectual clarity was not likely to despise intellectual effort. Wesley's attitude to theology was profoundly affected by the bent of his mind and by the nature of his mission. He was not an original thinker; his speculative powers were limited, and his interest in abstract theory was slight. His outlook was shaped by his ministry. He was a man of action, and he epitomised the protest of religious consciousness against the sterility of rationalism. His purpose was to help men find the way to salvation. He was interested in whatever promoted this objective; he was unconcerned about everything else. But he certainly did not count Christian theology as one of the indifferent things which could be neglected by men in a hurry to get to heaven. Truth was important; theory was not. He repeatedly referred to doctrines on which there could be no compromise. 'On the Godhead of Christ', he said, 'I *must* insist as the foundation of all our hope.'[1] 'But as to all opinions which do not strike at the root of Christianity, we think and let think.'[2] 'Orthodoxy, or right opinions, is, at best, but a very slender part of religion, if it can be allowed to be any part of it at all.'[3] Wesley thus drew a sharp distinction between essential doctrines and non-essential opinions, but he often spoke in a way which seemed to blur the distinction. He counted the Trinity among the beliefs which must be accepted. 'I do not know', he said, 'how anyone can be a Christian believer . . . till God the Holy Spirit witnesses that God the Father has accepted him through the merits of God the Son.' But he refused to bind men to the niceties of a precise theological formulation of this truth. 'I dare not insist upon anyone's using the word Trinity or Person. I use them myself because I know of none better, but if any man has any scruple concerning them, who shall constrain him to use them? I cannot.' He accepted the *fact*; he found the '*manner how*' incomprehensible, and therefore refused to make it a matter of contention.[4] He regarded original sin as a truth so essential that its denial vitiated the Gospel, but he did not feel committed to a particular theory about it. 'It is quite beyond my understanding', he said, 'it is a depth which I cannot fathom.'[1] In his famous sermon on the Catholic spirit, he made a strong plea for unity in Christian witness. Differences of conviction about worship or polity need not, and should not, hinder co-operation. 'Is thine heart right, as my heart is with thy heart? . . . If it be, give me thy hand.'[2] The case for generous forbearance in minor matters is vigorously stated, but never in such a way as to jeopardise essentials. 'What', asked Wesley, 'should a follower of Christ understand by [the question in the text] when he proposes it to any of his brethren?' and he gave his answer in more than two pages of searching examination of the great truths of faith and the chief duties of discipleship.[3] Wesley was obviously convinced that unity of heart presupposed considerable agreement in belief. He was concerned to maintain a proper balance between truth and its appropriation.

Wesley reacted against the excessive rationalism of his age, but he had no intention of depreciating the valid role of reason. Though some people had unduly magnified its powers there was no need to deny its value. Prevalent assumptions had obscured the limits of human knowledge, which are 'narrower than common people imagine or men of learning are willing to acknowledge'.[4] To Wesley it seemed as foolish to minimise the importance of reason as to exaggerate it. 'When you despise or depreciate reason, you must not imagine that you are doing God service; least of all, are you promoting the cause of God when you are endeavouring to exclude reason out of religion.'[5] Few of those who were most eager to exalt the dignity of reason had bothered to clarify its meaning, so Wesley defined it as 'the faculty of the soul which includes these three operations': simple apprehension, judgment, discourse.[6] Its powers are obviously great; do they extend to religion? Yes, said Wesley; 'it can do exceeding much, both with regard to the foundation of it and the superstructure'.[7] What he advocated was 'a religion founded on reason and everyway agreeable thereto'.[8] On this point he often spoke with an emphasis quite in keeping with the outlook of his age. 'It is a fundamental principle with us that to renounce reason is to renounce religion, that religion and reason go hand in hand, and that all irrational religion is false religion.'[1] Here is a God-given resource which we neglect to our impoverishment. 'Let reason do all that reason can: Employ it as far as it will go.'[2] Yet there is much that reason cannot do. 'And as it cannot give either faith, hope, or virtue, so it cannot give happiness.'[3] Though Wesley could 'earnestly exhort all who seek after God to use all the reason which God hath given them', he believed that unaided reason lacked the resources necessary to provide any kind of genuine religious knowledge. It 'has no ground whereon to stand, no materials to work upon'. Natural theology is not even a possibility, and unless God intervenes man can know nothing of any consequence about God.[4] Our reason may tell us that he exists; it cannot answer the much more important question, what is he like? Our own faculties cannot supply the knowledge we need. 'We could no more perceive him by our natural understanding than we could see him with our eyes.'[5] Revelation is absolutely necessary if we are to make any progress in divine truth. 'By what art will reason get over the immense chasm? This cannot be till the Almighty come in to your succour, and give you that faith you have hitherto despised.'[6] Nor 'should this seem a thing incredible' to us. 'Is it any more repugnant to reason, that spirit should influence spirit than that matter should influence matter? Nay, is not the former the more intelligible of the two?'[7]

To supplement reason with revelation and to interpret revelation by reason might seem a plea acceptable to a Latitudinarian. The distinctive character of Wesley's doctrine of authority emerges in his treatment of the Bible—the repository of revelation. He believed that God reveals himself in many ways, but that his supreme self-disclosure is in Scripture. Wesley first learned this lesson from William Law, and later, when challenging the value of 'the whole army of mystic authors', he reminded his former mentor of this fact. 'In religion', he wrote, 'I regard no writings but the inspired. . . . At a time when I was in great danger of not valuing this authority enough, you made that important observation: "I see where your mistake lies. You would have a philosophical religion; but there can be no such thing. Religion is the most plain simple thing in the world. It is only, We love him because he first loved us. So far as you add philosophy to religion, just so far you spoil it." This remark I have never forgotten since; and I trust in God I never shall.'[1] Wesley relied wholly on the method of salvation revealed in the Bible. Everything else was tested by this standard. 'The Scriptures are the touchstone whereby Christians examine all, real or supposed, revelations. In all cases they appeal "to the law and the testimony" to try every spirit thereby.'[2] 'My ground is the Bible', he wrote on another occasion; '. . . I follow it in all things both great and small'.[3]

Wesley believed that the Bible was simply and literally the Word of God. There were three possible theories of its origin, but since he could prove that neither good men or angels nor bad men or devils had written it, he drew 'this conclusion, that the Bible must be given by divine inspiration'.[4] This did not make Wesley a slavish literalist. No other book concerned men so deeply; therefore it was important to show them the right way of using it. He invoked reason, tradition and experience in order to clarify the meaning of obscure passages. He examined the literal sense of any passage both in the context in which it occurs and in the light of the total message of the Bible. Wesley was aware of the value of Biblical criticism—admittedly of an elementary kind—but he was convinced that all theories about the Bible must be kept subordinate to a firm expectation that the Holy Spirit would guide the reader into all the truth.

Wesley was satisfied that the believer would not be left in uncertainty about the essentials of his faith. 'The testimony of the Spirit', he said, 'is an inward impression of the soul, whereby the Spirit of God directly witnesses to my Spirit, that I am a child of God; that Jesus Christ hath loved me, and given himself for me;

and that all my sins are blotted out, and I, even I, am reconciled to God.'¹ His *Journal* shows that the authority of experience played an important part in his own discovery of the meaning of vital Christianity,² and having learned the lesson, he never forgot it. The appeal to experience is a constant ingredient in the literature of Methodism. There is no disposition to isolate or exalt certain emotional states, nor to imply that the irrational element in religion can claim any priority. What we encounter is an unvarying testimony that the truths declared in Scripture have been verified and confirmed in the believer's own life. God's blessings are accepted as a gift, they are never regarded as our achievement or discovery. Associated with this we have a vivid awareness of a personal reality which meets us in the midst of life's problems. This kind of experience usually grew out of a personal appropriation of what the Gospel offers, and it was invariably associated with what Jesus Christ said and did. It brought a man out of darkness and doubt but not beyond effort, and it was confirmed by the discovery that in the moral struggle we are constantly victorious.³

But Wesley never allowed experience to stand alone. It was always checked by the evidence of Scripture and by the judgment of his reason. Experience confirms authority, it does not establish it. It verifies the truth we have discovered, but it is not the source of that truth. Consequently we cannot authenticate our faith by appealing to our feelings. 'That some consciousness of our being in favour with God is joined with the Christian faith I cannot doubt; but it is not the essence of it. A consciousness of pardon cannot be the condition of pardon.'⁴ Wesley had too shrewd an understanding of human nature not to realise that emotions can be unpredictable and unreliable. Consequently he laid down the principle that 'you are not to judge by your feelings, but by the Word of God'.⁵

Wesley, it is clear, had built up a carefully balanced doctrine of authority.⁶ His appeal was to the Bible, interpreted by reason and confirmed by experience. 'I have endeavoured', he said, 'to describe the true, the Scriptural, experimental religion, so as to omit nothing that is a real part thereof, and to add nothing thereto which is not.'¹ His reaction to Hutcheson's moral theory is typical of his attitude to all the problems he encountered. 'I know both from Scripture, reason and experience that his picture of man is not drawn from life.'² The fact that the Holy Spirit speaks to us principally through the Bible endows the witness of Scripture with a unique vitality. This relegates to a subsidiary status all other authorities, but it does not deprive them of their proper role. In the hierarchy of authority, tradition comes well below experience, but it has its appropriate place. When Christianity is 'considered as an inward principle', he told Conyers Middleton, 'it is holiness and happiness, the image of God impressed on a created spirit, a fountain of peace and love springing up into everlasting life'. But, he added, 'I do not undervalue traditional evidence. Let it have its place and its due honour. It is highly serviceable in its kind and in its degree. And yet I do not set it on a level with this'.³ Tradition is the testimony of the Church; the same Spirit which spoke through Christians in the past speaks through their successors in every age, and we do well to heed what they say. The authority of the Church is a continuous and living force so long as the Church is sensitive to the guidance of the Spirit.

Wesley's view of authority is closely related to an inclusive doctrinal position. Even when most practical in their aim, his teachings were firmly placed within a theological framework. In suggesting to simple people some elementary rules for reading the Bible, he urged them constantly to watch for 'the connexion and harmony there is between those grand fundamental doctrines, original sin, justification by faith, the new birth, inward and outward holiness'.⁴ Though not a profound scholar, Wesley was an indefatigable reader of theological works. His *Journal* is full of comments on books he has been reading, and his *Christian Library* —issued in order that his followers also might read—reflects the breadth of his interests. These works also help us to identify his sources, and to understand the elements which he combined in his own system of thought. The practical mysticism which so profoundly affected his doctrine of perfection he learned from Law and Molinos. The characteristic cast of his Anglicanism he derived from Laud and the Caroline divines. The strain of Calvinism in his theology came from the Puritans. He reaffirmed the great doctrines of the Reformers (sometimes with characteristic modifications). He was deeply indebted to the Fathers, to Augustine and Chrysostom, to the Alexandrians and the Cappadocians. His aim, no less than his sources, was comprehensive. He was not satisfied with the neat antitheses which had dominated polemic theology. Because he exalted faith he saw no need to abase works. He had no intention of choosing between a doctrine of salvation and a system of ethics. He intended to have both. He has been described as an Arminian tinged with Calvinism and as a Reformed theologian who made concessions to the Catholic tradition.[1] He was not completely successful in reconciling his sources, but he was deliberately eclectic in his use of them. He was an evangelical Catholic, and this fact determines the characteristic quality of his thought.

The comprehensive framework of Wesley's theology is a doctrine of salvation. He was an evangelist who pondered the nature and implications of his task. He started with a realistic assessment of man's predicament, and he believed that it is most accurately described in terms of original sin. 'Our *old man*' (Paul's phrase in Romans vi. 6) is 'coeval with our being and as old as the fall, our evil nature; a strong and beautiful expression for that entire depravity and corruption, which by nature spreads itself over the whole man, leaving no part uninfected.'[2] 'We are all born', he wrote, 'with a sinful, devilish nature. By reason whereof we are children of wrath, liable to death eternal.'[3] But Wesley emphatically repudiated predestination, which has so often been a companion doctrine to original sin. He regarded it as contrary to the ordinances of God; it destroys the holiness and happiness of Christianity, and threatens the very being of all religion; it undermines our zeal for good works; it overthrows the whole Christian revelation. It is, in fact, 'a doctrine full of blasphemy'.[1]

Wesley's unyielding view of original sin, combined with his conditional doctrine of election, might seem to threaten complications. Yet it is an integral part of his distinctive theory of man and salvation. Wesley's emphasis on experience led him to the belief that guilt is incurred only when man consciously sins.[2] No one is damned unless by his own deliberate act he brings this fate upon himself. But original sin has so restricted man's choice that he is condemned to choose evil. How can he resist evil? How can he resist the impulse to which his nature irresistibly impels him? The answer to these questions follows from Wesley's doctrine of conditional election. Original sin does not inexorably lead to actual sin, because God's grace is at work and its goal is the salvation of all men. Prevenient grace anticipates man's repentance and antedates the creation of that new relationship which God promises and effects. 'By nature ye are wholly corrupted; but by grace ye shall be wholly renewed.'[3] 'A measure of free will' is 'supernaturally restored to every man, together with that supernatural light which "enlightens every man that cometh into the world".'[4] Man is thus enabled to seek God, and the great work of his restoration has begun. 'Salvation begins with what is usually termed *preventing grace*; including the first wish to please God, the first dawn of light concerning his will and the first slight transient conviction of having sinned against him.'[5] The first stage in Wesley's system thus makes man wholly dependent upon God for salvation, even for the initial impulse which bids him turn and be saved. But he has placed a co-ordinate emphasis on man's own responsibility. The new life is God's gift, but only those who co-operate with God receive it.

How we receive the new gift is defined by Wesley with precision and care. He presents us with an account of the origin and development of the Christian life which is basically orthodox, which is indebted both to Arminian and to Calvinist strains, and which reflects Wesley's distinctive concerns. In the Atonement he found the point at which God's redemptive purpose begins to be effective in transforming the sinner's life. 'Nothing in the Christian system is of greater consequence than the doctrine of Atonement.'¹ What Wesley set forth is a complex interpretation which integrates many different elements. He followed the Thirty-nine Articles with considerable fidelity; he thus incorporated the strain of Calvinism inherent in the articles, and placed a strong emphasis on the objective reality of the change Christ has wrought. He allowed a place for the effect of Christ's death in awakening in man an answering response. He included the victory over the powers of evil which Christ has won and in which we participate. This might seem to qualify him to agree with most Christians on the Atonement, but he consciously differed from Law, from Zinzendorf and from the Calvinists. None, he felt, was holding the fulness of the truth in a way that would explain and undergird the new life.

The new life, of course, begins with a revulsion from the old life. Before man can appropriate the benefits of what God has done for him in Christ he must be aroused to a consciousness of his need. Wesley believed that when a man was confronted with the demands of the moral law, God's grace would stir his conscience to recognise his sin, and to desire deliverance from it. Then Christ's atoning word becomes effective; man is brought into a new relationship with God, and the new life begins. Salvation, of course, is an intricate and complex process. Even if you contend that it takes place instantaneously, it is possible to distinguish elements which must be separated if you are to understand what has happened. 'This then is the salvation which is through faith, even in the present world: a salvation from sin, and the consequences of sin, both often expressed in the word *justification.*' This involves forgiveness; it is the fruit of the Atonement, and it is the result of that trusting response on the part of the believer by which Christ is *formed in his heart.* So that he who is thus justified, or saved by faith, is indeed *born again.* He is *born again of the Spirit* into a new life'.[1] Justification and sanctification, pardon for the past, strength for the future—these are central in Wesley's thought. 'If any doctrines within the whole compass of Christianity may be properly termed "fundamental", they are doubtless these two—the doctrine of Justification and that of the new birth.'[2] Wesley further defined the relation of these experiences to each other by indicating the different ways in which they affect the believer. 'Justification', he said, 'implies only a relative, the new birth a real change. God in justifying us does something *for* us; in begetting us again, he does the work *in* us. The former changes our outward relation to God, so that of enemies we become children; by the latter our inmost souls are changed, so that of sinners we become saints. . . . The one is the taking away the guilt, the other the taking away the power of sin.'[3]

A man who has experienced so decisive a change will have no doubts about the nature and results of this transformation. The witness of the Holy Spirit will be the source of his certainty. Its direct testimony will convince him of God's love and of the reconciled relationship into which he has entered. He will have the further confirmation (real enough though indirect) which comes from the conscious possession of the fruits of the Spirit. Both experiences are necessary, but the first will always precede the second. 'That this testimony of the Spirit of God must needs . . . be antecedent to the testimony of our own spirit may appear from this single consideration. We must be holy of heart and holy of life before we can be conscious that we are so. . . . But we must love God before we can be holy at all. . . . Now we cannot love God till we know that he loves us.'[4] This doctrine of assurance was one of Wesley's distinctive contributions to the presentation of religious truth. The thought was not original; the place it occupied was. It has been claimed that in his treatment of assurance Wesley made theology do the work of psychology. He would probably have regarded the distinction as unreal. At least he had no doubt that here he was touching the dynamic which made his movement so revolutionary a force.

Wesley's theological interests were practical rather than theoretical. This explains the very important place which he assigned to sanctification. The power of God's Spirit, which effects the miracle of the new birth, is no less responsible for the believer's growth in grace. 'Our main doctrines', wrote Wesley, 'which include all the rest, are three—that of repentance, of faith, and of holiness. The first of these we account, as it were, the porch of religion; the next, the door; the third, religion itself.'[1] In his sermon on 'Scriptural Christianity' he traced the experience of a hearer moved to repentance by Peter's sermon at Pentecost. The new convert responds in love to the Gospel, and manifests this love in all his relationships. 'It did not satisfy him merely to abstain from doing evil. He soul was athirst to do good.'[2] Faith has missed its true goal unless it works by love. The injunction, 'Believe and thou shalt be saved', points neither to a speculative theory nor to a remote and heavenly reward. It means 'Believe and thou shalt be holy; believe in the Lord Jesus Christ, and thou shalt have peace and power together; . . . thou shalt both do and teach all the commandments of God . . .; thou shalt teach them by thy life as well as thy words.'[3]

This particular emphasis was fortified by Wesley's controversy with the Antinomians. In Protestant thought there had consistently been a strain which exalted faith to such a degree that in effect it depressed morality. It equated concern about conduct with the legalism from which the Gospel has set us free. Wesley made it quite clear that nothing can call in question the primacy of faith, but he insisted that obedience to the law must not be confused with the legalism which makes its hope of salvation dependent on works. He found this error lurking in the Moravians and in the Calvinists.[4] To Wesley it was clear that there is a moral law which the Christian is obliged to obey. The mark of his freedom is not that he is emancipated from its demands but that he is empowered to fulfil them. 'Now this law is an incorruptible picture of the High and Holy One that inhabiteth eternity. . . . It is the face of God unveiled. . . . It is the heart of God disclosed to man.'[1] We are not committed to a ceremonial code, nor does the faith release us from all moral constraint. There is a valid intermediary position. 'We are justified without the works of the law, as any previous condition of justification; but they are an immediate fruit of that faith whereby we are justified. So that if good works do not follow our faith, even all inward and outward holiness, it is plain our faith is nothing worth.'[2] Wesley believed that the new doctrine confirmed the true content of the moral law, and that the new life would fully correspond to its demands. But the law can be fulfilled only with the aid of the resources of belief. Faith is subservient to love. The one is the means, the other the end. True religion means 'righteousness' or 'holiness'—love to God and to our fellow-creatures—and 'happiness'—peace, assurance of adoption, and joy in the Holy Ghost.[3]

This general view of religion is sharpened in his description of the members of his societies. In 'The Character of a Methodist' he gave as the first quality to be observed in one of his followers that 'the love of God has been shed abroad in his heart'. This explains the joy which radiates his life: he is 'happy in God, yea, always happy'. Hope, too, is the outcome of his love to God. Yet this is only half the picture. He keeps all the commandments of God, 'and that with all his might'. His end in all things is God's glory, and he will permit none of the customs of the world to obstruct his purpose. 'He is inwardly and outwardly conformed to the will of God. . . . His soul is renewed after the image of God, in righteousness and in all true holiness. And having that mind that was in Christ, he walks as Christ also walked.'[4] This is the practical demonstration of an important truth: sanctification involves the ethical transformation of the believer. Because he is changed in heart, he is also changed in the pattern of his outward life.

The characteristic means by which Wesley enforced this truth was his doctrine of Christian Perfection. He believed that perfection was the natural consequence of the total process of salvation, and he saw it as God's special gift to the Methodist people. In some respects the doctrine proved to be an embarrassment; Wesley himself was not always consistent in his statements about it, and both his preachers and his followers sometimes found it difficult to interpret and apply. But the problems inherent in perfection could not be regarded as sufficient grounds for neglecting it, and to the end Wesley insisted that it be given its proper place in the life of his societies. This, indeed, is the most constant strain in his thought. He dealt with it in his sermons, his *Journal*, his letters and his hymns. It was frequently debated at the early meetings of the Conference. With great care he gathered together most of what he had said or written on the subject in *A Plain Account of Christian Perfection, as believed and taught by the Reverend Mr. John Wesley, from the year 1725 to the year 1777.*[1] He traced back his conviction on this matter to a period at least thirteen years before the quickening of his own religious life, and he made clear his debt to Jeremy Taylor, Thomas à Kempis, and William Law. His initial obligation was to the practical mystics, and he saw no reason to repudiate—or even seriously to modify—what they had taught him. The essence of perfection, he believed, 'is "perfect love"', and the Bible speaks of it so often that we are without excuse if we do not earnestly strive to understand its meaning and to appropriate its reality.

Wesley felt that the first step is to indicate, with considerable precision, what perfection is and what it is not. Obviously Christians are not delivered from many of the defects in which they inevitably participate as a result of their human limitations. 'They are not perfect in knowledge. They are not free from ignorance, no, nor from mistakes. . . . They are not free from infirmities, such as quickness or slowness of understanding, irregular quickness or heaviness of imagination.'[2] Or, as he expressed it elsewhere, 'we willing allow and continually declare, that there is no such perfection in this life, as implies either a dispensation from doing good, and attending all the ordinances of God, or a freedom from ignorance, mistakes, temptation, and a thousand infirmities necessarily connected with flesh and blood'.[1] This perfection is not absolute in nature, it does not confer infallibility, and it may be forfeited. In stating what Christian perfection is, Wesley's most succinct definition is that 'it is perfect love'.[2] But he expanded this statement on various occasions. It is clear that he included at least three primary ingredients: purity of intention, which dedicates the whole of life to God; the possession of the mind of Christ, so that we may walk as Christ walked and may find our nature renewed in the image of God; an unreserved love of God and of our neighbour. Perfection thus includes consecration, sanctification, and active love. Wesley defined it as a life purged of all evil and joyfully expended in service. 'In retirement or company, in leisure, business, or conversation his heart is ever with the Lord.'[3]

Perfection is a difficult concept, fraught with serious hazards. Wesley knew that those who claim too much fall into pride and pharisaism, but those who expect too little usually claim less than they are entitled to receive of the effective power which transforms life. On this subject Wesley did not find it easy to avoid confusion. He modified his views even on so important a subject as sin. Initially he taught that perfection involved complete victory. 'Q. Does this imply that all inward sin is taken away? A. Undoubtedly. . . .' But, though this kind of categorical statement agrees with his earlier pronouncements, Wesley modified it: 'yet sin remains in him, yea, the seed of all sin, till he is sanctified throughout'.[4] The believer is saved from outward sin, but the carnal mind remains. In part, the weakness of Wesley's position is related to the fact that he uses sin in more than one sense, but never with sufficient subtlety. He speaks of 'sin properly so called (that is, a voluntary transgression of a known law)' and contrasts it with 'sin improperly so called (that is, involuntary transgression of a divine law, known or unknown)'.[5] He believed that Christians would be saved 'not only from outward sins, but also from the sins of their hearts; from evil thoughts and from evil tempers';[6] from involuntary transgressions they would not be delivered. Yet even here Wesley was not always consistent, and certainly he did not probe sufficiently the nature of those secret, subtle sins of which we are scarcely conscious.[1] He was careful not to insist on *sinless* perfection. The phrase was open to misunderstanding, and he did not propose to contend for mere words. He did not claim that the Christian would be above criticism and free from all faults. He was defending a biblical concept: 'they that love God with all their heart and all men as themselves are scripturally perfect'.[2] 'This', he said, 'is the doctrine which we preached from the beginning and which we preach at this day.'[3]

Wesley believed that he taught the fundamentals of the Christian faith. He was concerned to maintain the truth in the form in which the Church of England had always received it; at most he restored to their rightful position certain essentials which had been obscured by neglect. But when even his own followers sometimes misinterpreted his views, he could scarcely hope to avoid controversy with those who differed from him. His bitterest struggles were with those most akin to him in aim and outlook. The relations of Methodists and Evangelicals prove the truth of the observation that nothing divides so bitterly as common convictions held with a difference. In many respects, John Wesley and George Whitefield were more akin than any two other religious leaders of the age, and each generously acknowledged his debt to the other. But they disagreed in theology. Because their contention was sharp, and because it expanded into an acrimonious controversy, it is important not to forget the extent of their agreement. Wesley found himself in a delicate position. He was not a Calvinist, but he was committed to an order of salvation (repentance, conversion, assurance) which was usually associated with a strictly Calvinistic interpretation of justification by faith. Wesley strongly enforced doctrines which were common property to all who seriously affirmed their loyalty to the Reformation. In his letter to James Hervey, he made it clear that in many respects he agreed with the Calvinist doctrine of the atonement.[1] Wesley certainly did not dispute the central place assigned by the Calvinists to the sovereignty of God. He believed that he had overcome the danger of misconstruction by his doctrines of prevenient grace and sanctification.

Wesley parted company with the Calvinists on the doctrine of the 'eternal decrees' of God, and he stated his disagreement in the most unequivocal terms. 'How uncomfortable a thought is this, that thousands and millions of men, without any preceding offence or fault of theirs, were unchangeably doomed to everlasting burnings!'[2] After epitomising what he conceived to be the Calvinist view of predestination, he exclaimed, 'I could sooner be a Turk, a Deist, yea an Atheist, than I could believe this. It is less absurd to deny the very being of God than to make him an almighty tyrant.'[3] Even more explicit was his denunciation of Calvinism as 'the direct antidote to Methodism. . . . All the devices of Satan, for these fifty years, have done less toward stopping this work of God, than that single doctrine. . . . Wherein', he asked, 'lie the charms of this doctrine? . . . It seems to magnify Christ, although in reality it supposes him to have died in vain. For the absolutely elect must have been saved without him; and the non-elect cannot be saved by him.'[4]

In reply, Whitefield frankly avowed his full acceptance of the doctrine of reprobation. He believed 'that God intends to give saving grace, through Jesus Christ, only to a certain number, and that the rest of mankind, after the fall of Adam, being justly left of God to continue in sin, will at last suffer that eternal death which is the proper wages of sin'.[5] Point by point he met Wesley's argument. Election, so far from making preaching vain, presupposes that the Gospel will be proclaimed. It does not destroy the comfort of religion or the joy of Christianity; indeed, Whitefield found it his daily support, and 'a comfortable assurance of eternal salvation'. It does not exclude charity, and it is the inspiration of all good works. It does not overthrow Christianity, and none of the contemporary enemies of the faith—Deists, Arians, Socinians—accept it. Both Wesley and Whitefield acquiesced in the fact that neither could convince the other. 'The great day will discover why the Lord permits dear Mr Wesley and me to be of a different way of thinking.' 'When his time is come', said Wesley, 'God will do what man cannot, namely, make us both of one mind.' Though they differed with intensity, they treated each other with the great respect great men can accord to each other, and Wesley paid a noble tribute to Whitefield when he preached his funeral sermon. But lesser men fought with greater bitterness, and the Calvinist controversy plunged forward through mounting intensity to unbridled acrimony.

> What image of their fury can we form?
> Dullness and rage. A puddle in a storm.[1]

Issues which had often been debated in the past were revived. Are a specific number predestined to eternal life?—and are the rest inevitably damned? What is the relation between justification and sanctification? Is Christ's righteousness imputed to the believer or imparted to him? Is it possible to fall from grace, or is final perseverance certain? Do the workings of divine grace allow any scope for the free exercise of our wills? Does Christ's saving work apply to all men, or only to the elect? The debate was inconclusive, but it was not the less intense on that account.

The Calvinists' emphasis on their orthodoxy became increasingly shrill. Augustus Toplady devoted two volumes to an elaborate proof that the official theology of the Church of England was, and always had been, Calvinism.[2] The ineffectiveness of the Church's witness and the listlessness of its spiritual life were due to its having forsaken its true faith. 'Our liturgy, our articles, and our homilies, it is true, still keep possession of our church walls: but we pray, we subscribe, we assent, one way; we believe, we preach, we write, another.' Then, changing his figure of speech, he affirmed, 'without hesitation . . . that Arminianism is the poisonous wood to which the waters of our national sanctuary are primarily indebted for their embitterment'.[3]

173

Whitefield's friends were careful to emphasise that 'he was zealous, steady, and unshaken in the great and fundamental truths of the Gospel'. 'The great doctrines which he taught and insisted on were : (1) Original Sin; (2) The New Birth; (3) Justification by faith in Christ; (4) The final perseverance of the saints; (5) Eternal and unconditional election. And if I am not mistaken', added Mr Elliot, 'he held and taught the first three in a very different manner from some who would be thought to hold and teach them too.'[1] But it is the last two topics which Elliot expounded with greatest care. Popular expositions of Calvinism multiplied in number. James Hervey's stilted and sententious dialogues, *Theron and Aspasio*, sold very widely. William Wilberforce claimed that the 'grand radical defect in the practical system of . . . nominal Christians is their forgetfulness of the peculiar doctrines of the religion which they profess—the corruption of human nature—the atonement of the Saviour—and the sanctifying influence of the Holy Spirit', and he interpreted each in a distinctly Calvinist manner.[2]

The position occupied by these men is more readily defined in terms of emphasis than of content. They claimed to represent authentic Christianity—primitive, reformed, and Anglican. It seemed to them that many of their contemporaries had been beguiled into accepting too genial a view of human nature. In retrospect, Thomas Scott found that the epitome of his youthful folly lay in his clinging to a view of man which was wholly Arminian, and which trembled on the brink of Pelagianism, even of Socinianism. Surely God's justly offended wrath must have been stayed by an unimaginable mercy![3] After pages of patient exposition, Henry Venn felt that he had paved the way for an adequate definition of man's natural state. 'From this proof of the total depravity of man in his temper towards God, his natural guilt and sinfulness appears in a glaring light.'[4] To William Wilberforce, the listlessness of popular Christianity could be traced to an apathy which refuses to treat a serious subject in a serious way, to an indifference which ignores our true hope, to a confidence which takes salvation for granted, and to a readiness to trust in works without faith. But most serious of all is the neglect of man's actual nature. Wilberforce confronts the genial estimate of our natural state with 'the humiliating language of Christianity. From it we learn that man is an apostate creature, fallen from his high original, degraded in his nature, and depraved in his faculties; indisposed to good, and disposed to evil; prone to vice, it is natural and easy to him; disinclined to virtue, it is difficult and laborious; that he is tainted with sin, not slightly and superficially, but radically and to the very core.'¹ Such a view of man's state required a proportionate emphasis on God's grace, the only cause (in any ultimate sense) of man's salvation. And it presupposed a doctrine of the atonement in which Christ's sacrifice accomplished on man's behalf what man himself could never do. Salvation, thus provided by God's mercy, is appropriated by men through justification by faith. Again, the distinguishing point is a certain kind of emphasis. The preaching of the Cross acquires a new urgency. Grace is seen as 'the cardinal point on which the whole of Christianity turns', and the only possible response on the part of man is 'an absolute and unconditional surrender of soul and body to the will and service of God'.²

Even more characteristic of the Evangelicals was their deliberate effort to maintain a heavenly frame of mind. A man like Toplady consciously turned his thoughts to spiritual things. If he sang hymns during his private devotions, and found it profitable, he noted the fact in his diary. 'I can testify, by sweet and repeated experience, that singing is an ordinance of God, and a means of grace. Lord, fit my soul to bear a part in that song for ever new. . . .' Too much company provoked the comment, 'How unprofitable are worldly interviews!' In the midst of his annual tithe dinner, while entertaining his parishioners and collecting his dues, Toplady snatched a few moments to converse with a kindred soul 'on the best subjects, particularly the decrees of God and the spiritual impotence of man's will'. His finger was seldom off his own spiritual pulse. While riding home—and he precisely identified the exact spot—'my soul was in a very comfortable frame. O the unutterable sweetness of a sensible interest in God's election, the covenant of grace, and the righteousness of Christ! I trust I can say they are all mine.' The record was not always so encouraging. 'At night before I went to bed, was much troubled with coldness and wanderings in secret prayer.' His attention, of course, was not always fixed on himself, and one of the marks of evangelical piety was its adoring concentration on Jesus Christ. 'My shortcomings and my wrong-doings, my unbelief and want of love, would sink me into the nethermost hell, was not Jesus my righteousness and my redemption. There is no sin which I would not commit, was not Jesus, by the power of his Spirit, my sanctification.'[1]

Experience, it is apparent, occupied a very important place in the Evangelical's understanding of religion. Toplady decided to keep a diary in order to record 'God's gracious dealings with my soul in a way of spiritual experience'. On reading a work on predestination he was evidently impressed by its contents, but he was more concerned with his active appropriation of its spiritual meaning. 'How sweet is that blessed and glorious doctrine to the soul, when it is received through the channel of inward experience.'[2] From this particular emphasis there followed consequences which were sometimes desirable, sometimes deplorable. Experience was closely related to emotion, and the Evangelicals at least saved religion from the arid intellectualism of an excessively rationalistic age. Wilberforce was aware that his critics would claim that he was 'degrading the worship of the understanding, and . . . substituting and raising up a set of mere feelings in its stead'. But was it not time, he added, to point out that the rational and the emotional are not true opposites; therefore it is possible to enlist both in the service of faith. Surely it is a very restricted view which proposes 'to exclude from the service of religion so grand a part of the composition of man' as the whole range of emotion. It is the peculiar glory of Christianity that it brings 'all the faculties of our nature into their just subordination and dependence; that so the whole man, complete in all his functions, may be restored to the true ends of his being, and be devoted, entire and harmonious, to the service and glory of God'.[1]

This was an elementary plea on behalf of a basic integrity of life. When Wilberforce wrote, others were already groping, along different paths, towards the same goal,

> To those sweet counsels between head and heart
> Whence grew that genuine knowledge, fraught with peace.[2]

After the desiccated rationalism which had so often done service as religion, the protest of the Evangelicals was sorely needed. But unfortunately emotion, so long suppressed, often erupted with an embarrassing exuberance. At its best, it was intense, yet disciplined and controlled.

> 'Twere new indeed to see a bard all fire,
> Touched with a coal from heav'n, assume the lyre,
> And tell the world, still kindling as he sung,
> With more than mortal music on his tongue,
> That He, who died below and reigns above,
> Inspires the song, and that his name is love.[3]

At its worst, it was morbid and maudlin. Then the Evangelical showed signs of inducing religious experience because he believed that the righteous man is expected to feel the appropriate fervours. James Hervey's *Meditations Among the Tombs* are an extreme but not an exceptional example of the way bathos and platitude can struggle indecisively for mastery. Imagination is encouraged to speculate about the past history and the present state of the dead. 'Here enemies . . . dwell together in unity. They drop every embittered thought, and forget that they once were foes. Perhaps their crumbling bones *mix*, as they *moulder*; and those who while they lived stood aloof in irreconcilable variance, here fall into mutual embraces, and even incorporate with each other in the grave.' Here, too, we see, without inhibition, the Evangelical preoccupation with death. 'Doubtless', wrote Hervey, rhapsodising over the grave of a young man, 'it would have pierced one's heart to have beheld the tender parents following the breathless youth to his long home. Perhaps drowned in tears and all but overwhelmed with sorrows, they stood like weeping statues, on this very spot. Methinks I see the deeply distressed mourners attending the sad solemnity. How they wring their hands, and pour floods from their eyes.'[1] Warburton might speak contemptuously of 'such weak but well-meaning rhapsodies as Hervey's Meditations',[2] but they were surprisingly popular.

The Evangelicals emphasised experience. Consequently they kept religion closely related to life. Venn began his *Complete Duty of Man* with an epitome of theology, but his purpose was to provide a suitable foundation for Christian conduct. If you separate belief and action, both suffer. 'All treatises, therefore, written to promote holiness of living must be deplorably defective, in which the Cross of Christ is not laid as the foundation, and constantly kept in view, and every duty enforced as having relation to the Redeemer.'[3] The title of Wilberforce's work (*A Practical View*) is important. He believed that 'the practical precepts of Christianity grow out of her peculiar doctrines and are inseparably connected with them'.[4] His aim was to prove that if 'a principle of true religion should in any considerable degree gain ground, there is no estimating the effect on public morals, and the consequent influence on our political welfare'.[5] It is the great glory of the Evangelicals that they put their theories into practice. In the abolitionist struggle Wilberforce and his friends proved that there is, indeed, no predicting what dedicated men can accomplish in political reform. The various philanthropic efforts which were so conspicuous a feature of the age owed a great deal to the Evangelicals. The preoccupation with the individual's conversion was thus balanced by a growing sense of social responsibility. The evils of society and the needs of the weak and the exploited increasingly engaged the attention of the Evangelicals. In addition they promoted various enterprises— the Church Missionary Society, the Religious Tract Society, the

British and Foreign Bible Society—designed to disseminate the light of truth. Hannah More's struggles to establish schools in the Mendip villages is an excellent example of what a practical faith was willing to attempt and able to achieve.

But a practical faith is often tempted to reinforce its demands with the aid of regulations. The Evangelicals were the descendants of the Puritans; the spirit of the fathers reappeared in the children. Conduct was hedged about with negative restraints. Amusements were regarded with suspicion; in certain forms they were forbidden. In her *Thoughts on the Importance of the Manners of the Great to General Society*, Hannah More courageously attacked the prevailing obsession with cards and gambling, and she had an appreciable effect on social customs. But this kind of witness too readily degenerated into mere insistence on certain inflexible conventions. Respect for the Lord's Day hardened into a rigid Sabbatarianism. Even the simplest pleasures were banished. When a messenger brought Toplady a letter from his mother and two London newspapers, he put them aside with evident regret. 'I hope', he said, 'to read [them] to-morrow; but dare not do on God's day.'[1] It was with the utmost reluctance that Wilberforce permitted even urgent public duties to disrupt the Sabbath peace. He found Swift's *Letters* distinctly shocking: 'What a thoroughly irreligious mind—no trace of Sunday to be found in his journals or letters to his most intimate friends.' Wilberforce himself delighted in the devout activities of the Sabbath day. 'There was nothing of affected seriousness in his deportment or manner on this day', observed a friend; 'all was easy, natural and cheerful.'[2] Unfortunately this was far from universal among the Evangelicals; the serenity of the Sabbath was often overcast with gloom. We are already on the threshold of an age in which a cultivated man like Ruskin could cover his Turner paintings on Saturday evening lest they disturb the serious thoughts appropriate to Sunday.

One consequence of the practical strain in Evangelical thought was a tendency to depreciate intellectual effort. This was reinforced from a variety of directions. All human aids to salvation were irrelevant, and learning might prove to be dangerous because it is so easily confused with merit. In reaction against the exaggerated, but very prevalent, reliance on reason, it was easy to assume that none of the works of reason could contribute to the well-being of man's spirit. Certain areas of thought lay beyond the range of interest of the Evangelicals. Their exclusive authority was the Bible; they were relatively unconcerned about the doctrine of the Church. They were intensely preoccupied with the conversion of the individual; they were little interested in his sacramental incorporation into the Church. They believed in the sanctifying power of the Holy Spirit; they emphasised its personal rather than its corporate aspects. Even the characteristic form of the Evangelical emphasis on 'the foolishness of preaching', though entirely compatible with much earnest and excellent preaching, tended to make homiletics a substitute for theology. The permanent value of the literary work of the Evangelicals stands therefore in sharp contrast with its contemporary popularity. To Bishop Hurd, Hervey's writings might seem 'puerile trifles', but they reached an extensive public. Wilberforce's *Practical View* sold seventy-five hundred copies in a few weeks, and passed through some forty editions in England and America. Wilberforce represented the Evangelical tradition at its best; at its worst it showed a tendency to elicit a desired response by the use of stock phrases. It developed a characteristic idiom of speech instead of fashioning a distinctive pattern of thought.

The strength of the Evangelical witness sprang from the vigour with which its positive views were proclaimed. Inward conviction was sustained by complete reliance on divine aid. During the closing years of the eighteenth century the Evangelicals grew both in numbers and in influence. Earnestness and religious devotion found a congenial refuge in their party, and by the close of the century it was the most active group in the Church of England. It has always been easy to criticise some of their views; it has never been easy to emulate much of their witness.

CHAPTER VII

THE AUTHORITY OF THE STATE AND THE CLAIMS OF THE CHURCH

THE seventeenth century had been a troubled period; it seemed apparent to the Age of Reason that religious strife had caused this turmoil. The results had been aggravated by the perennial problem of the relations of Church and State. The seventeenth century had made its distinctive contributions to this subject; the next generation would not appropriate, but could not ignore, them.

The Restoration period reacted violently against both the principles of the Commonwealth and the theories of Thomas Hobbes. Hobbes believed that one of the first tasks of the State must be to define correctly its relation to religion. The crux of all political theory is the problem of sovereignty. In the past it had often been founded on a divine sanction, derived, perhaps, from Noah or Melchizedek; Hobbes relied on reason and argued from 'the principles of Nature only'. Nor would he allow the Church even a co-ordinate authority. Dualism is always fatal; no man can serve two masters, and, since the civil ruler is also the supreme pastor, no man needs to try. 'Temporal and spiritual are two words brought into the world to make men see double, and mistake their lawful sovereign. . . . Seeing there are no men on earth whose bodies are spiritual, there can be no spiritual commonwealth among men that are yet in the flesh. . . . Men's actions proceed from their opinions; if the sovereign give away the government of doctrines, men will be frightened into rebellion with the fear of spirits.'[1] There is no escape from the stark Erastianism of Hobbes' position. The 'power ecclesiastical' is completely subject to the temporal ruler; spiritual tyranny and priestly arrogance are swept aside with high-handed confidence, and Presbytery, Prelacy and Papacy are dismissed as the successive 'knots on Christian liberty'. Such doctrines won few devotees; for years to come every champion of the Church broke his lance against the 'atheist of Malmesbury'. But it was easier to vilify Hobbes than to escape his influence. The reliance on reason, the appeal to nature, the resistance to sacerdotal claims, a secular rather than a textual method of debating—these were the marks of his work and they were qualities certain to reappear.

For a generation, however, the divine right of kings and the duty of passive obedience held the field. Submission to royal authority was the distinguishing mark of the Anglican Church and was treated as its peculiar glory. The theory was useful as a stick with which to beat the dissenters and, in due course, the Whigs. It had originally been devised to withstand papal encroachments; it was a natural weapon against opponents of the royal prerogative. But it had lost touch with reality. When James II rashly put the theory to the test, it collapsed, completely and irrevocably.

The vacuum thus created was filled by John Locke. To the new age he transmitted the elements in the thought of his own century which were destined to achieve greatest permanence. He reflected the mounting impatience with the authorities to which men had recently given their allegiance. In a series of profoundly influential works he explored the significance of freedom in all its forms; intellectual liberty in the *Essay*, political liberty in the *Treatises on Government*, religious liberty in the *Letters on Toleration*. The *Letters* proved to be his most significant contribution to social theory. He regarded religion as an individual matter; he saw each man as the fittest judge of the things that conduce to his salvation. He had a modest estimate, of course, of the individual's capacity for forming true judgments in religion, and he was far less persuaded than many of his contemporaries of the immorality of holding convictions which deviated from the accepted norm. His work, in fact, was a standing protest against the arrogance of those who demand certainty where only probability can be attained. But he had no intention of dissolving religious societies by insisting on the right of unrestricted personal choice. Separate nationalities justified national churches. Locke did not object to a religious establishment, provided it embraced all who sought the consolation of faith. He believed that most ceremonies are indifferent; in sacerdotalism he found one of the great enemies of charity. Persecution only encourages hypocrisy, while freedom is the best guarantee of truth. It was necessary therefore to recall the national religion to the essential simplicities of the Gospel; it would be found that these were few and reasonable. Church and State can be linked in a union from which both will benefit, if the state accepts Christianity as the foundation of its life, and if the Church be made sufficiently tolerant and comprehensive to embrace all men of goodwill. Such an establishment would be in effect the nation organised to promote goodness. Yet Locke was careful to avoid any blurring of the essential distinctiveness of Church and State. They might co-operate; they would never coalesce, since each has its own nature and its own sphere. These two societies 'are in their original, end, business, and in everything, perfectly distinct and infinitely different from each other. . . . If each of them would contain itself within its own bounds, the one attending to the worldly business of the commonwealth, and the other to the salvation of souls, it is impossible that any discord should ever have happened between them.'[1]

In this respect, as in so many others, Locke's views were a justification of the Revolution settlement. Reinforced by his immense prestige, they profoundly modified both the thought and the practice of the eighteenth century. The appeal to simplicity, the claim that Christianity is essentially reasonable, the assumption that the State rests on a natural law which has been secularised in spirit—all these became the axioms of the succeeding generation. Those who agreed with him accepted his presuppositions and expanded them, his critics ignored the duty of developing a theory of the state in Christian terms, and 'fought a rearguard action for the undermined Church–State idea'.[1] The first example of this appears in the defence of the Non-juror position.

In the seventeenth century, the Church of England had been so completely committed to the Stuart cause that the fall of James II confronted the clergy with an agonising choice. When required to swear allegiance to the new monarchs, few of the clergy wanted to refuse and so forfeit their positions; but after a generation of enthusiastic preaching of the doctrines of the divine right and indefeasible hereditary succession few felt comfortable about taking the new oaths. Those who could not compromise seceded. Numerically the Non-jurors were a small group; in ability, learning, and sincerity they were a serious loss to the Church of England. Their loyalty to conscience gave their witness a specious appearance of superior consistency; actually the overtones of their witness were more largely political than religious. They contended that when the government deprived the bishops who refused the oaths it invaded an ecclesiastical realm in which it had no right to interfere. In fact, the government was revoking what the government had conferred; it was doing what James II had done (without protest), and consequently the issue was not really the interference of the State in Church affairs, but the legitimacy of the exercise of the civil power in this particular case.[2] 'But see, my Lord', wrote White Kennett to the bishop of Carlisle, 'this schism is nothing but a political faction arising out of the deadly feud, and abhorrence of the Revolution, and of the Protestant succession. . . .'[3] The Non-jurors were concerned with a general theory as well as with a particular grievance, and in the writings of Charles Leslie and George Hickes the broad outlines of the one are often obscured by the peculiar character of the other.

The Church of England, according to Leslie, was exposed to a twofold danger. On the one hand its safety was threatened by an alliance between those who wished to curtail its free activity (i.e. Whigs and Moderates) and those who sought its overthrow (i.e. dissenters).[1] But, on the other, it was threatened by the consequences of a mistaken view of its essential nature. The Church is a spiritual kingdom; as to spiritual authority it must be independent of all earthly powers.[2] The issue had been confused by the artificiality of Whig theories. There is nothing to prove that freedom is man's birthright, nor is there any reason to suppose that the relations of Church and State were ever settled by compact.[3] Actually the one has invaded the rights of the other. This is a matter of record, but not a case of necessity. In his teaching, Christ left the independence of each intact. The two powers do not conflict, since they run in channels which are parallel but distinct. Confusion arises only when the one tries to thrust 'its sickle into the other's harvest'.[4] Because all the nonconformists magnify their spiritual independence, 'the people run to them, and look upon the Church of England as a parliamentary religion and establishment of the state'.[5] Both Leslie and Hickes agreed that the civil power can exercise over bishops and priests only the authority to which all citizens are subject, but 'the church is left wholly independent of the state as to her purely spiritual power and authority'.[6] The Church of England, they insisted, had subsided into a very compromising position regarding appointments to episcopal sees which were not canonically vacant. The solution was simple: 'the supremacy and power of the state over the church' should be 'reduced to what our laws before-mentioned have limited and explained it, viz., to extend only to a civil power, though in ecclesiastical causes and over ecclesiastical persons'. The application of such a measure was urgent; in itself the remedy was perfectly feasible. Christ gave his church no greater 'authority than was necessary for carrying on those ends for which he did institute it. And therefore to lessen that must certainly, so far, deprive us of those benefits which Christ designed to the world in the erecting his church among men.'[7]

The case for the subordination of the Church to the State was presented in its starkest form by Matthew Tindal. He was an uncompromising Erastian who knew the high church position from within. Indeed, as a young man, this future champion of Deism believed that his convictions pointed to Rome as his true spiritual home. His cool, detached mind soon reacted against what he termed 'the absurdities of popery', and for the rest of his life he was a vigilant foe of sacerdotal pretensions in any form. One of his earliest works was an *Essay on the Power of the Magistrate and the Rights of Mankind in Religion* (1697); nine years later he followed it with *The Rights of the Christian Church Asserted.*

Tindal assumed the essential validity of Locke's contract theory. Government is based upon agreement. 'As government at first was founded on the consent of the parties concerned, so it still continues on the same foot.'¹ Society needs religion, and cannot subsist without it. If the Church is a part of the organised community, and claims the benefits of that fact, and if the magistrate is responsible for all that happens in society, his power must extend to the Church and to those who serve it. His authority, it is true, is restricted; it includes whatever touches the public interest—'under which I reckon the determining of all those things which the good of the society will not permit to remain uncertain'²—but it does not authorise persecution on account of questions of belief. It is impossible for two independent powers to subsist in the same society. The clergy, therefore, cannot claim any rights which exempt them from the state's control. Tindal, of course, discussed power exclusively in terms of political and legislative sovereignty. He had at least this justification, that the high churchmen were currently claiming that convocation possessed independent powers of precisely this kind. Tindal insisted that every jurisdiction, in Church or State, derives from the king and parliament. There is no preserve where ecclesiastical authority is unchallenged. The king can suspend or deprive bishops; he can revoke their spiritual censures, 'nay can by his proclamation pardon all excommunication and restore people to the communion of the Church: it shews that there's no branch of spiritual jurisdiction which is not vested in him, and that all the jurisdiction which the archbishop, bishops, or any other inferior ecclesiastical judges have, is derived from him.'[1] So much is a plain matter of record. When you examine the legal constitution of the Church, it is clear that the Church has no independent jurisdiction, and the claim to 'an independent or divine power in the clergy of making and depriving ecclesiastical officers and ministers is . . . inconsistent with the laws'.[2] The kind of authority the Church is demanding is incompatible with its status as an established body; the clergy could have what they wanted if they were willing to be a 'private society'. Clerical ambition has aggravated a relatively simple problem; moreover it poses a constant threat. 'Any notion which is for the interests of the ecclesiastics, if once suffered to take root, will quickly grow and spread.'[3] To this theme Tindal devoted the greater part of a lengthy chapter: 'the clergy's pretending to an independent power has been the occasion of infinite mischief to the Christian world, as it is utterly inconsistent with the happiness of human society'.[4] Consequently those who try to extend priestly rights are binding the Church in 'ecclesiastical tyranny'.[5]

The theories debated by Non-jurors and Erastians became matters of acute contention in the Convocation controversy. The Church's nature and the measure of its dependence upon the State suddenly acquired explosive political significance. Throughout the latter part of the seventeenth century, convocation had been virtually in abeyance. It had been silenced by the counsels of its friends. After Archbishop Sheldon and the Earl of Clarendon agreed, in 1664, that clerical taxation should no longer be voted by the clerical assembly, there were no urgent reasons why convocation should sit and there were often sufficient causes why it should not. In 1689, when it was summoned to consider the proposed comprehension of dissenters, its temper was so refractory that William III saw little reason to repeat the experiment. It was Francis Atterbury, a clergyman as vehement in his political sympathies as in his religious convictions, who projected the question of convocation into the midst of general debate. Though a superficial scholar, Atterbury was a notable pamphleteer, and that in an age when experts like Swift and Hoadly had raised the dubious art of political propaganda to its highest point. *A Letter to a Convocation Man*[1] not only initiated the controversy but determined the lines along which it would develop.

Christianity, said Atterbury, was seriously endangered by its foes. The ills of the age were manifold and acute: 'an open looseness of men's principles and practices . . . a settled contempt of religion and priesthood'. It was a time 'when heresies of all kinds, when scepticism, deism, and atheism itself overrun us like a deluge . . . when the power of the magistrate and of the Church is struck at, and the indifference to all religion is endeavoured to be established by pleas for the justice and necessity of an universal unlimited toleration. . .'.[2] A deep-seated conspiracy was aimed at the Catholic faith itself. Only convocation could check heresy and cleanse Christianity of corruption. The bishops' courts and the universities would not do so; parliament was unfit even to attempt it. There are, said Atterbury, two kinds of authority within the nation; corresponding to each there is an appropriate representative body. The religious society is answerable solely to its head, who is Christ. He has provided officers for its government, and for the first three hundred years of its life the church was ruled by these officers alone. 'From hence it follows that such spiritual jurisdiction cannot be in its own nature necessarily dependent on the temporal; for then it can never have been lawfully exercised till kings, states and potentates became Christian.'[3]

Atterbury pitched his argument on a high plane. 'The Church then is a society instituted in order to a supernatural end; and as such must have an inherent power in it of governing itself in order to that end.' In the exercise of this power, a vital place was reserved for Convocation, which is 'an ecclesiastical court or assembly, essential to our constitution, and established by the law of it'.[4] At this point, Atterbury passed from his high theoretical grounds to his immediate practical concerns. He was anxious to establish an exact parallel between parliament and convocation. Each consists of two houses, the royal summons applies to both alike, and in each freedom of debate should be axiomatic. 'It is plain that convocations ought to be held as often as parliaments'; moreover, 'the liberties of the Church do in a great measure run parallel to those of the State'.[1]

The strength of Atterbury's case lay in the vigour of his plea for the spiritual independence of the Church.[2] This involved a matter of principle; Atterbury grasped it clearly and stated it cogently. But he was not a disinterested servant of the truth; he had a patently political motive, and in reality he was almost as erastian as many of the Whig Latitudinarians whom he despised. Once he had descended to their level, his weakness in constitutional history delivered him into their hands. His mistakes were promptly exposed by William Wake. Wake subsequently explained that his initial reply to Atterbury had been completed in great haste and in spite of illness and the pressure of many other duties;[3] in a surprisingly short time he published a sequel, a massive folio of nearly four hundred pages. Whereas Atterbury set forth little learning with the maximum effect, Wake almost buried his most telling points under an exhaustive examination of the historical evidence. A State Church presupposes that civil power extends, in some degree, to religious societies. Wake frankly accepted the fact and made no attempt to minimise it. 'That Christian Princes have a right not only to exercise authority over ecclesiastical persons, but to interpose in the ordering of ecclesiastical affairs too, neither our own articles and canons, nor the consent of the universal church . . . will suffer us to doubt.'[4] This is the basic thesis of the work. Step by step Wake established his case. The Christian prince has the power to call ecclesiastical synods; he therefore 'has a right to prescribe to his synods the matters on which they are to deliberate; but is moreover at liberty to determine both the manner and the method of their proceeding in them'.[5] If he chooses to do so, he can sit in them;

if he prefers, he can preside at their sessions.[1] Their decisions, when completed, carry no authority until he gives his approval; 'for though the faith of Christ neither depends upon the authority of man, nor is subject to the power either of synods or princes, as to what concerns the truth of it: yet what that faith is which shall be allowed to be professed in every community by the laws of it, and receive not merely protection but encouragement from the civil power, must be left to the prince to determine'.[2]

Thus far Wake has been laying down general principles; he now interjects, almost casually, one of his most damaging arguments against Atterbury's case. Two forms of summons were used to call together clerical assemblies; from this it follows that there were two kinds of council.[3] 'It is therefore as plain as anything can well be, that the convocation of the clergy considered as called by the parliamentary writs and sitting by virtue of them, and the convocation, considered as summoned by the convocation writ and the orders of the archbishop thereupon, are in their nature and constitution two different assemblies, and which by no means ought to be confounded together.'[4] The elaborate argument which Atterbury had based on the parallel between parliament and convocation split on this basic error. Wake still had to deal with Atterbury's claim that only convocation could meet the threat posed by heresy. The bishops, he pointed out, are immediate spiritual judges; they are invested with the authority to cope with heresy and they have at hand the necessary means. If they fail, the power of the magistrate is in reserve. 'The authority of the king in all these matters is, by law, very great and extensive; and I believe few evils can happen to the church which may not, in good measure, be provided for by it.'[5]

Atterbury realised the force of Wake's argument about the two types of convocation, and with great ingenuity tried to twist the evidence to suit his own needs. He still claimed that the clergy constituted 'an estate of the realm, assembling jointly with the parliament, and obliged by the rules of our constitution to attend always upon it'.[6] This fact, he insisted, laid bare the usurpation of power which underlay the archbishop's control of convocation. Atterbury did not really answer Wake, but he skilfully obscured the outlines of the argument, and in an intricate subject the public regards the most specious disputant as the victor. Wake, moreover, had alarmed even his friends by the inflexible Erastianism of his approach. To White Kennett (subsequently bishop of Peterborough) it was therefore clear that the whole issue needed restatement in clear and simple terms. In his *Ecclesiastical Synods and Parliamentary Convocations in the Church of England* Kennett showed that the position maintained by the bishops implied a higher, not a lower, doctrine of the Church's authority than that advocated by Atterbury and his friends. He placed as little emphasis as possible on the prince's authority over the Church, and as much as possible on the Church's right 'to assemble and agree upon the common measures of faith and unity'.[1] Atterbury, he claimed, had confused civil and ecclesiastical assemblies because he had not distinguished between the original ecclesiastical synod and the parliamentary convocation summoned by the king for purposes of taxation. As a result of this mistake, Atterbury had weakened the Church's claim to essential independence.

Atterbury's campaign was successful; his agitation resulted in a sitting convocation. He and his friends were consequently faced with the responsibility of turning their victory to some constructive use. His opponents had always questioned the feasibility of permitting convocation to sit. Wake had prophesied that the meetings would breed nothing but turmoil.[2] Bishop Burnet had foreseen that if the spirit reflected in Atterbury's pamphlets gained wider expression the results would inevitably be serious. 'A meeting of men of that temper would give but too much occasion to renew all the complaints that Nazianzen made of the synods and councils in his time; and would, I doubt, be a greater prejudice to the common concerns of the Christian religion than could be balanced by anything in it that the best of men might promote.'[3] The turbulent sessions of Convocation fully confirmed Burnet's estimate of 'the roughness and acrimony' that would result; they also showed that the controversy had entered a new phase. Once the right of Convocation to sit had been established, the debate shifted to the question of the authority exercised by the archbishop as the presiding officer. Atterbury, attacking Edmund Gibson, affirmed *The Power of the Lower House of Convocation to adjourn itself.* Gibson strenuously defended *The Right of the Archbishop to continue or prorogue the whole Convocation.* The paradox of the controversy had clearly emerged: those who had championed the spiritual independence of the Church were now undermining its essential nature. The whole character of the Church of England as an episopal church seemed to be at stake. Bishops are 'invested with the authority of imposing spiritual censures; in which authority all synodical acts are founded, and by which they must be enforced. Whereas the lower clergy, having no such authority in themselves, cannot exercise any power that must depend upon it.'[1]

The bitter wrangling which had made convocation a cockpit of indecisive and unedifying strife had brought clerical debates into serious disrepute. This was the damage which Wake had foreseen and foretold. To him it seemed a particularly cogent proof of the futility of this kind of contention. 'There is something in the nature of controversial writing so corruptive of morality, so apt to destroy some of the noblest graces of a Christian life, that I look upon the case to be much the same in that, as in other wars, and that nothing less than an absolute necessity ought to engage a good man in either.'[2] But this was not merely a struggle about Church government. It was an aspect of the bitter political feud which raged throughout the reign of Anne, and left no part of national life untouched. Atterbury and his friends could betray the cause for which they struggled only because they were contending for temporal as well as spiritual power.

An important by-product of this bitter struggle was the appearance of a massive work on ecclesiastical law.[3] Edmund Gibson had been one of the most erudite of Atterbury's opponents. He

had learned by painful experience the importance of 'the promoting of ecclesiastical order and discipline'.[1] But it was
impossible to codify the laws of the Church without clarifying
the relationship of the Church to the State—the origin of these
laws. 'The Church of England (considered not only as a spiritual
society, but also as a national church) tho' as national it hath the
same common head with the State, is yet of a different nature and
governed by different laws.'[2] Any legal terminology which suggests that 'all ecclesiastical authority is in the crown and derived
from thence', was originally devised to exclude 'the usurped
power of the Pope' and in no way vitiates that spiritual authority
which belongs to the bishop as such. The legal power certainly
comes from the king, but parliament has always recognised the
rights of the Church, by virtue of its inherent authority, to deal
with spiritual matters.[3] Having thus paved the way, Gibson
offers one of the most precise statements that this age provided of
the exact relation between the two powers. 'Having cleared the
divine right of the Church to the exercise of spiritual discipline, and
acknowledged that the external administration of that, and of all
ecclesiastical matters, in established courts and established forms,
is by authority from the Crown and in subordination to the royal
supremacy; and so taken off the reproach, on the one hand, of the
church being a mere creature of the State, and on the other of her
affecting an independence' which is unreal, he shows how 'the
administration of ecclesiastical matters (under the prince as
supreme head of the Church) stands distinguished by the law and
constitution of England from the administration of temporal
matters (under the same prince, as supreme sovereign in the State).
And how these two administrations flow from the same fountain,
and each is designed by the constitution for its own proper ends,
and limited to its own proper channel' can also be demonstrated.[4]

Gibson realised that such claims would in all probability be
challenged, and he cautiously defended himself against the charge
that in clarifying ecclesiastical law for the benefit of churchmen he
had infringed the prerogatives of the civil and the common law.[5]

But this mild answer failed to turn away wrath. Sir Michael Foster, an eminent judge, replied with *An Examination of the Scheme of Church-Power laid down by the Codex Juris Ecclesiastici Anglicani*. The uncompromising Erastianism of the Hanoverian age found no more convinced exponent. His basic contention rests on the doctrine beloved of all who magnify the power of the State at the expense of the Church. Christ's kingdom is not of this world; it is 'an empire of truth and righteousness in the hearts of his faithful subjects'.[1] Any one who tries to establish any kind of ecclesiastical jurisdiction is reviving the gross perversions of popery. The distinction often drawn between spiritual and temporal jurisdiction is false and unreal. The clergy love it, because it seems to substantiate their claims, but it has no foundation whatsoever.[2] The authority of bishops is not derived from the Word of God, and the powers which Gibson ascribes to the bishops are incompatible with the English constitution.[3] 'All the power of our bishops for correction and discipline is the creature of the State.'[4] It has been conferred by the temporal power, and is exercised only within such bounds as the civil ruler permits. The Reformation established this pattern. Our forefathers, having abrogated papal jurisdiction 'went to the root of the evil and declared that all jurisdiction as well ecclesiastical as civil is invested in, and exercised by delegation from, the Crown'.[5] A minute examination of Tudor statutes shows that there is virtually no limit to the authority ascribed to the sovereign in spiritual matters, and Foster triumphantly concludes his pamplet by reaffirming the absolute extent of the temporal power which the State rightly exercises over the Church.[6]

The ingredients which had hitherto contributed to the debates on Church and State were many and diverse; most of them coalesced in the fierce controversy precipitated by Bishop Hoadly of Bangor, and known by the name of his see. The views of the Non-jurors had gained fresh prominence because of an unhappy coincidence. Shortly after the suppression of the first Jacobite rebellion, Hickes' work on *The Constitution of the Catholic Church* was posthumously published, and angered all supporters of the Revolution settlement. Fear of Stuart absolutism and resentment against priestly pretensions made the Erastians doubly suspicious of any attempt to magnify the claims of the Church at the expense of the rights of the State. Convocation was inevitably involved. The Bangorian controversy intensified the turmoil in which its proceedings had recently been embroiled, and was directly responsible for its suppression.

Contention had made Hoadly famous. He had not won pre-eminence among Whig pamphleteers without making himself feared and hated by Tories and High Churchmen. He became, noted Whiston, 'a great writer of controversy, one of the most pernicious things to true Christianity in the world ... and indeed this Bangorian controversy seemed for a great while to engross the attention of the public'.[1] In his *Preservative against the Principles and Practice of the Non-jurors* (1716), Hoadly refuted Hickes' position. In the following year he preached, and by royal command published, his notorious sermon on *The Nature of the Kingdom or Church of Christ*. Hoadly abruptly dismissed the argument that the non-juring bishops had been unlawfully deprived. The supreme power can revoke what it has bestowed;[2] even if it had not conferred the sphere of jurisdiction it could still withdraw it, since 'every government hath a right to everything necessary for its own defence and preservation'.[3] Hoadly, whose perceptions were far keener in political than in religious matters, claimed that his position rested on 'a few uncontested principles of civil government and on the plain and express declarations of the gospel itself'.[4] Since God himself had instituted civil government, he could not extend to ecclesiastical rulers any powers likely to jeopardise his primary gift of political order.[5] The jurisdiction which bishops exercise is subordinate in nature, and can never be allowed to conflict with the sovereign power of the State.[6] 'In all your civil concerns, the public good, the peace, the happiness of that society to which you belong will easily and safely conduct you both to know and to do the will of

God.'¹ In religious matters, the words of Christ will be our sole and sufficient guide. The rights of the individual conscience thus supersede the authority of the Church.² His view of the relation of Church to State is far from precise, but it is clear that he tends to blur the lines of demarcation between them. The pre-eminence of the State reduces the Church to a subordinate and dependent position, and makes the difference between citizenship and church membership extremely vague.

Hoadly equated the Church with Christ's kingdom, and the text of his sermon ('My kingdom is not of this world') provided him with his point of departure. There are no vicegerents of this kingdom among men. There is no visible human authority: if Christ is the king, he is the only lawgiver, the sole judge over his subjects.³ No one else is entitled to offer rewards or affix punishments; if he should do so he would infringe Christ's exclusive prerogative.⁴ The laws and sanctions of the Church have no relevance to the affairs of this world; they are 'declarations relating to the favour of God in another state after this'.⁵ In spiritual matters reliance on outward constraint is wholly out of place, and the attempt to apply the methods of this world to a kingdom which does not belong to it has resulted in incalculable harm.⁶ His contemporaries noted with dismay that Hoadly's definition of the Church excluded any possibility either of ascribing to it real authority or of permitting it to exercise effective discipline. He went further: he virtually dissolved the Church as a corporate body. He insisted that there is no such thing as a visible Church of Christ.⁷ He conceived of a religious society in the most tenuous and incoherent terms. Apparently he visualised the Church as a vaguely defined spiritual body, composed of those who think alike and who individually yield themselves to Christ's rule. The essence of Christianity lay in unfettered private judgment. From this he drew an important corollary: sincerity is the chief virtue which Christ demands of his followers. The mechanics of the good life, like the structure of the divine society, are inconsequential; a man's 'title to God's favour' depends 'upon his real sincerity in the conduct of his conscience and of his own actions under it.[1] Hoadly believed that it is possible to recover 'Christianity in its first simplicity'; in essence it concerned a religious relationship between God and the individual, and would express itself in appropriate conduct.

Hoadly's sermon plunged both the Church and the nation into a maelstrom of controversy. Dr Snape of Eton maintained that Christ had appointed ministers in his Church who had authority to act in his stead. Hoadly denied absolute authority to the apostles themselves.[2] Snape accused Hoadly of sophistry and equivocation, and charged him with keeping a Jesuit in his household. This may indicate the mounting confusion which enveloped the debate; it gives no conception of its expanding scope. Most of the issues which divided the Whigs and Tories made their appearance in the controversy and most of the prominent writers on either side were drawn into it. A couple of hundred books and pamphlets were published, and the catalogue of them, in Hoadly's works, fills fifteen folio pages. The bitterness of the struggle gave Hoadly a strong claim to an unenviable primacy among those who have been hated and vilified. But he had ardent partisans of his own. Balguy believed that Hoadly made a pre-eminent contribution to a more enlightened political theory. He had demolished 'the wild schemes of patriarchal and despotic power'; he had erected 'in their stead that glorious pile of solid reasoning and sound politics which protects our just liberties and deserves to be reckoned among the principal bulwarks of our constitution'.[3] But praise was drowned in an uproar of abuse. Convocation appointed a committee to study his views. Its report declared that Hoadly's recent publications tended to subvert all government and discipline in the Church of Christ: they would also undermine the authority of the legislature to enforce obedience in matters of religion. The government had no intention of seeing its clerical favourite censured and the prorogation of Convocation ended, for many a decade, its participation in religious life. Hoadly answered at great length the criticisms of Convocation;[1] he carefully ignored the far more serious challenge posed by William Law's attacks.

In his first two *Letters*, Law was content to prove that Hoadly's views endangered the constitution of the Church as a regular society. Hoadly's basic premise about sincerity might establish a man's moral integrity, but it did nothing to distinguish between truth and error. A man can be sincere in defending falsehood; by Hoadly's definition God should be as well pleased with a person who rejected Christ as with one who accepted him—provided both were sincere.[2] His treatment of authority, said Law, is superficial; he has dealt with the ministry and with all its offices in a way which ignores the fundamental acts of a religious society. He has not only dissolved the Church as a corporate body, he has undermined all organised societies of every kind. In the name of individual freedom he has created social chaos. In his third and longest *Letter* Law offered a defence of the Church as a visible society, entitled to discipline its members and endowed with authority sufficient for all its distinctive purposes. With the remorseless logic which marks all his controversial works, Law cut through the cloud of words and the tangle of qualifications with which Hoadly enveloped serious religious themes.[3]

Hoadly's insight was far greater in politics than in religion. The exaggerated individualism of his theory of the Church carried, as its natural corollary, the necessity of toleration and without demur he accepted this consequence. All who belong to Christ's church, regardless of their position in the world, are equally his subjects, 'and no one of them more than another hath authority, either to make new laws for Christ's subjects, or to impose a new sense upon the old ones; or to judge, censure, or punish the servants of another Master in matters relating purely to conscience or salvation'.[4] Earlier writers often anticipated his theories; few of his contemporaries, either among Whig statesmen or Anglican bishops, so consistently advocated toleration as a desirable policy. Hoadly's supporters often echoed his views; even his opponents conceded that toleration is an axiom of good statesmanship, and were ill at ease when defending policies which seemed to infringe it. To Latitudinarians like Sykes and Jackson, toleration is a consequence of natural law. It is a right 'common to all mankind, and such as no man can give up to or lawfully restrain in another'. It is true that it is hedged about with limitations. No one can 'do, in consequence of such doctrines, anything inconsistent with other men's rights, whether religious or civil, or the public good'. It must not be pushed to extremes; neither must it be infringed. Persecution is an affront to reason and good government.[1] John Rogers, though he had little sympathy with Hoadly and his followers, agreed that the decisive consideration is whether or not the views which claim toleration are detrimental to the public welfare, and this 'leaves the whole question of toleration entirely to the magistrate's judgment'. This conviction coincided perfectly with the prevalent belief that the justification of an established church is its contribution to security and public order. Since a State religion is the great bulwark of social stability, the magistrate must be free to check the expression of views that challenge its privileges, especially when religious disputes seem likely to endanger public peace. A man can worship as he wishes in his own house; no one can compel him 'to go abroad to the public rites', but he must not invoke conscience as a pretext for interfering with the faith and practice which the State has authorised. No one can be allowed to proselytise among the adherents of the established church.[2]

As far as the dissenters were concerned, the practical implications of this attitude seemed clear enough. Once the excitements of Queen Anne's reign were past, few Anglicans advocated the repeal of toleration, but it was generally agreed that no further concessions should be made. Changes disturbed the *status quo*, and the position of the Church seemed so precarious that sober clerics were apprehensive of anything that might disrupt the constitutional arrangements. A touch of irritation marks their references to the insufficient gratitude of the nonconformists. 'The moderation and indulgence which have been used towards them deserves a better return.' Sometimes a veiled threat is mingled with the resentment. 'I hope the greater and wiser part of our dissenters are satisfied with the liberties indulged them by law. Whiles they are so, I know no wise man who desires they be taken from them.'[1] But the nonconformists were not content with 'few and reasonable limitations'. They believed that their loyalty to the Whig party and to the house of Hanover merited a better return than suffrance, and they freely said so. Their demand for the repeal of the Corporation and Test Acts raised in a practical form the just limits of toleration. Hoadly and Sykes claimed that the objectionable laws did far more harm than good. They embittered religious feelings; they jeopardised economic progress; they ought to be repealed. On the contrary, said Bishop Gibson; the acts were designed for the security of Church and State and ought to be retained.[2] Those who advocate repeal talk much about 'natural rights' and about the way existing legislation infringes them. 'But is not society and government itself founded in the abridgment of natural rights?' Consider how many are debarred from the franchise, how few can qualify to sit in the House of Commons. If these restrictions are just, why not those which protect the national church?[3] Thomas Sherlock stated the same point with even stronger emphasis. The controversial laws were designed to protect the Church as an integral part of the constitution, and this could best be done if the foes of the establishment were excluded from positions of power.[4] To receive the sacrament was not a qualification for office, but merely a proof that the recipient qualified.[5] Was it legitimate to restrict official positions to those who favoured the established constitution in Church and State? Of course, he replied; after all, self-preservation is the basic law of political life. If the nonconformists again seized power they would undoubtedly be prompted by a spirit indistinguishable from that of Cromwell, and 'hence the necessity was urgent to protect the mass of the nation from the enthusiasm of the few'.[6] In doing so there was no difference in principle between imposing an oath and requiring the reception of the sacrament. Both appealed to a religious sanction; the sacrament was merely the more effective barrier. The need to preserve the unity of society was beyond dispute; this unity expressed itself in two forms—politically in the State, religiously in the Church. Sherlock believed that those who stood outside the constitution might expect suffrance, but nothing more. Nonformists might be tolerated; they should not be encouraged.[1]

The defence of the discriminatory laws had raised the question of the exact status of an established church. What was its theoretical justification, and what were its rights and privileges? Anglicans of all schools agreed that a strong case could be made for a State church, and a certain similarity marks their arguments —always excepting the views of that perverse and wayward genius, William Warburton. Gibson stated the basic issue succinctly enough: it was 'whether a civil power *can* establish a national church; and if it can, whether it is or is not conducive to the ends of religion and of public peace and order that such a church be established.'[2] Anglican apologists believed that the answer to the first question was Yes. In the answer to the second they found the strongest argument for a state church. Natural law was the foundation of civil law; to both the preservation of order was a paramount necessity, and the chief bulwark of the public well-being was the influence of religion. 'The universal experience and practice of mankind' prove 'that civil government cannot subsist without regard to the will of God, or, in other words, without the sanctions of religion'.[3] The magistrate must consequently take account of anything that weakens Christianity, since it will inevitably weaken the State. To promote this necessary and beneficent relationship between civil order and the beliefs which maintain it, he may decide to establish a particular church. He cannot compel anyone to share his views, but he can restrain those who resist them. Writers of all schools insisted that though the magistrate's right to establish a church was beyond question, his dictates could extend only as far as the due scope of civil acts permits. He cannot override conscience. He must not expect uniformity: our position as men, as Christians, as Protestants, as Anglicans shows that it is unobtainable, and the fact that Scripture never specifies it as a desideratum of Christianity suggests that it is not desirable. The coercive powers of the Church are strictly limited, since discipline has too often answered 'no end but of establishing hypocrisy by law and beating down of all supports of truth and honesty'.[1] The powers of the magistrate are extensive; law touches life at many points, including the organisation and worship of the Church. He holds the gift of office in his hand; he grants it to whom he pleases—as a sign of favour, not as a requirement of justice. But though the established Church should be comprehensive, and should permit such liberty and latitude as basic human rights require, the magistrate is justified in preventing any infringement of privileges, and he can curtail any 'public disputations' that may endanger peace.[2]

Warburton was too distinctive, and from the point of view of his contemporaries too important, to be included among the ordinary champions of the establishment. He characteristically affirmed that those who support a State church and those who oppose it are alike wrong: 'while the arguments of both are bottomed on the same mistaken foundation, the one defends a test on such reasonings as destroy toleration; and the other opposes it on such as conclude equally against the very essence and being of a natural religion'.[3] With his customary arrogance, he declared that he alone was right; with his love of paradox, he undertook to defend both complete toleration and restrictive legislation.[4] His method was simple. First he defined the nature of both Church and State; then he defined the compact which united them; in the light of this he proved the validity of a test act. Reason and nature show that both Church and State are necessary to human life, and are interdependent. Religion could not remedy moral disorders without the aid of government, and government would be ineffectual without the support of religion. At every point the one needs the other; they perform different functions, in different ways, from different motives, for different ends.[1] It is often assumed that the hinges of society are rewards and punishments; but the State can punish, but cannot really reward, while the Church can reward but cannot really punish. So religion and government perforce are partners, ever assisting each other, and complementary at every point.[2] Civil society was established for one primary purpose—to provide 'security to the temporal liberty and property of mankind'.[3] The State is not concerned with the salvation of souls nor with the means to this end—therefore it supports toleration, but with proper and necessary limitations. The magistrate can permit no denial of 'the three fundamental principles of natural religion, namely, the being of God, his providence over human affairs, and the natural essential difference of moral good and evil. These doctrines it is directly his office to cherish, protect and propagate; and all oppugners of them it is as much his right and duty to restrain as any the most flagrant offenders against the civil peace'.[4] In restraining them he acts from political and not from religious motives.

The nature of the Church, said Warburton, is indicated by the ends it serves—'first to procure the favour of God, and secondly to advance and improve our intellectual nature'.[5] The first does not require an organised society, but the second does. From the nature of the societies which he has described, Warburton deduced the nature of the compact which united them. Bishop Hurd remarked that Warburton used the idea of an alliance because of the great popularity which the contract theory enjoyed in contemporary political thought; 'the meaning', he added, 'is this, that our church establishment is such as in equity it must have been, had the terms of it been settled by mutual agreement between the two parties. Which . . . is only saying that those terms are just and reasonable.'[6] The Church is concerned with the soul, the State with the body; if they are to deal with the whole man, they must unite. Since each is free, this must be done by mutual compact. An established church is 'indeed no other than a politic league and alliance for mutual support and defence'.¹ Each side is prompted by strong motives. Each looks for solid advantages. The State needs the sanctions which only religion can add to duty and obligation—and especially to oaths. The Church possesses no civil power; left to itself it would have no security against external violence. The 'great preliminary and fundamental article' of the alliance is that 'the Church shall apply its utmost influence in the service of the State, and the state shall support and protect the church'. This means that a 'mutual communication of their respective powers is necessary'; and since the Church is the weaker body she resigns her independence to the State.² In return she receives a public endowment for her ministers, a 'place for her representatives in the court of legislature', and the right of maintaining courts for the reformation of manners. In return for such extensive gifts, the State is entitled to proportionate concessions and these are epitomised in the phrase 'supremacy in matters ecclesiastical'. By 'resigning up her independency', the Church has made 'the magistrate her supreme head, without whose approbation and allowance, she can administer, transact, or decree nothing'.³ Every political right which the Church exercised as an independent body before the agreement was concluded, has been resigned to the State. Warburton did not minimise the scope of this abdication, nor did he feel that it required any defence. The arrangement was admirably designed to achieve its purpose, viz., 'that the Church should serve the State, and the State protect the Church'.⁴

Warburton claimed that he had elaborated a theory 'formed solely on the contemplation of nature and the unvariable reason of things'. He admitted that it bore 'an amazing agreement with our own happy establishment'.⁵ This was a coincidence; the magistrate is not committed to one type of religion, and no State church has an inalienable right to its privileges. In making an alliance, the State is always prompted by considerations of utility. If there are more churches than one, it selects the strongest, extends to it the benefits of establishment, and grants toleration to the rest.⁶ It follows, however, that the State church is protected from attack by members of the other churches, since, from the Church's point of view, this was the sole purpose of the covenant made with the State. Enemies could most effectively injure the Church by securing places of power in the State. Hence a test-law is the inevitable consequence of the alliance between Church and State.

Warburton's work was too arrogant in tone and too paradoxical in character to be generally acceptable. Bishop Horsley, indeed, claimed that it showed 'the general good policy of the establishment and the necessity of a test for its security upon principles which republicans themselves cannot easily deny'.[1] Hurd was closer to the truth when he remarked that 'it was neither calculated to please the high church divines nor the low'. Yet few works reflect so accurately the temper of eighteenth-century debate. Here we find the self-confident spirit of the age, its prudential ethics, its intellectual view of religion, its argumentative spirit, its interest in enquiry, even its persuasion that it favoured toleration in a suitably restricted form. *The Alliance* was characteristic of the period in basing its argument on deduction, not on fact. When Warburton was asked for a copy of the agreement between Church and State, he felt it was sufficient to reply that it was 'in the same archive' as the compact between the magistrate and the people.[2] His hypothesis was no more arbitrary than that of Locke. In politics (which is an 'artificial system'), the strength of a theory is 'estimated not according to its agreement with fact but right reason'.[3] Even Warburton's contemporaries were uneasy about a defence of the establishment which relied so exclusively on the usefulness of the Church to the State.[4] But at least he believed that 'truth and public utility coincide', that 'truth is productive of utility, and utility indicative of truth'.[5]

The debate about Church and State involved the issue of toleration; the two controversies became intertwined, and both owed their peculiar urgency to the presence of the nonconformists. Churchmen were defending positions which were actually under attack. Everyone, of course, paid lip-service to toleration, but some Anglicans sought ways of curtailing it in practice while defending it in principle. The nonconformists claimed that the theory, if consistently applied, would involve an extension of the privileges they enjoyed, and to such an extension they felt themselves fully entitled. The Revolution and the Act of Toleration had receded into the middle distance. The excitements of the reign of Anne—the embarrassments caused by Defoe, the hazards of the Occasional Conformity and Schism Acts, the controversy precipitated by Calamy—were half-forgotten. The struggle for the principle of freedom had given way to a political opportunism sporadically manœuvreing to induce the government to grant further concessions. The dignity of the earlier struggle had largely vanished, and even in the narrow sphere of bargaining it registered few gains. For much of the period, most dissenters accepted small favours from the government, and made the best of a toleration modified by partial civil disability. The diffident apologetic of this stage is faithfully reflected in the works of Samuel Chandler. Chandler did not object to the principle of establishment but only to the form in which Rogers and others defended it. Yet the true nature of religion, in its inwardness, is something that cannot be established.[1] Nor dare one claim that it has ever been strengthened when positions of power and authority have been entailed upon its representatives. The policies of State churches, and their actions, give the unpleasant impression that the purpose of an establishment is not the conversion of the many but the aggrandisement of the few.[2] On Roger's principles, at his trial Christ would have been stripped of all defence, and his judges have been fully vindicated; the early Christians deserved all the persecution that was visited upon them; the Reformers were irresponsible trouble-makers, and most missionaries are misguided idealists.[3] When religion is established, the spirit of persecution insinuates itself into public life. Trivialities provide the pretext for repression: 'hard words, technical terms, and inexplicable phrases, points of mere speculation, abstruse questions and metaphysical notions. . .'.¹ But Chandler wrote with an irenic purpose. The time is long past, he said, when matters like gowns, crosses or godfathers were sufficient to keep Christians apart.² Many of the charges which the Anglicans bring against the nonconformists are unfounded, and the spirit of controversy is out of place. Could not a more flexible attitude prevail in the established Church? Need the demand for subscription so often prove a barrier? 'And I hope I shall be forgiven if I say that the circumstances of the present times point out to men of all parties that have a regard for religion and the happiness of these kingdoms seriously to think of methods that will tend to their common union.'³

Such sentiments are above exception; the spirit behind them is mild and charitable. Such an attitude neither re-animated the ancient debate about freedom nor wrung from a reluctant government any significant concessions. Its ideal was to achieve 'the desirable mean, to preserve strict liberty without licentiousness, and strict order without encroaching on natural rights'.⁴ But nonconformity was redeemed from this amiable apathy by the genius of two men, Isaac Watts and Michaijah Towgood, who succeeded in giving a new turn to the controversy. It was natural for Watts to protest against 'an imposing spirit' and the persecution in which it always issues.⁵ It was characteristic of him to remind his fellow dissenters that they could not boast of spiritual privileges unless they had already vindicated them in the quality of their lives. There must be no controversial spirit, no presumptuous comparison of the relative merits of the two sides. The real aim of nonconformity should be to assert true freedom, and only the humble in spirit could effectually promote it. To set the dissenting position in its proper perspective, Watts first considered the nature of civil government. Order is the prime requisite of social existence. 'Mankind have been led by the principles of reason and self-preservation to join themselves in distinct civil societies; wherein, as by a compact, expressed or implied, every single person is concerned in the welfare and safety

of all the rest.'¹ Government takes account of religious issues
only in so far as they 'have a most vivid evident reference to the
natural and civil welfare of men in the present life'. Rulers are
concerned with religion as a guarantee of social stability, not as a
means of obtaining salvation. 'The common acknowledgment
of the one living and true God, both by the princes and people,
by the governors and the government, is by far the best and surest
bond of government and the common peace.'² Watts believed
that rulers might reasonably promote training in natural religion
and basic morality. He admitted that the magistrates might wish
to undergird their programme with public worship organised 'as
an act of natural religion', but 'it is difficult to find how this may
be done in any nation without intrenching on the liberty of mankind and imposing upon the conscience of some of the inhabitants
of the land'.³ Nor have the rulers any right to impose a particular
faith or a pattern of worship on those whose consciences compel
them to dissent. Since the distinguishing peculiarities of any sect
are never essential to the well-being of a state, the magistrate
cannot command others to practise the religion which he himself
professes. Nor has he any right to divert public funds to support
his own form of faith. 'I cannot yet see any sufficient reason why
a state should appoint the peculiarities of any revealed religion or
the special rites and ceremonies of any particular worshippers, or
the men who celebrate them to be supported at the public charge.
For these peculiarities are not necessary to the preservation of the
state, nor to the common outward civil welfare of a people;
and I think the power of the magistrate reaches no further.'⁴
Above all, Watts insisted that the State has no right to penalise
the subject because of his faith. It can ask whether he holds views
which prevent him from discharging the duties of his citizenship or
which nullify the obligations of public vows, but it must not lay
any public odium or civil incapacity upon him merely because
of his beliefs. Every member of a state has the same right to
office as any other member, 'nor is it reasonable or just that a
capacity of preferment should be taken from him by law, but

for some civil crime or misdemeanour'.[1] Watts objected to a state religion because it involved an incongruous mixture of things human and divine: 'the laws and rights of God and of Caesar, persons and ordinances temporal and spiritual . . . powers sacred and human. . .'.[2] The results are lamentable; 'while we hold forth this confused mass and mixture of things divine and human and call it the religion of Christ, we tempt the men of infidelity to establish themselves in their unbelief'.[3]

Watts argued his case with considerable restraint. He admitted that where one church embraces the majority of the population the magistrate naturally will fill most political offices from among its members. He was at pains to emphasise how deeply conscious the nonconformists were of the benefits which they derived from living under the British constitution. He strongly objected to what he considered the discriminatory consequences of a doctrinaire view of the right relations of Church and State. In effect Watts argued, in a reasonable spirit but on high grounds, against the civil establishment of a national church. The moderate dissenters had once looked for equality through comprehension. Watts foreshadows a new position; in due course nonconformity will seek equality through disestablishment.

The next stage in the controversy is represented by the letters of the Rev. John White on the one hand, and of the Rev. Michaijah Towgood on the other. White was a popular but pedestrian exponent of a view which tried to embrace most of the emphases current in Anglican circles. The Church of England constituted at least 'one half-part of the constitution';[4] yet it was wholly independent of the State in essential spiritual matters. To oppose it was tantamount to treason; the Test Act was a necessary safeguard, and partial disability was the best that dissenters could expect. His book was not an impressive performance and is notable only because it inspired 'one of the enduring monuments of the polemics of dissent'.[5] Towgood was a powerful controversialist, and he systematically pulverised White's *Letters*.

Towgood began, as was natural for a nonconformist, with a

plea for freedom. He found it an affront to human dignity that church authorities should limit man's search for the truth.[1] Like all dissenters he regarded the Test Act as an infringement of the essential rights of the citizen. It is shocking that the sacrament should thus be degraded; it is worse that the Church, through its champion, Mr White, should defend this abuse as a necessary bulwark of the Church. 'What Church, alas! must that be which cannot be preserved but by an acknowledged prostitution and perversion of a holy sacrament! Surely it cannot be the Church of Christ!'[2] Nor is there any indication that God, who is the source of civil order, ever intimated that it must be defended by such a profanation of sacred things.[3] Is this not 'making that a political instrument to divine Christians which Christ instituted as a religious instrument to coalesce and unite them?' How offensive it must be to God to see a sacrament 'thus prostituted, perverted, made an engine and tool of state, employed to strengthen and perpetuate differences amongst good Christians'! To the nonconformist the Test Act seemed 'a most unrighteous restraint upon us, and an undoubted violation of our natural rights'.[4] 'All I plead for', he said, 'is the removal of the incapacity under which they [the dissenters] unjustly lie, the breaking of a disgraceful yoke which the test hath put upon their needs, and the restoring them to their native freedom, and honour, and right; that the State may have liberty, if it thinks it needs their faithful services, to avail itself of them.'[5]

Towgood was essentially concerned with more fundamental problems. The basic question, he claimed, concerned the nature of the Church. White consistently evaded this issue; nor would he state precisely to whom God had committed the power to define terms of communion or determine controversies of faith—to the king and parliament, to the clergy in convocation, to each bishop in his diocese, or to the whole body of Christian people?[6] The entire controversy really depended on a single point: 'Is there any other lawgiver or king in the Church of God to whose authority and command, as to things religious, Christians are bound to submit, BESIDES Jesus Christ? Or is there not?' The magistrate has no right to interfere with the pattern of worship or with the substance of belief. 'When the powers of this world take upon themselves authoritatively to interpret and prescribe in things of religion, which are Christ's kingdom and province, they act beyond their sphere; they invade the throne of another prince; the rights of Christians are violated, the unity of the Church is broken, and a gate is opened for innumerable superstitions to enter.'¹ To Towgood it was clear that 'no civil magistrate has ever had, or ever can have, any right, authority or power over the conscience and religious opinions of Christians'; to God alone belongs 'the glory of dominion over conscience, and all authority in religion throughout all churches, in all ages'.² With such a view, said Towgood, contrast the Erastianism prevailing in Anglican circles. He seized on Warburton's admission that 'the Church has, by contract or alliance, resigned up her supremacy in matters ecclesiastical and her independency to the State'. The evidence of facts is unmistakable: 'the Church of England is really a parliamentary church . . . not properly an ally but a mere creature of the state. It depends entirely upon the acts and authority of parliament for its very essence and frame. The qualification of its ministers, their power to officiate, the manner in which they are to administer the sacraments are all limited and prescribed by authority of parliament'.³ Is it not strange that the 'presumed successors of the apostles' can be suspended or even removed by the civil power?⁴ So Towgood returned repeatedly to the question how such a situation had emerged. 'How came the civil magistrate by this authority in the Church of Christ? Who gave him power to decree rites in Christian worship, which Christ never decreed, and to make articles of faith which Christ never made? Neither Christ nor the apostles ever gave him this authority: from whence then is it derived?' 'You are silent and cannot say.'⁵ The contrast between the actual and the ideal is too sharp to be ignored. 'Now here, Sir, I am pressed with an insuperable difficulty how to reconcile this constitution of the

211

Church of Christ. Are they not most indisputably two different societies, subject to two different, sometimes opposite, authorities, animated and governed by two different heads? In Christ's Church, himself is the only sovereign and head: he only hath the power to decree ceremonies and rites, to fix terms of communion and authority in points of faith: nor hath any earthly prince power to make laws in his kingdom.'¹

From his argument Towgood drew certain inferences. If the magistrate does not control the outward life of the Church—if it is not 'now become entirely and absolutely a civil system'²—it is not a State church and has no right to persecute, or even to rely on discriminatory laws. But if the magistrate has such power, the establishment is preserved at the cost of the essential Christian character of the Church. While not explicitly a plea for disestablishment, Towgood's *Letters* clearly implied that there was no other escape from the dilemma. Meanwhile he reaffirmed the nonconformists' position. They take their stand on 'the sufficiency of Scripture, the right of private judgment (our distinguishing principles as dissenters)', and they note that when the Anglican Church contends with Rome it occupies the same ground.³ The dissenters believe in freedom and they claim a fuller toleration; and concerning their historic witness 'they rejoice . . . that they have entered their protest against the impositions and inventions of men, which have corrupted the simplicity, enervated the vigour, deformed the beauty, and broken the communion of the body of Christ'.⁴

Towgood carried the debate as far as the presuppositions of his age permitted. But gradually conditions changed. The activities, the interests, the methods and the temper of nonconformity changed as well. The radical dissenters of the later eighteenth century seized the initiative, and the defenders of the established Church were thrown on the defensive. This belongs, however, to a later phase of our story, to the demand for reform and Burke's massive resistance to it in the name of tradition. One figure, however, who chronologically belongs to the later period fittingly

closes this phase of the discussion. William Paley was the embodi-
ment of many of the virtues which the eighteenth century prized
most highly. He was so reasonable that he often seems merely
pedestrian. Common sense never found a more persuasive
exponent. His wariness of 'enthusiasm' kept him close to the
realities of political and ecclesiastical life. He summed up the
debate with a notable freedom from doctrinaire theories.

Paley published his *Principles of Moral and Political Philosophy* in
1785. At the outset he saluted, across the intervening century, the
venerated figure of John Locke. 'The credit of that great name,
the courage and liberality of his principles, the skill and clearness
with which his arguments are proposed, no less than the weight
of the arguments themselves, have given a reputation and currency to his opinions of which I am persuaded, in any unsettled
state of public affairs, the influence would be felt.'[1] Though
Paley was perhaps the last great representative of the Whig and
latitudinarian spirit, at certain points he refused to follow Locke's
lead. In his approach to Church and State, he was soberly
utilitarian. 'A religious establishment is no part of Christianity',
he said; 'it is only the means of inculcating it.'[2] The New
Testament, unlike the Old, gives us no guidance on church
government. Christ issued no commands; an appeal to the
apostles yields inconclusive results. We can infer that church
order took shape in response to the needs of the times; it did not
develop because of any conscious intention of devising a sacrosanct system. So Paley reached the conclusion which governs
all his thought on this subject: 'the authority therefore of a church
establishment is founded on its utility'. The decisive consideration should always be, what is most likely to promote 'the
preservation and communication of religious knowledge'? If
anyone questions the wisdom of this modest approach, let him
consider the results to which more ambitious theories have led.
'Every other idea, and every other end that have been mixed
with this, as the making of the Church an engine, or even an ally
of the State, converting it into the means of strengthening or

diffusing influence, or regarding it as a support of regal in opposition to popular forms of government have served only to debase the institution and to introduce into it numerous corruptions and abuses.'[1]

There are three distinguishing characteristics requisite in any national church. You must have a clergy; there must be 'a legal provision for their maintenance'; this support must be restricted to 'the teachers of a particular sect of Christianity'. Paley realised that the third point is the most contentious, especially since he reluctantly concluded that inevitably there must be resort to some kind of 'test'. Such imposed requirements check enquiry, violate liberty and ensnare the consciences of the clergy; therefore they should be as simple as possible, and 'should never reach farther than is strictly necessary'.[2] At every point the sober utilitarianism of Paley's position emerges. It is wise to have inequalities in the ministry since the Church thereby corresponds more nearly to the society in which it functions—and 'prizes of different value' provide a valuable incentive. The hypothetical compacts which Locke and Warburton posited are beyond historical verification, so Paley argued from the more pedestrian ground that what works well must be good. He reached 'the unreserved conclusion that the jurisdiction of the magistrate is limited by no consideration but that of general utility'.[3] 'The general tendency to the public happiness' will govern policy. It will dictate that toleration shall be as wide as possible, and that any limitation placed upon it must be imposed only because of the proven social perniciousness of certain views. It is desirable as well as right that dissenters should enjoy full rights as citizens and complete freedom to worship as they choose.

This represented the conclusion to which the Age of Reason brought the debate on Church and State. Common sense and utility dictated the pattern. Extravagent claims and highflown theories were banished. Liberty was given the widest possible scope, and peace was to be promoted by mutual forbearance. But the answer was already an anachronism. The radical dissenters were placing the problem in a different context. The fear of change was raising up opponents of even moderate reform. Before long the French Revolution would shatter the presuppositions of the departing age. Paley represented the Indian summer of eighteenth-century assumptions. His own summary of his own conclusions may serve as the epitaph of its aspirations. 'That a comprehensive national religion, guarded by a few articles of peace and conformity, together with a legal provision for the clergy of that religion; and with *complete* toleration for all dissenters from the established Church, without any other limitation or exception than what arises from the conjunction of dangerous political dispositions with certain religious tenets, appears to be, not only the most just and liberal, but the wisest and safest system which a state can adopt; in as much as it united the several perfections which a religious constitution ought to aim at: liberty of conscience, with means of instruction; the progress of truth, with the peace of society; the right of private judgment, with the care of the public safety.'[1]

CHAPTER VIII

THE APPEAL TO THE AUTHORITY OF SCIENCE

THE eighteenth century was not a period notable for scientific advance. It was, however, an age profoundly affected by the scientific outlook. The influence of Newton was all-pervasive. In each of the languages of western Europe, popular expositions made the essentials of his system accessible even to the common man. The results of the new attitude appeared in a variety of ways. The authority of science combined with the prestige of reason to challenge every form of 'superstition'; traditional views were suspect till they had been scrutinised and tested. In particular, it seemed imperative to re-examine the nature of man. Thus the new science inspired a new psychology. It was no longer sufficient to argue from conventional assumptions about the workings of man's mind, and David Hartley opened a new chapter by relating psychological states to physiological processes. This was a position adopted and amplified by Joseph Priestley. Moreover, the pattern of man's conduct is affected by the pattern of his thought, and thus the influence of the new science can be traced in the development of a new ethic. The eighteenth century was profoundly interested in moral theory. In Hartley, psychology was related to physiology, and both were invoked to support his ethical principles. In Godwin, a new understanding of nature, combined with a new conception of man, issued in a moral theory suffused with confidence and hope.

Hartley made no secret of his indebtedness to others. The initial impulse, he tells us, came from 'The Rev. Mr Gay', who 'asserted the possibility of deducing all our intellectual pleasures

The Appeal to the Authority of Science

and pains from association'.¹ So Hartley began to ponder the implications of association, and what he had already learned from Locke convinced him that herein lay an important clue to the working of the human mind. Hartley, of course, developed this principle in his own way, and he diverged from his predecessors because of what he had learned from Newton, the other great mentor of the eighteenth-century mind. In the preface to the *Principia Mathematica*, Newton had suggested that 'the same kind of reasoning from mechanical principles', which he had employed in this work, might profitably be extended to the study of 'the rest of the phenomena of Nature', since, doubtless, the same laws underlay them all. In the *Opticks* he had held out the hope that the methods used in natural philosophy, if wisely applied, might greatly extend the bounds of moral philosophy. 'The proper method of philosophising', wrote Hartley, 'seems to be to discover and establish the general laws of action, affecting the subject under consideration, from certain select, well-defined, and well-attested phenomena, and then explain and predict the other phenomena by these laws. This is the method of analysis and synthesis recommended and followed by Sir Isaac Newton.'² But Hartley was indebted to Newton for a great deal more than general principles of this kind. If Locke and Gay prompted him to consider the meaning of association, it was Newton who inspired him to examine nervous impulses—'the performance of sensation and motion'³—and so to reach his other characteristic doctrine: the theory of vibrations.

Hartley's work consists of two principal parts. In the first place he elaborated a doctrine concerning the human body and mind, and the mutual connections and relations of both. In the light of this he discussed the duties and expectations of mankind. The various elements in his system were loosely co-ordinated, and this, as he himself admitted, was largely due to the somewhat casual methods he employed. He began with the idea of association and worked back to discover its 'physical cause' in the structure of man's body; he was also led forward 'to examine . . . its consequences in respect of morality and religion'. Matters which might seem extraneous to the subject 'intermixed themselves', and finally, arranging all his 'separate papers' in the best order he could achieve, he published his observations. He did not claim to be a 'system-maker'; he did not start with a theory and find facts to support it, 'but was carried on by a train of thoughts from one thing to another, frequently without any express design or even any previous suspicion of the consequences that might arise'.[1] The strength of his work was its experimental basis; its weakness, its unco-ordinated discursiveness. The former won Priestley's hearty approval. The latter explains why Priestley could dismember the book and re-publish only one part without feeling that he was thereby weakening the effectiveness of Hartley's case.

The human mind, said Hartley, is a blank until sensation initiates the process which produces ideas. Sensations 'are those internal feelings of the mind, which arise from the impressions made by external objects upon the several parts of our bodies'.[2] Such impressions set up vibrations in the minute particles of the medullary substance of the nerves, 'motions backward and forward of the small particles of the same kind as the oscillation of the pendulum and the trembling of particles of sounding bodies'.[3] This 'medullary substance', uniform throughout the nerves, spinal marrow and brain, is continuous and soft, and as a result it does not obstruct the operation of the aether, 'a very subtle and elastic fluid' which is 'diffused through the pores of gross bodies as well as through the open spaces that are void of gross matter'.[4] Hartley was indebted to Newton for this idea, and in its light he developed the details of this theory of vibrations. The small particles of bodies emit this thin elastic fluid called aether, which 'is extremely susceptible of vibrations and pulses'. Since it has 'a repulsive force in respect of the bodies which emit it'[5] it sets up a process of action and reaction. 'The vibrations thus excited in the aether and particles of the sensory nerves will be propagated along the course of these nerves up to the brain.'[6] When vibrations are moderate, they produce pleasure; when they are sufficiently violent to break the continuity of the nerves, they cause pain.

Vibrations communicate an impression to the brain; they fade, but not immediately, and they leave behind them a tendency to fainter vibrations of a similar kind. For the sake of clarity these can be termed 'vibratiuncles', and they correspond to 'simple ideas of sensation'.[1] Simple ideas coalesce, by the power of association, into complex ones. Hartley thus co-ordinated his two fundamental postulates. From vibration and association he was able to construct the whole of man's mental life. He applied them first to 'each of the sensations and motions in particular'. He showed that feeling, taste, sight, smell and hearing could be satisfactorily explained on his principles, and, as he believed, on his principles alone. He found that sexual desire fitted into his scheme, and that involuntary actions (coughing, sighing, the beating of the heart) fell naturally into place. Memory could be explained as 'that faculty by which traces of sensations and ideas recur, or are recalled, in the same order and proportion, accurately or nearly, as they were presented'.[2] The course of reminiscence is sometimes immediately dependent on outward sensation, but often it is due to the fact that there are always vibrations in the brain because of its heat and the pulsing of the arteries. And here each man's past, in conjunction with the influences operative at the moment, provides the pattern of the ideas which memory resuscitates. Hartley also believed that he had found a means of explaining imperfections in the rational faculty of man. 'Deviations from sound reason and alienations of the mind' became intelligible on his principles; could any other theory, he asked, claim as much?

Hartley has considered in detail the phenomena of the senses. He has studied the rational faculties of man, and now turns to examine the emotions. In dealing with conscious life, he constantly used a phrase for which he was indebted to Locke—'the association of ideas'—and it is necessary to consider the sense in which he used it. Actually Hartley presupposed an association, not of ideas as normally understood, but of sensations, and he treated sensations as identical with vibrations. Whereas Locke believed that ideas of reflection point to the constructive function of the mind, Hartley made the law of association correspond to nerve processes. What he is concerned to establish is a physiological, not a psychological law of association. After pages of detailed argument about particular sensations and their corresponding ideas, he epitomised his view in a definitive formula. 'If any sensation *A*, idea *B*, or muscular motion *C* be associated for a sufficient number of times with any other sensation *D*, idea *E*, or muscular motion *F*, it will, at last, excite the simple idea belonging to the sensation *D*, the very idea *E*, or the very muscular motion *F*.'[1] There is one thing, Hartley admitted, that association cannot do: it cannot provide sensation *D*. Hartley was not content to prove that we have certain sequences of ideas; he was anxious to show that man is really a microcosm. Our lives are ruled by laws which operate both within us and without. Hartley regarded man as an organism; it was with the uniformity of his life that he was concerned. As a proponent of association Hartley had had predecessors, but in his *Observations* he did what no one else had done: he used the principle to elaborate a comprehensive psychological theory. For the first time he provided a methodical survey of the phenomena of mental life. In detail and with great care he showed how the more complex mental states are elaborated, by means of association, from the simpler ingredients. Hartley's psychology might have attracted greater contemporary attention if it had not been so intimately related to a physiology which failed to gain favour. This also explains the neglect of Hartley's appeal to association as a means of explaining the genesis of man's moral ideas. This occupies, however, an important place in his thought and illustrates the way in which he believed that a scientific understanding of human nature would illuminate the fundamental problems of man's behaviour.

Having 'despatched the history and analysis of the sensations, motions and ideas', Hartley felt that his 'next business' was 'to enquire particularly into the rise and gradual increase of the pleasures and pains of imagination, ambition, self-interest, sympathy, theopathy, and the moral sense'.¹ Sensation thus provided him with his point of departure, though he admitted that his interpretation of association and its consequences need not necessarily derive its validity from his distinctive theory of vibrations. Because of the place occupied by sensation, the whole range of pleasures is firmly rooted in our experience of the world about us. But Hartley skilfully devised a system by which we pass from simple to complex experiences, and from lower to higher pleasures. Imagination opens delights to which sensation alone cannot introduce us. It makes us aware both of the beauties of the natural world, and of the charms of the world of art. It explains our delight in 'the three liberal and sister arts of music, painting and poetry'.² It leads us on to consider 'the pleasures arising from the study of the sciences'; it makes us aware of 'the numerous connections of truth of all kinds with those most amiable and important doctrines which religion, natural and revealed, teaches us'.³ It embraces invention ('the art of producing new beauties in works of imagination and new truths in matters of science') and the pleasures of mirth, wit, and humour. When sensation and imagination combine we are introduced to the pleasures and pains of ambition. We discover that our fellow men either approve or disapprove of us and of our conduct. Here are 'principal sources of happiness or misery'.⁴ Association teaches us to seek what produces the one and to avoid what results in the other. Here we can clearly recognise the tendency of virtue to generate its counterpart, and of vice always to discourage vice. 'And thus it comes to pass, that praise and shame have a strong reflected influence upon themselves; and that praise begets the love of praise and shame increases the fear of shame.'⁵ Ambition leads on to the pleasures and pains of self-interest. Here the progressive character of morality is even more conspicuously apparent. From 'gross self-interest' we pass to 'refined self-interest'; in the former we are content with the pleasures of 'sensation, imagination and ambition', in the latter we pursue those of 'sympathy, theopathy and the moral sense'. But a third stage awaits us: 'rational self-interest, or the pursuit of a man's greatest possible happiness, without any partiality to this or that kind of happiness, means of happiness, means of a means, etc.'.[1] To understand this kind of pleasure and pain we can do no better than study our anticipations of death and of a future state. Moreover, we have at this point an exceptionally clear instance of the way in which association modifies our initial reactions. These hopes and fears are 'the strongest of our selfish affections and yet at the same time the chief foundation of the pure disinterested love of God and of our neighbour, and the chief means of transferring our associations, so that we may love and hate, pursue and fly, in the manner best suited to our attainment of our greatest possible happiness'.[2]

By steady progression, said Hartley, we advance from simple reactions to complex ones and from a preoccupation with selfish fears to an appreciation of altruistic pleasures. At each stage association is the key to the process, and the means by which the next advance is made. This is particularly evident when we consider the intellectual pleasures associated with sympathy, theopathy and the moral sense. Under sympathy, Hartley considered generosity, sociability, compassion, mercy and their opposites. Even in childhood, association is at work to identity pleasures with 'mutual affability' and pain with malice, anger or envy. It teaches us 'to forgo great pleasures or to endure great pain for the sake of others', and it lifts us above 'explicit expectation of reward, either from God or man'. 'And this', adds Hartley, 'I take to be a proof from the doctrine of association that there is, and must be, such a thing as pure disinterested benevolence'.[3] Theopathy (the love of God) likewise has its distinctive fears and pleasures. When awe blends with love to create reverence, fear assumes a legitimate guise; in superstition and atheism it appears in its corrupt but commoner forms. The pleasures which attend theopathy are gratitude, confidence and resignation; enthusiasm is 'a degeneration of it'. It must not be assumed that the love of God arises inevitably or appears initially in its final form. With great skill and insight, Hartley examined the emergence in the child's mind of the love of God. In summarising the stages of growth as he had indicated them, Hartley claimed that 'amongst Jews and Christians, children begin probably with a definite visible idea of God; but that by degrees this is quite obliterated, without anything of a stable precise nature succeeding in its room; and that by farther degrees, a great variety of strong secondary ideas . . . recur in their turns, when they think upon God, i.e. when this word, or any of its equivalents, or any equivalent phrase or symbol, strikes the mind strongly, so that it dwells upon them for a sufficient time, and is affected by them in a sufficient degree'.[1]

All the preceding stages culminate in the pleasures and pains of the moral sense, which leads us 'to the love and approbation of virtue and to the fear, hatred and abhorrence of vice'. This cumulative quality in morality explains its distinctive authority, and enables it to mobilise the force of 'the whole nature of man against any particular part of it that rebels against the determinations and commands of the conscience or moral judgment'.[2] It is the moral sense which makes us recognise in the pure love of God 'our highest and ultimate perfection, our end, centre and only resting place'. It teaches us to seek the satisfaction of rectitude simply because we should, and to avoid the seductions of evil for the same wholly sufficient reason.

With considerable skill Hartley has elaborated a complete theory of man's conscious life, but he had an eminently practical purpose in mind. A study of man's emotional development might culminate in the moral sense, but this in turn would have to be embraced within a comprehensive interpretation of man's life. This is what Hartley attempted to provide in the second part of his work. His governing motive was clearly religious. 'Whatever be our doubts, fears or anxieties', he said, '. . . our only hope and refuge must be in the infinite power, knowledge, and goodness of God.'¹ This was not merely a formal avowal; his correspondence reveals Hartley as a man of strong religious feeling, but his statement of theological principles is curiously conventional in character. He reproduced the customary arguments for the existence of God, and detailed the truths of natural religion in a tone and manner indistinguishable from a score of rationalist theologians of the first half of the century. He treated revelation and the truths of the Christian religion as any Latitudinarian might have done and reached much the same conclusions. He argued that faith should issue in practice, that belief ought to result in a rule of life. Here he could relate his theology to his psychology, and he surveyed each of the stages of man's emotional development in order to show its bearing on the formation of our rule of life. It seemed obvious that the principles which he had originally discerned were not merely confirmed but greatly clarified by being brought into close conjunction with religious insights. He advanced a further stage: a rule of life actually presupposes a rule of faith, and examination proves that the beliefs of Christianity are necessary 'for the purification and perfection of our natures'.² In this part of his work Hartley combined conventional theological arguments with the application to man's life and conduct of the novel and startling implications which he drew from his material.

To his contemporaries the strangest feature of Hartley's system was his assumption that an orthodox theological superstructure could rest on the foundation of a mechanistic view of man. He was quite conscious of the criticism to which his theories were exposed, and he could easily understand why this was so. He himself had seen the implications of his thought only relatively late in his enquiries, and he had accepted them with considerable hesitancy. 'I was not at all aware', he wrote, 'that [the doctrine of *necessity*] followed from that of association, for several years after I had begun my enquiries; nor did I admit it at last without the greatest reluctance.'³ Hartley was here dealing with a subject which invited misunderstanding, and he realised that clear definitions were essential. 'By the mechanism of human actions', he said, 'I mean that each results from the previous circumstances of body and mind in the same manner and with the same certainty as other effects do from their mechanical causes.'[1] Did this leave any latitude to free will? Again Hartley felt that much depended on the way in which terms were defined. He did not believe that man has power to initiate motion; this would overthrow his whole theory of 'vibrations'. But this was a conviction which only philosophers maintained; free will in 'the popular and practical sense' was a very different matter. If it 'be defined as the power of doing what a person desires or wills to do, of deliberating, suspending, choosing, etc., or of resisting the motives of sensuality, ambition, resentment, etc., free will ... is not only consistent with the doctrine of mechanism, but even flows from it'.[2] Hartley regarded as frivolous the objection that materialism is inconsistent with the ethical consciousness. The whole gist of his theory pointed to the conclusion that material impulses create ideas, but out of the resultant ideas, the higher ones evolve directly from the lower ones. Self-regarding impulses give way to disinterested attitudes. Hartley did not reduce the moral life to non-moral elements. He derived the higher from the lower; because the connection was clear, the conclusion was inescapable: 'the moral sense is therefore guaranteed necessarily and mechanically'.[3] Much of the argument revolves around the way in which present motives are determined by past influences. If the causal sequence is at work, we choose as we do because our desires are shaped by everything that has made us what we are. Hartley felt that we can treat free will as opposed to mechanism only if a man feels that 'he can do different things while the motives remain the same'. But this would create confusion. We have no choice but to admit that our actions are determined by our motives; when a motive is insufficient it is because one of greater power is actually at work, and the direct sequence which leads us back to mechanical impulses remains unbroken.[4] But necessitarianism need not result in moral lassitude. Hartley believed that we would and should do everything in our power to modify for the better the circumstances which control our lives. One of the striking features of his discussion of the development of our emotional life is the insight with which he analyses the attitudes of little children. 'A parent who believes the doctrine of mechanism may, consistently with it, or rather must necessarily, in consequence of this belief, exhort his child.'[1]

Hartley's position, it will be observed, seems clear and definite, but he kept some surprises in reserve. He was unequivocally committed to determinism, but he declined to say that necessity involves materialism. More than once he seemed to presuppose as much, but at the end he side-stepped the issue. His theory, he felt, was independent of metaphysical presuppositions, and in any case he was quite convinced of the immateriality of the human soul. He believed he had evolved a system which satisfied the demands of reason and of faith. It was consonant with science and confirmed the truths of natural religion. It did not contradict Scripture nor the insights of revelation. And it explained and enforced the precepts of morality. Hartley, it is apparent, stood in the tradition represented in an earlier day by Newton and Boyle. The works of creation—this time in the fashioning of man's body and mind—declare the glory of God.

The uncertainty about Hartley's true meaning arises in part from the problem of exact definition of words which can sustain a variety of interpretations. He regarded himself as a materialist, but not in any sense which would conflict with a genuinely religious interpretation of life. Hence, though some of his critics claimed that his theories involved a materialistic sensationalism, he demurred.[2] But some of the problems of interpretation are inherent in Hartley's theory, and cannot be dismissed as a confusion about words. It may be argued that what Hartley really affirmed is a parallelism, not a materialism. As we have seen, 'a change is made in the medullary substance proportional and correspondent to every change in the sensations'. There is a likeness in kind between the physical and the psychical elements in man's life, but not an identity.[1] He was apparently as much concerned to prove that human life is determined by circumstances as he was to urge men to change the pattern of their lives. Fate and duty are held in uneasy balance. What is and what must be are offset by what should be. In this he was typical of his age. The materialists of the eighteenth century consciously accepted the obligation to struggle to achieve a perfection which might now be out of reach but which could ultimately be grasped.

In Hartley we see the scientific outlook in alliance with a buoyant and optimistic temper. In this respect he anticipated both the attitude and the spirit of Priestley and Godwin. His theory of association was also linked with utilitarianism, and here Hartley anticipated Bentham and Mill. He accepted the principle of utility and applied it. He anticipated John Stuart Mill in claiming that qualitative differences can be detected in pleasures. But his theological preoccupations always limited the extent to which he was prepared to accept utilitarianism as a ruling principle. In actual conduct he believed that we should be ruled by the precepts of Scripture rather than by a calculation of consequences. He was perhaps the first to appreciate the problems inherent in the hedonistic calculus. 'It is impossible', he said, 'for the most sagacious and experienced persons to make any accurate estimate of the future consequences of particular actions, so as . . . to determine justly what actions would contribute most to augment happiness and lessen misery'.[2]

Hartley's merits as a writer were augmented by the spirit in which he approached his task. His sincerity and candour are everywhere apparent. He made no exaggerated claims on behalf of his work. The task was difficult and the subject matter obscure; his pages, he said, would indicate as much, and he threw himself on the 'great indulgence' of his readers. On some points he admitted that he had perhaps been 'too hasty and censorious', but at least he had set forth the truth as honestly and faithfully as he could. Some readers would blame him for going too far and saying too much, but he felt that to muffle the truth 'would have been a disingenuous procedure'.[1] It is equally obvious that in developing his theories his method was often more important than his results. His aim was to apply 'the method of analysis and synthesis recommended and followed by Sir Isaac Newton'.[2] By doing so he might discover a single principle which would account for all mental phenomena in the same way as the law of gravitation explained all events in the physical world. His theory of vibrations did not bridge the dualism of mind and body in the way he hoped. Even association proved a less fruitful hypothesis than he expected. His failure in detail does not make his professed purpose less significant. His attempt was in keeping with the consistent aim of his life. 'From his earliest youth', wrote his son, 'his mental ambition was preoccupied by pursuits of science.'[3] Herein lay his importance; for the first time a serious effort was made to apply the methods of science to the study of man's mental processes. He took the first step toward resolving complex intellectual processes into simple ones, and the means he used was the law of association.

Hartley's intention was often better than his performance. His method was right, but he did not always adhere to it. At times he subordinated his observations to his preconceptions, and allowed his theories to govern his findings. But this does not seriously detract from his significance. In the history of thought he stands as the originator of a psychology based on the study of physiology. Hitherto there had been little serious attempt to explain mind and body by relating the one to the other; even the possibility of doing so had hardly been suspected. Hartley's hypothesis of 'vibratiuncles' suffered from serious defects and even his supporters tacitly abandoned it. They did not realise that behind its crude form lay an important insight: that mind and body are intimately related, and that the operations of the one produce a corresponding effect on the other. At certain points also Hartley clearly anticipated a comparative method of dealing with various types of phenomena. He was handicapped by his own limitations; he had no conception of the need of relating sociology to ethics.

The Appeal to the Authority of Science

But in the area where he was most at home, he moved with ease and with a notable freedom from restricting prejudices, and his discussion of the intellectual faculties of animals is a remarkable achievement.[1]

It is easy to find fault with Hartley's work. His theories were defective. He attempted to assimilate elements which no amount of ingenuity could combine. He lacked a comprehensive system of philosophy. He did not recognise the difficulty of applying his favourite theories in a way that would account for judgment, assent or belief. He himself made no exaggerated claims on behalf of his book. He conceded that it lacked unity and coherence. He confessed that he had gathered together materials written at various times over a long period. Most of his views have been repudiated or ignored, yet few of his contemporaries had a more fruitful influence on subsequent thought.

What David Hartley initiated, Joseph Priestley extended and developed. As a young man Priestley read *Observations on Man* and was deeply impressed. In due course, and as a means of disseminating principles which he accepted, he re-published the section of Hartley's work which dealt with association.[2] This, he felt, contained the heart of the matter; the theory of vibrations (while not necessarily wrong) would distract attention from the central issue, while the theological passages could be excised because they were loosely related to the central doctrine of association. But Priestley did not omit the religious portions of the work because he considered them out of place. The two men shared a common outlook; what was more important, they were agreed in basic purpose. Both of them represented and maintained the characteristic English partnership between scientific interest and religious zeal. Priestley was one of the founders of modern chemistry, but he regarded his research as the peripheral interest of a mind dedicated to religious truth. He detected no incompatibility between his religious avocation and his scientific pursuits; clearly both the cast of his thought and the character of his convictions were affected by this balance between two great areas of intellectual endeavour. Though he treated science as a marginal activity in a very busy life, it certainly determined his approach to every question. He felt that he was committed to a rigidly scientific view of the universe. Its laws necessarily limited the measure of freedom man might claim; association and determinism seemed to him inferences which a scientific understanding of our life in the world must prompt. In the opening pages of his *Disquisitions relating to Matter and Spirit* Priestley made it clear that he intended to erect his philosophical and theological systems on a strictly scientific foundation. Newton had demonstrated the laws which govern the universe, and 'for my part', said Priestley, 'I profess an uniform and rigorous adherence to them.'[1] Here we can clearly detect a tendency to replace the traditional methods of metaphysical enquiry with new ones more in keeping with scientific principles.

In addition to his scientific purpose, certain definite presuppositions underlay Priestley's work. He treated the existence of God as an unquestioned fact. He was equally certain that God is good. On the strength of these convictions he advanced to the belief that God's purpose for mankind is unquestionably beneficent. From this in turn it followed that the goal before the human race is unlimited happiness. The future is bright with hope. Here Priestley's scientific outlook coalesced with his confident optimism. This is a combination which he inherited from Hartley and transmitted to the future. In due course it became the secular faith of the nineteenth century. Everywhere, he declared, 'the minds of men are opening to large and generous views of things'. The reign of superstition and darkness would be overthrown and the kingdom of light would be ushered in. 'Whatever was the beginning of this world, the end will be glorious and paradisiacal beyond what our imagination can now conceive.'[2] Twenty years after writing these words, Priestley hailed with delight the changes effected by the French Revolution. His apocalyptic hopes had always been political in character; now their revolutionary implications became transparently clear.

The Appeal to the Authority of Science

'How glorious then is the prospect, the reverse of all the past, that is now opening upon us and upon the world!'[1] There was a bland assurance about Priestley's optimism which was particularly infuriating to his critics. It could not be dismissed merely as the buoyancy of a sanguine temperament. Priestley's confidence sprang from his necessitarian principles; his political millennium had the inevitability of the final term in a scientific demonstration. Progress had been written into the constitution of the universe by God himself. Man need only await, with joyous expectation, the culmination of God's beneficent purpose.

Priestley, as we have seen, adopted Hartley's principle of association, and with it the general theory of the development of conscious life which Hartley had advocated. Priestley, however, definitely pushed the doctrine of ideas in a materialistic direction. The identification of psychical with physical processes became more intimate still; psychology was even more closely related to the physiology of the nervous system. He categorically rejected Hartley's view of the mind as an immaterial principle; 'mental powers', he said, are the result of 'such an organical structure as that of the brain'. To establish his point he explained that matter is composed of minute particles which he called atoms (akin to molecules in more modern terminology), whose essential quality is the power of attraction and repulsion. Popular misconception regarded matter 'as solid and inert, being incapable of the powers of sensation and thought',[2] but this is as false as the view which treats the human soul as incorporeal. Actually the sentient principle in man is always associated with the material substance of the brain. 'The powers of sensation and thought, as belonging to man, have never been found but in conjunction with a certain system of matter.'[3] Both in men and in animals we can detect the same close interrelation of the conscious life and its physical base; the differences between them are of degree, not of kind. If we postulate an immaterial soul for men, must we not do the same for animals? This, said Priestley, is only one of the problems which his doctrine of materialism resolves.[4]

Priestley used his materialism to account for man. Since he refused to concede that human nature can be explained in terms either of immaterial spirit or of inert matter, we might expect him to interpret man as a living organism, but his theory made the metaphor of a machine more congenial. By eliminating the usual concept of soul, Priestley destroyed that element in man which had been regarded as akin to the divine. Having made man material, would he attempt to do the same for God? That God occupied a fundamental place in Priestley's thought is obvious. Natural religion presupposed a first cause and a creative principle; revealed religion demanded a God who could disclose himself and who would authenticate doctrines so essential to Priestley's system as the resurrection. But though materialism might explain man's nature, Priestley refused to imply that it might also encompass God's being. He reminded his readers that we know the properties of matter by observing how it acts; its nature becomes intelligible in the light of its powers.[1] In the same way we can only claim to know God when we study the attributes and properties which his mighty acts declare. 'All we can pretend to know of God is his infinite wisdom, power and goodness.'[2] About his being we are necessarily ignorant. We believe there must be a first cause; 'but of the nature of the existence of this primary cause, concerning which we know nothing but by its effects, we cannot have any conception. We are absolutely confounded, bewildered and lost when we attempt to speculate concerning it'.[3] To those who argued that atheism was the corollary of materialism, Priestley replied that our practical knowledge of God does not depend on any particular theory about the divine essence, and therefore it can neither be confirmed nor refuted by any doctrine concerning the nature of man. Priestley defined God as an intelligent first cause; the world must have had such a maker, since its ordered symmetry indicates a purpose and a design. But this purpose, even as reflected in man's nature, supplies no grounds for dogmatism about God himself.

The Appeal to the Authority of Science

It is obvious that Priestley felt no need to push his theory to its logical conclusion. He had taken Newtonian physics as his point of departure, and essentially his doctrine of materialism was merely a demand for a theory of human nature in conformity with the principles of science. But this theory had to be compatible with a Christian theology cleansed of all corruptions, and it is this aim which inspired his exposition of necessity. He acknowledged his indebtedness to Hartley, but he felt free to press beyond the position of his preceptor. Here, also, he believed that he was propounding both the new science and the true faith. In Priestley, as in so many other eighteenth-century rationalists, the contemplation of the gospel of enlightenment awakened something akin to evangelical exaltation. The sinister bondage of Calvinism had been broken, and men were free to move into a world beneficently ruled by strict necessity. At first sight the difference, at this point, between the faith which Priestley had known as a boy and that which he accepted as a man, might seem relatively slight; he himself was convinced that it was both extensive and important. Calvinism paralysed moral incentive; necessitarianism gave it free scope. Predestination made a mockery of any attempt to convert a man to better ways; a belief in necessity provided all the inducements that he could possibly require.[1] The reason for the difference is simple but far-reaching. The moral life owes its character and quality to the motives which inspire it. Priestley believed that necessitarianism made it possible to isolate the proper motives and present them in their full effectiveness. The controversy about free will between Priestley and his opponents was complicated by ambiguity of terms. Popular views and technical theories attached the same words to very different concepts. Moreover, in psychology freedom of the will meant the ability to reach your own decisions; in contemporary metaphysics it meant that will or decision had no cause. Priestley denied freedom in the latter sense; he conceded it in the former. 'I would observe', he wrote, 'that I allow to man all the liberty or power that is *possible in itself*, and to which the ideas of mankind in general ever go, which is *the power of doing whatever they will or please.*[1] This view, of course, distinguished between popular and technical views. Priestley thus repudiated 'philosophical liberty' (which is really bondage) and exalted necessity (which at times sounds very much like freedom). Herein, of course, lies the seeming paradox of progressive eighteenth-century thought. The most ardent champions of liberty found the philosophical support of their position in the doctrine of necessity. The explanation is relatively simple: the acceptance of necessity seemed to be the corollary of a belief in the scientific interpretation of the universe. The counterpart to the laws which controlled the stars was the necessity which governed human life. 'In short it is my firm persuasion that the three doctrines of *materialism*, of that which is commonly called *Socinianism*, and of *philosophical necessity*, are equally parts of *one system*, being equally founded on just observations of nature and fair deductions from the Scriptures.'[2] The enlightened person, Priestley felt, could as reasonably challenge the law of gravitation as repudiate any of these views. He might, like Priestley himself, be forced to devise some ingenious expedients to justify his position, and he might ingenuously try to make the best both of the old interpretations and of the new. It was disconcerting, of course, that a person so enlightened as Richard Price—and one so similar in general outlook to Priestley himself—should miss the essential relationship between necessity, freedom, and morals. Price defended the free agency of man and maintained the unity and immateriality of the soul. But Price was a Platonist; what was more, he was a mathematician and an economist rather than a scientist. But though Priestley and Price seemed to argue at cross purposes, they proved that a genuinely candid controversy could be conducted in perfect charity by men who disagreed profoundly about metaphysical principles.[3]

Nowhere did the application of an enlightened spirit seem so important as in religious thought. Priestley's consuming passion was to expose and eradicate the superstitions which had corrupted faith. But it is his approach to the problem which is significant. The seemingly multifarious activities of his long and busy life were unified by his desire to bring the light of truth to bear upon every area into which his interests led him. His experimental investigations, his studies of history and government, his incursions into politics, his dissertations on philosophy, his treatises on doctrine—all had a common purpose. All, too, found their motive in Priestley's religious zeal. His views were highly distinctive, yet at the same time representative. In his own intellectual pilgrimage he epitomised the forces at work in dissenting circles. He began life in a family where Calvinism, though held with moderation, was a living creed. In due course he passed to Arminianism, then to Arianism, and so to Socinianism. Of his intellectual pilgrimage he left a candid and convincing account in his *Memoirs*. What he did not indicate is the extent to which Presbyterianism was travelling the same road at the same time. But at least the reader can understand why the 'old dissent' was so open to change. Their traditions, the structure of their congregational life, their freedom from inhibiting social restraints, all were reinforced by the fact that men and churches who yielded to the prevailing currents of thought had very little to lose. To their more cautious contemporaries it seemed clear that they were actually forfeiting their faith, but to Priestley this was entirely a matter of definition. Though others believed that he was attacking the very citadel of Christian belief, he was convinced that he was merely removing 'the corruptions of Christianity'. This phrase provided the title of his most representative work in this field. The chief distortions of true belief make, he believed, a very melancholy catalogue: 'a trinity of persons in the godhead, original sin, arbitrary predestination, atonement for the sins of men by the death of Christ, and (which has perhaps been as great a cause of infidelity as any other) the doctrine of the plenary inspiration of the Scriptures'.[1] Priestley did not merely state his thesis; he undertook to prove it by an appeal to the past. In the *History of the Corruptions of Christianity* he traced back the course of each offending doctrine till he discovered the point at which it had deviated from the simple and original truth. The test he applied was the belief of the primitive Church, and he found it relatively simple to isolate in Scripture the beliefs of the early Christians. One of the gravest distortions of truth concerned the person of Jesus Christ. From this cardinal error there followed in due course all the grotesque misconceptions associated with the atonement. It was clear, he felt, that Jesus Christ was neither infallible nor impeccable, and he subsequently expanded his preliminary exploration of this subject into the detailed examination of the Incarnation and the Atonement which he provided in *A History of Early Opinions Concerning Jesus Christ*.

For this particular task Priestley had certain genuine qualifications and a number of serious disabilities. He felt free to follow his argument in whatever direction its implications might lead him. He recognised that doctrine had grown and taken shape slowly over many decades, and in this respect he was a genuine pioneer. He saw that the only final court of judgment was the verdict of further investigation: such problems are ultimately settled by research. He believed that modern interpretations of Scripture often rest on little more than an appeal to private judgment and are consequently worthless; the speculations of the Fathers are subject to the same criticism and carry no greater weight. The proper method, therefore, was to penetrate to the mind of the earliest believers and so reach the meaning attached in the first instance to the phrases which Christians still use. Unfortunately Priestley vitiated his method by the way he applied it. He did not try to conceal his personal bias, which is an advantage; but he also made no attempt to suppress his sectarian aims. He professed to be pursuing a scientific objective, but he frankly wrote as a partisan. He had decided in advance what was authentic Christianity and what were its corruptions; with these presuppositions firmly established in his thought he turned to history to find the support he needed. He did not consult his sources in order to base his verdict on what he found in them. He reached his conclusions first and then used his authorities to substantiate his preconceptions.

Priestley's interests were too diverse for him to be a finished scholar in any of the fields which he explored. He believed that he was right about essentials; he did not bother to be scrupulously accurate about details. But a man who is inexact about points which can easily be verified is often assumed to be wrong about more important matters. This well-known fact determined Horsley's line of attack in the famous controversy between the two men. The method was not novel; Bentley had used it with brilliant effect to prove that Collins was so often wrong about details that his argument as a whole did not deserve serious consideration. Horsley deliberately set himself 'to destroy the writer's credit and the authority of his name';[1] he had little difficulty in suggesting that Priestley had been so slipshod in handling his sources that no reliance need be placed on his conclusions. Horsley also implied, of course, that by discrediting his opponent's facts, he had vindicated his own contention that the ante-Nicene church had been unanimous in affirming that Christ was consubstantial with the Father. Having made his point, Horsley claimed the victory and retired from the field; when Priestley continued the battle, Horsley announced (from the vantage point of an episcopal see) that he had no intention of even reading his opponent's work. This was a fate which Priestley often suffered. As a controversialist he was not easily discouraged, but his antagonists usually refused to follow him through the mazes of debate. As we have seen, Horsley treated the matter at issue between them as closed, though Priestley was fuming with eagerness to pursue it further. Hume had passed beyond Priestley's reach when the *Letters to a Philosophic Unbeliever* appeared, and surely the frustrated author got little satisfaction from his confident verdict that 'compared with Dr Hartley I consider Mr Hume as not even a child'.[2] When Priestley tried to tempt Gibbon into the lists, he drew upon himself a snub in which eloquence of expression was nicely balanced by supercilious contempt.

Priestley's religious views, of course, made many enemies and gained few friends. For some of his contemporaries, he believed too little; for others, he believed too much. He had a curious gift for removing with one hand what he had apparently given with the other. At first sight his definition of the Christian faith seemed comprehensive enough. It was, he said, 'a belief of all the great historical facts recorded in the Old and New Testament, in which we are informed of the creation and government of the world, the history of the discourses, miracles, death and resurrection of Christ; and his assurance of the resurrection of all the dead to a future life of retribution; and this is the doctrine that is of the most consequence to enforce the good conduct of men'.[1] But this excluded most of the theological inferences which orthodoxy had drawn from biblical sources, while his materialism and determinism impressed most of his contemporaries as incompatible with any religious system. On the other hand his more emancipated friends were amazed that so intelligent a man should still cling to the tattered vestiges of an outworn creed. Like Aesop's bat, which was repudiated by birds and beasts alike, Priestley was regarded with suspicion by both sides. But he believed that he had found a tenable position between credulity and scepticism, and he considered it the true alternative to complementary forms of error. That he was attacked from both sides did not surprise him. He regarded atheism and religious superstition as natural allies: each, by its errors, promoted the progress of the other. Blind credulity drove thoughtful men to unbelief, but the extremes of atheism sent them back for sanctuary to the haven of mystery and authority.

Nor was Priestley really typical of his period in the unquestioning confidence which he reposed in reason. Powerful forces were at work to modify the assurance which had marked the early part of the century. Hume's scepticism had shown how narrow were the limits within which reason can operate. 'Wesley's appeal to the submerged masses proved that there were satisfactions in religious experience which had a validity of their own. Priestley was unmoved. While attacking the sceptics on the one hand and the Methodists on the other, he stoutly reaffirmed his own position. 'Things *above* reason may, for anything we know to the contrary, be true, but things expressly *contrary* to our reason, as that *three* should be *one*, or *one three*, can never appear to be so.'[1] This is still the language of an earlier phase, and the apparent lag in Priestley's awareness of current trends was possibly related to the nature of his own preoccupations. He is one of the clearest examples of the initial attempt 'to supplant metaphysical by scientific methods'.[2] But he did not wholly abandon metaphysics; he merely continued to operate in this area with concepts which were unaffected by recent changes.

In many respects, however, Priestley reflected certain of the most admirable qualities, alike in mind and spirit, of the latter part of the eighteenth century. He accepted the pursuit of truth as a moral duty, and his investigations in science, theology, philosophy, history and government were all inspired by an inflexible resolve to probe to the heart of the truth. His methods often lagged behind his aims, but even his most infuriating qualities were never wholly unrelated to his ultimate objectives. Even when he seemed most doctrinaire in his dissent from accepted standards, he believed that he was responding to an irresistible constraint. 'Truth', he said, 'makes it impossible merely to go along with the majority on anything.'[3]

The principles and methods of the new science carried immense authority. Hartley applied them to psychology. Priestley used them to refashion theology. William Godwin invoked them as the foundation of a new theory of government. It is obvious, he felt, that those who understand man's nature, will also understand the problems of man's corporate life.

It is unusually easy to identify the sources on which Godwin drew. Many of the ideas which had been generally current in the eighteenth century reappear in his pages, but he also reflects new tendencies which were refashioning accepted views. His inspiration was the Newtonian system. His aim was to apply the principles of science to the study of man and society. 'Abstractedly considered', he wrote, 'it [science] conduces to the happiness and virtue of the individual, as well as to the improvement of our social institutions.'[1] He acknowledged his debt to Locke, both in human psychology and in the theory of government. From 'the celebrated Hartley' ('one of the most acute philosophical writers') he borrowed his account of the mechanism of the human mind. 'The sagacity of Hartley', he added, 'in having arranged and analysed the phenomena of mind, and shown the practicability of reducing its different operations to a simple principle, cannot be too highly applauded.'[2] The political writings of Swift persuaded him that 'monarchy was a species of government essentially corrupt'; the Latin historians confirmed his suspicions. To the French *philosophes* his obligations were even more pronounced: he tells us that he 'derived much additional stimulus from several French productions . . . the *Système de la Nature*, the works of Rousseau, and those of Helvetius'.[3] Seldom openly avowed, but never wholly absent, was the influence of Godwin's dissenting background. His father and his grandfather had been nonconformist ministers. He himself was trained for this profession; he even practised it for five years—till the *philosophes* destroyed his faith. Hazlitt aptly described him as 'the metaphysician engrafted on the dissenting minister'.[4] His intellectual outlook was fashioned by a dissenting academy, and traces of dissenting attitudes can be found throughout his writings. He was indebted to Priestley, Price, and Kippis. His ardent advocacy of freedom, equality and justice was in the best tradition of dissent. His zeal in attacking iniquity carries the distinctive marks of the 'nonconformist conscience'. But if the emotional foundation of his thought was provided by his dissenting background, his mature convictions represent at many points a conscious revolt against religious beliefs. Yet even in the midst of his reaction we can trace the influence of rational dissent: in advocating materialism he used arguments provided by continental philosophers, but he relied on a type of approach which he had learned among the nonconformists.

The Appeal to the Authority of Science

The pattern of his thought reflects in detail the general influences to which he was exposed. For his theory of ideas he was indebted to Hartley. Locke had shown that innate ideas do not exist. Sensations from the outer world give rise to simple ideas; complex ideas, added Hartley, are the product of association. Godwin adopted the principle of association and elaborated it in his own way. The science of mind provided him with the exact foundation he needed for his social theories. He began with the general proposition that 'it is the business of science to carry this task of generalisation to its furthest extent, and to reduce the diversified events of the universe to a small number of original principles'. He then turned his attention to the human mind. 'Can the intellect be made a topic of science?' If so, the principles of connection which operate in the other areas will be found at work here as well.[1] But Godwin, while accepting association as an explanation of the way the mind operates, objected to 'the scheme of material automatism' with which Hartley had 'unnecessarily clogged' it.[2] He defined thought as 'the medium through which the motions of the animal system are generally carried on'.[3] Though psychology was not Godwin's main concern, his theory of ideas bore directly on his primary interest. Environment is responsible for sensation, which imprints on the blank sheet of the mind the character it subsequently bears. If innate ideas are discredited, argued Godwin, original sin must be abandoned. If a change of environment can produce new impressions, a reformation in society will accomplish a parallel reformation in human character.

The theory of ideas inevitably involved an interpretation of reason. There is a 'law of reason', said Godwin; as gravitation holds the physical universe together, reason unifies the moral world. He believed that 'whatever can be adequately brought home to the conviction of the understanding, may be depended upon as affording a secure hold upon conduct'. Here, again, Godwin was concerned with the practical rather than with the theoretical implications of his beliefs. The 'thinking principle' is 'in every respect the proper subject of education and persuasion'. Educate a man with wisdom and persuasiveness and he can be improved far beyond the measure of our pedestrian expectation: 'sound reasoning and truth, when adequately communicated, must always be victorious over error'. In this process of human improvement, reason is the supreme arbiter and guide. It determines the proper choice when alternative courses face us. It sits as judge among the forces which seek to shape the social life of men. 'Reason, though it cannot excite us to action, is calculated to regulate our conduct, according to the comparative worth it ascribes to different excitements. It is to the improvement of reason, therefore, that we are to look for the improvement of our social condition.'[1]

To the power of reason Godwin paid unquestioning reverence. At this point, he recapitulated earlier trends and in an excess of enthusiasm destroyed their results. The psychological realism of his account of man's conduct is undermined by the exaggerated role he assigned to reason. He believed that in the age of justice, sexual desire would wither away. 'Reasonable men then will propagate their species, not because a certain sensible pleasure is annexed to this action, but because it is right that the species should be propagated, and the manner in which they exercise this function will be regulated by the dictates of reason and duty.'[2] He believed that the way to secure incorruptible civil servants was to give them no salary. He regarded family affection as an irrational, because a non-universal, emotion. Reason, it is clear, has become so dominant that it has excluded common sense.

The primacy of reason was one of Godwin's basic presuppositions; the all-pervading influence of necessity was another. His intellectual ancestry predisposed him to accept it as an indubitable fact; the trend of his sociological theories made him exalt it as a factor of primary importance. He was careful, of course, to interpret it in his own way. Holbach had expounded a doctrine of necessity based on pure determinism, but to Godwin this ignored the vital part played by the human will. Exact definition was obviously the initial need. 'To the right understanding of any arguments that may be adduced under this head, it is requisite that we should have a clear idea of the meaning of the term, necessity. He who affirms that all actions are necessary, means that the man who is acquainted with all the circumstances under which a living or intelligent being is placed upon any given occasion, is qualified to predict the conduct he will hold, with as much certainty as he can predict any of the phenomena of inanimate nature.'[1] Observation of the physical universe teaches us to expect 'a uniformity of events', and we learn to regard certain regular sequences as 'a ground for future expectation'.[2] Why an appropriate result always follows a particular cause we do not know; causation remains an impenetrable mystery. But this does not, in the slightest degree, invalidate our inference from one event to another, or 'affect the operations of moral prudence and expectation'.[3] When science, which investigates this kind of phenomena in nature, extends its consideration to man's social life, it reveals similar sequences. Cause inevitably produces effect. 'The idea of moral discipline proceeds entirely upon this principle. If I carefully persuade, exhort, and exhibit motive to another, it is because I believe that motives have a tendency to influence his conduct.'[4] Human will is itself an important casual factor. What Godwin really meant by necessity is the conviction that we can predict reactions and events in the realm of human conduct as well as in the natural world, and that we can confidently act on this assumption. 'The voluntary conduct of our neighbours enters for a share into almost all those calculations upon which our plans and determinations are founded. If voluntary conduct, as well as material impulse, were not subjected to general laws, and a legitimate topic of prediction and foresight, the certainty of events in the material universe would be productive of little benefit.'[5]

To defend his view of necessity, Godwin attacked free will. He saw it as a 'blind and capricious principle' which would interject chance into human experience and make life uncertain, precarious and unpredictable. This is how he interpreted 'the philosophical notion of free will'; and this is why he repudiated it with such vehemence. In opposition to this view, he insisted that the voluntary actions of men are governed by their moral judgments. Involuntary acts may be affected by material factors —climate or environment—but every voluntary act springs from certain motives and looks forward to certain ends. Reason's task is to enlarge the domain of voluntary action and to reduce that of involuntary action. The enlightened mind inevitably chooses what is good (since evil is prompted only by ignorance) and thus in the upshot Godwin's necessity closely approximated to the will to be enlightened—and this is what many people meant by free will. It was Godwin's aim to 'unite in one system scientific predictability and moral choice'.[1] But Godwin did imply that what we shall choose is largely determined for us. 'This view of things', he claimed, 'presents us with an idea of the universe, as a body of events in systematical arrangement, nothing in the boundless progress of things interrupting this system, or breaking in upon the experienced succession of antecedents and consequents. In the life of every human being there is a chain of events, generated in the lapse of ages which preceded his birth, and going on in regular procession through the whole period of his existence, in consequence of which it was impossible for him to act in any instance otherwise than he has acted.'[2]

Godwin was a convinced utilitarian. It has been debated whether he was also a consistent one, but at least Hazlitt claimed that he was the author of the first full-fledged system based on utility. The test of virtuous conduct is the extent to which it benefits the community. A good society, said Godwin, is one in which the actions of individuals promote the well-being of the greatest number. 'Morality is that system of conduct which is determined by a consideration of the greatest general good.'[3] Utility is 'the only basis of moral and political truth'.[4] Godwin's avowed intention was to discover 'that form of public political society, that system of intercourse and reciprocal action, extending beyond the bounds of a single family, which shall be found to conduce to the general benefit'.[1]

The counterpart of utilitarianism was hedonism. The well-being of society would surely result in the happiness of its members. To promote it must be the object of all study and endeavour, for 'the happiness of the human species is the most desirable object of human science to promote'. Among his basic principles, Godwin laid it down that 'the true object of moral and political endeavour is pleasure or happiness'. But happiness, of course, must be defined in sufficiently comprehensive terms. It begins with the simple 'pleasures of the external senses'; it ascends to 'the secondary pleasures'—those of intellectual feeling, or sympathy, or self-approbation—and it finally embraces altruism and the sense of rectitude.

One other assumption, shared by Godwin with other leaders of progressive thought, conditioned his political theories. It was a commonplace among the advocates of reform that mankind is capable of a degree of progress far beyond anything thus far achieved. Once we comprehend the laws which control man's thought, his behaviour, his moral principles, his social structures, humanity can be progressively transformed. When man's scientific progress was refashioning his material world, was it unreasonable to look for similar triumphs in other fields? 'Are vice and misery . . ., in all their extent and with all their disgustful circumstances as they now exist in the world, entailed on us forever; or may we hope ultimately to throw off, or greatly diminish, the burthen? In other cases of an eminent nature, what the heart of man is able to conceive, the hand of man is strong enough to perform. . . . For myself, I firmly believe that days of greater virtue and more ample justice will descend upon the earth.'[2] Progress is inevitable because it is inherent in man. Godwin was convinced that 'vice is nothing more than error and mistake reduced into practice, and adopted as the principle of our conduct'.[3] Enlightenment will inevitably banish evil, because 'sound reason and truth, when adequately communicated, must always be victorious over error'. 'Truth is omnipotent'; consequently 'man is perfectible'.¹ Godwin did not imagine that man would immediately become perfect; in spite of his naïveté, he was not so devoid of realism as to expect the impossible. But it was reasonable to look for steady improvement, and this was what he really anticipated. 'By perfectible', he said, 'it is not meant that [man] is capable of being brought to perfection. But the word seems to be sufficiently adapted to express the faculty of being continually made better and receiving perpetual improvement.'² The attainment of perfection would be the culmination of progress; and for the moment Godwin had his attention fixed on the means, not on the end.

Godwin was oppressed by the contrast between man's intellectual triumphs and his moral failures. His theories about human nature served as prolegomena to a consideration of the proper method of safeguarding human values. His doctrine of perfectibility eliminated as a cause any inherent defects on the part of man. The trouble lay in man's institutions, not in his nature. Governments have fostered and fortified the power of error. They have created a massive system of deception. 'They poison our minds before we can resist, or so much as suspect their malignity.'³ Everything Godwin says about government is informed by suspicion and hatred. It was 'forced upon mankind by their vices'; it has 'commonly been the creature of their ignorance and mistakes'. It was 'intended to suppress injustice, but its effect has been to embody and perpetuate it'. 'The only sufficient reason that can be offered for the institution of government is a fatal and indispensable necessity.'⁴ He quoted with obvious approval Paine's dictum: 'Society is produced by our wants, and government by our wickedness. Society is in every state a blessing; government even in its best state but a necessary evil.'⁵

Political power corrupts, but we need not acquiesce in its pernicious results. All other sciences have progressed; cannot moral science do likewise? Other arts can be improved; why not social institutions? 'The very conception of this as possible, is in the highest degree encouraging.'¹ Godwin consequently felt compelled to study the science of government, and his theories of reason, necessity, and perfectibility encouraged him to pursue his studies with hope. The existing situation was admittedly depressing, but the error lay, 'not in tolerating the worst forms of government for a while, but in supposing a change impracticable, and not incessantly looking forward to its accomplishment'.² He abhorred the way governments interfered with political liberty, set up established churches to curtail religious freedom, provided educational systems that fostered ancient prejudices and condemned reform. Governments encourage error and evil to consolidate their empire over the minds of men. But mankind has not been 'rendered incapable of the exercise of reason'. 'The real enemies of liberty in any country are not the people, but those higher orders who find their imaginary profit in a contrary system. Infuse just views of society into a certain number of liberally educated and reflecting members; give to the people guides and instructors; and the business is done.'³ It must be done gradually, of course, for Godwin advocated reform not revolution, but no one need despair of the coming of a better day. A slow process of moral education would 'correct public opinion'. As experience proved that government was superfluous, it would gradually be eliminated. Like Paine, Godwin believed that as common sense increased and virtue extended its rule, government would wither away. His ideal was anarchism.

The way ahead might be long and tedious. Progress would be hastened if certain simple moral principles were accepted and observed. Sincerity was the first requisite. Even minor social deceptions must be checked; to have the servant report that you were not at home simply because you wished to avoid an unwelcome caller was to retard the overthrow of error and injustice. The force of public opinion must be rallied to restrain evil and to reform the man who commits it. War must be repudiated; it is tolerable only as an instrument of policy. The institution of property must be administered in a more equitable spirit. Even marriage is an abuse, and ought to be abandoned. At every point duty exercises its inflexible constraint. In the hypothetical case of the fire in the Archbishop of Cambrai's palace, he had no hesitation in postulating that a conscientious man would save Fénelon (for the welfare of mankind) in preference to the maid (who might be his own mother or sister). Morality was reason undeflected by passion. The theme of Godwin's greatest work was political justice; and by this phrase he meant 'the adoption of any principle of morality and truth into the practice of a community'.

Political Justice was fortunate in the date of its publication. It caught the tide of excitement created by the French Revolution and achieved astonishing success; a little later, it would have been completely swamped by the backwash of reaction. Indeed, Godwin's momentary fame was soon overwhelmed by the passions of a new day. Within a few years it was generally assumed that he must be dead, and Shelley discovered with amazement that he was still alive. Later, Hazlitt described him as the prime example of the vagaries of popular taste. He had long outlived his fame; 'no one thinks it worth his while even to traduce and vilify him, he has scarcely friend or foe . . .; he is to all intents and purposes dead and buried'. His eclipse was partly due to faults inherent in his work. It may be unjust to claim that his devotion to reason was arid because it was completely divorced from emotion, but there is no denying the doctrinaire quality of much that he advocated. His most ardent disciples could not accept all his views; to the unconverted much of what he said was patently absurd. Certainly he pressed the claims of reason to a point where the distinction between what is feasible and what is not became painfully apparent. By his exaggerations he made it clear that there is much that reason cannot do; and so the last great champion of eighteenth-century rationalism hastened the reaction which finally eclipsed it.

A greater book might have won a more enduring fame; it would possibly have had a less striking immediate effect. Godwin gathered together ideas which had been current for a generation or more and out of them he fashioned a manifesto which inspired a group of brilliant and impressionable young men. In due course Wordsworth, Southey and Coleridge shed their devotion and took refuge in conservatism and the Romantic revival. Shelley's more enduring zeal won for Godwin's ideas an immortality which Godwin himself could not have given them, even though Godwin's unhappy relations with his son-in-law have clouded his own good name. But Godwin's influence was not confined to poets. No book of the period had a comparable impact on the philosophic mind of England. *Political Justice* may have been a strange and wayward amalgam of psychology, ethics, metaphysics and political speculation, but it fused together popular rationalism and the last ardours of Puritan zeal. The resultant product became the gospel of philosophical radicalism. Godwin gave cohesion and confidence to the rising school of thought. And to a much wider public he bequeathed a more enduring legacy—his faith in the power of reason and in the duty of private judgment, his indignation at imposture, intolerance or injustice, his belief in human benevolence and his trust in man.

CHAPTER IX

THE AUTHORITY OF TRADITION AND THE DEMAND FOR REFORM

B y the middle of the eighteenth century the debate on Church and State had apparently exhausted its resources. The various alternatives had been thoroughly explored, and there was little need to restate the positions which repetition had made familiar. The earlier controversies, however, had raised certain problems which now demanded attention. Locke had made liberty an issue of paramount importance. The prestige attaching to his theories meant that any appeal to them attracted attention; yet in form his works had become 'a political text capable of sustaining any gloss'. Freedom, he had taught, is the right of the individual; it is also a privilege which must be exercised within a wider context. Hume and Bentham expanded Locke's view and contended that utility is the decisive factor in shaping social patterns. Montesquieu and Burke saw that the traditions which mould the life of a community are compounded of many elements—religious and moral as well as political and economic—and that all of them are blended in an indissoluble unity.[1] But what happens when the forces of tradition thwart a growing desire for change? Can venerable forms be allowed to block the fuller expression of man's free sprit? The eighteenth century thus found itself faced with the competing claims of tradition and reform. In both Church and State the clamour for change confronted the demand for stability.

The point of initial attack was subscription in the Church. The temper of the new age was critical of compulsory oaths. The debate about nonconformity had made thoughtful men suspicious of tests which admitted to office those who were ready to swear their acceptance of prescribed opinions, and excluded from it those who were not. The question attracted national attention in the second half of the century; by then it had behind it a long history of intermittent debate. Subscription became a problem whenever radical views were advocated. William Whiston was one of the first to demand that existing regulations be modified. His contemporaries often doubted his common sense; they never questioned his ability or his sincerity. He was a logical rigorist who pushed his convictions to their ultimate conclusion, and then insisted that the authorities take note of the disconcerting results. ' 'Tis the poor man's misfortune', wrote Bishop Hare, '. . . to have a warm head and to be very zealous in what he thinks the cause of God. He thinks prudence the worldly wisdom condemned by Christ and his apostles, and that 'tis gross prevarication and hypocrisy to conceal the discoveries which he thinks he has made.'[1] In a long series of works, Whiston attacked the 'Athanasian heresy' and called for a return to the simplicities of the primitive Christian faith.[2] The first step in a practical programme of reform, he believed, would be to require assent to no more than the Scriptures clearly required. His disinterested candour was unique; his opinions and his demands were not. As the celebrated Dr Clarke became more clearly Arian in his sympathies, he experimented with liturgical changes in his own parish. He believed that subscription was simply an undertaking to conform one's views to the true sense of Scripture.[3] The redoubtable Dr Waterland retorted that 'the Church requires subscription in *her own sense* because she judges *no other* sense to be agreeable to Scripture'.[4] But it was clear that many of the clergy interpreted the demand in a very flexible way. Men who were Arminian by conviction swore to Articles which were Calvinist in content; even when Unitarian in sympathy, they accepted creeds which were Trinitarian in form.[5] Thoughtful men were shocked; the whole cause of religion was discredited and demoralisation spread throughout the Church.[6] 'The forms of orthodoxy, the articles of faith', remarked Gibbon, 'are sub-scribed with a sigh, or a smile, by the modern clergy.'[1]

In moulding eighteenth-century thought both the evangelicals and the high churchmen played a relatively unimportant part. The major influence in the middle years of the century was exerted by men of liberal outlook. Their demand for reform—credal, liturgical, institutional—grew steadily more insistent. At length, in 1766, Francis Blackbourne's *The Confessional* provided them with an effective statement of their case. The problem of sub-scription, to which he primarily devoted his attention, did not concern the Anglicans alone. The dissenters, too, were obliged to take oaths which now often outraged their consciences, but at least the authorities were more likely to overlook their failures to fulfil the law.[2] In one form or another all were involved in the degradation of the sacrament into a test for holding office, and from a religious point of view no more hateful requirement had ever been imposed in a Protestant land.[3] Surely history pointed a moral: every party, when victorious, urges the magistrate to exclude dissenters from office, and every party, when overthrown, protests 'against the practice as an unreasonable, unchristian and wicked tyranny—the very practice which they themselves, in their prosperity, endeavoured to support by every claim of right and to defend by every argument of utility and experience'.[4] In actual practice men of all parties have usually claimed that the articles they dislike were intended to be interpreted with latitude, but that the remainder must be accepted in their literal sense.[5] Subscription could not achieve the results which its champions claimed on its behalf. Men took the oaths in so many senses that the only constant factor seemed to be the desire to secure pre-ferment. The need for reform was obvious; few would dispute the general proposition, and Blackbourne felt that the time had come to specify some of the points at which changes were necessary. 'For my own part', he said, 'I am neither afraid nor ashamed to call for a review of our Trinitarian forms as what, I think, is quite necessary for the honour of the Church herself.'[6]

Yet the crucial points could easily be obscured by too comprehensive a programme, and Blackbourne felt that the urgent matter was to concentrate on 'the stumbling block' which should be 'removed out of the way with the utmost expedition', namely 'the case of subscription to human creeds and confessions, and other ecclesiastical forms, which are required to be assented to, as being "agreeable to the Word of God" '.[1]

The practical upshot of Blackbourne's work was the Feathers Tavern Petition, presented to parliament and debated in February 1772. Its plea was that the clergy might be allowed to interpret the Bible in whatever sense appealed to them, and that they should not be bound by creeds and formulae. Behind the movement was the conviction that the laity should be encouraged to take a more active interest in the vital issues of worship and belief. Intelligent people were being alienated from the Church; they felt that its theology was petrified, its laws antiquated, and its attitude to other Christians exclusive and intolerant. Reform was necessary; to bring the forms of public worship into closer conformity with the prevailing standards of belief should be the initial step.

The petition may have commanded a good deal of general support, but, because it was organised by men who moved in academic and clerical circles, it was presented with relatively few signatures. Doubtless this fact affected its ultimate fate; it did not prevent it from prompting an important debate in the House of Commons. To Gibbon, a silent backbencher, the affair had comic overtones. The 'rebellious sons' of 'our dear Mamma the Church of England', he wrote, had tried to 'set aside her will on account of insanity'; but her loyal defenders, 'though they allowed the thirty-nine clauses of her testament were absurd, supported the validity of it with infinite humour'.[2] But the debate was not the amusing pantomime that Gibbon implies. For the first time a proposal had been advanced aimed at bringing the worship and the doctrinal standards of the Church of England into closer conformity with prevailing attitudes.[3] Edmund Burke contributed a major speech, 'an example of the highest performance of a man of letters, who is likewise a man of the world'.[1] He was largely responsible, indeed, for the defeat of the petition. He had no sympathy, he said, with the irresponsible arguments used by some of the opponents of the petition. He was not necessarily hostile to change. If you altered the symbols of the Church you would not destroy her being.[2] The Anglican liturgy doubtless had defects, and possibly the Articles of the Church needed revision, but 'the ground for legislative alteration of a legal establishment is this, and this only—that you find the inclinations of the majority of the people, concurring with your own sense of the intolerable nature of the abuse, are in favour of a change'.[3] Reform should follow popular demand. 'But if you have no evidence of this nature, it ill becomes your gravity, on the petition of a few gentlemen, to listen to anything that tends to shake one of the capital pillars of the State and alarm the body of your people upon that one ground in which every hope and fear, every interest, passion, prejudice, everything that can affect the human breast are all involved together. If you make this a season of religious alterations, depend upon it, you will soon find it a season of religious tumults and religious wars.'[4] To Burke it seemed clear that the petitioners wanted to enjoy the preferments of the establishment without submitting to its discipline. By the provisions of the Act of Toleration they were free to believe as they wished; if they wished they could secede and establish new congregations. 'Dissent, not satisfied with toleration, is not conscience but ambition.'[5] But the constitution has deemed it wise to extend public support to those who accept such forms and doctrines as the legislature, in the name of the people, prescribes. 'If you have religion publicly practised and publicly taught', he said, 'you must have a power to say what that religion will be which you will protect and encourage, and to distinguish it with such marks and characteristics as you in your wisdom shall think fit.'[6] Some test is necessary; the petitioners admit as much by suggesting that Scripture should be the standard, but Scripture is a test exceedingly difficult to apply.[7]

The house of Commons rejected the petition by 217 votes to
71. It was difficult for the majority to consider the matter purely
on its merits. Antipathy to nonconformity clearly swayed some
members: behind any move to secure relaxation of existing laws
they detected the shadow of dissent. Others saw the demand for
reform as one phase of a persistent drift toward Arian, Socinian
and Unitarian heresies.[1] So in part it was, and this explains the
reluctance of Anglican dignitaries to countenance any efforts to
achieve reform. After the failure of the Feathers Tavern movement, a group of priests approached Archbishop Cornwallis
with a plan to alter 'those parts of the Liturgy and Articles which
all reasonable persons agreed stood in need of amendment'.[2]
The attempt was rebuffed, and as the century progressed the most
militant advocates of change were usually the radical nonconformists. Doctrinal tests, wrote Dr Priestley, 'suited perfectly
well with the times of darkness and bigotry', but they had no
place in the age of reason. When men could not accept the findings of science 'without being satisfied, from proper evidence,
with respect to their truth', it was intolerable that they should
be less scrupulous about religion.[3]

Within the Church of England there persisted a tenuous witness in favour of reform. Its chief representative was Richard
Watson, Regius Professor of Divinity at Cambridge and bishop
of Llandaff. He described himself as 'a Christian Whig', which
meant that he was a liberal both in political and ecclesiastical
affairs. As a defender of the Revolution settlement he was convinced that England did not need a revolution, but he believed
that it would greatly benefit from changes both in Church and
State.[4] His ideal was 'a temperate reform', and he advocated it
long after most of his contemporaries had been frightened into
silence or reaction. He was interested in politics because of the
'political bend of my mind in favour of civil liberty', and his
enthusiasm survived the discovery of 'the selfish and lowminded'
motives which inspired eighteenth-century politicians.[5] The basic
problem in public life, he believed, was to raise the prevailing

tone. Statesmen gave the impression that their services were for sale, and the common man concluded that 'patronage is a scandalous game played by public men for private ends and frequently little better than the selfish struggle for power'.[1] Apparently everyone had his own ambition and his own price; unfortunately the Crown had 'the means of gratifying the expectation of them all'. So far from being a 'patriot king', George III was himself the source of all corruption in the State.[2]

A reformer on the bishops' bench could assess the need of reform in the Church; he might even hope to effect some changes. Within six months of his elevation Watson had explored, 'in the most prudent ways I could think of', the possibilities of action. The revenues of the different sees ought to be adjusted to remove flagrant inequalities; only thus could the bishops be delivered from the degrading servitude to politicians in which their hopes of translation bound them. As matters stood, it was impossible to dispute d'Alembert's judgment that high office was a pyramid whose summit could be reached only by eagles or reptiles. Under altered circumstances, bishops would not need to hold commendams. They could reside in their dioceses, and exercise due oversight over their clergy. They could discourage pluralism and non-residence, and they could gradually attack these problems at their root—the serious inadequacy of clerical stipends. Watson was realistic in his assessment both of the existing situation and of the prospects for change. A reformer like Luther, he felt, could transform the structure of church life within five years. Lacking such an impetus, a dormant national conscience made no demands of politicians, and without public clamour there would be no change. Even a gradualist like Watson was a marked man in the eyes of those who dispensed rewards; he was denied the translation which he blamed others for seeking, and his tone of injured virtue grew more querulous year by year.[3]

It was not only the organisation of the Church that needed reform. Watson felt that its doctrinal position was seriously in need of re-examination. He had little patience with tradition;

age alone could not invest with authority the pronouncements of the past. He saw no value in doctrines which had grown out of speculation on the divine nature. He therefore accepted the need to modify the terms of subscription, and he was quite prepared for drastic credal changes.[1] With the Duke of Grafton he agreed on a proposed measure for expunging the Athanasian creed from the liturgy of the Church, and only the upheavals caused by the French Revolution prevented them from introducing it in the House of Lords. 'I certainly dislike', he wrote, '*the imposition* of all creeds formed by human authority; though I do not dislike them as useful summaries of what other *compilers believe* to be true either in natural or revealed religion.'[2] This he said, was an emphasis demanded by the temper of the age. It was foolish and unnecessary to defend all inherited truths; the wise strategy was to defend the things which could be conserved. To this end he was prepared to sacrifice the mysteries which the common man could not understand. Only thus could the Church retain the loyalty of its educated laity. A new age demanded new methods. 'I do not, indeed, expect much success in propagating Christianity by missionaries from any part of Christendom, but I expect much from the extension of science and of commerce.'[3]

Watson believed that his mind was 'wholly unbiased'. 'I had no prejudice against, no predilection for, the Church of England, but a sincere regard for the *Church of Christ*, and an insuperable objection to every dogmatical intolerance.'[4] He was sensitive therefore to the discrimination from which the nonconformists suffered. The Test and Corporation Acts were antiquated and unjust; he believed they ought to be repealed. 'There appear to me but two reasons for excluding any honest man from eligibility to public office—want of capacity to serve the office and want of attachment to the civil constitution of the country. That the dissenters want capacity will not be asserted; that they want attachment to the civil constitution of the country is asserted by many but proved by none.'[5] Watson realised that at this point he parted company with Pitt and Burke. He also knew that 'the

cause of the dissenters was much injured by some indiscreet
expositions of Dr Priestley relative to the approaching fall of all
civil and ecclesiastical establishments'.[1] Here he touched on two
factors which require separate and detailed study: the role of the
radical dissenters as advocates of change, and the nature of the
reaction which overwhelmed all proposals for reform.

In the early part of the century the nonconformists were a subdued and tractable group. They dutifully supported the Hanover-
ians, hopefully looked for relief from discriminatory laws, and
stressed their loyalty to the British constitution. Doddridge's
famous *Course of Lectures* touched briefly on political questions
and treated them with a caution which would have disarmed even
the most suspicious critics. Yet unconsciously Doddridge was
helping to foster a new spirit. The dissenting academies, as
Joseph Priestley pointed out, encouraged the habits of free
enquiry and of informed discussion. In due course the nonconformists ceased to be content to trace their political ancestry to
Sidney and Locke while they faithfully supported the reigning
house. Their new attitude altered their sympathies and intensified
their interest in reform. It sprang naturally from convictions
wholly in keeping with their traditions.

The basic principle to which the radical dissenters appealed was
man's natural right to freedom of conscience. This represented
the continuity which linked them with their Puritan ancestors.[2]
Their emphasis on liberty gave a distinctive quality to their
works. 'The very existence of [their] dissent' was founded on
certain cardinal principles, and among these freedom stood pre-
eminent.[3] For Christians, liberty in general becomes 'that
liberty of conscience and freedom of enquiry which is essential
to the proper discharge of the duties of their profession'.[4] It is
consequently impossible to proceed to the discussion of any
Christian doctrine without first establishing the primacy of
Christian liberty; 'for . . . if this preliminary doctrine of right be
disallowed, voluntary piety is the dream of an enthusiast, the
oracles of God in the Christian world . . . are sounds convertible

to sensatorial sense. . . .'¹ When Dr Philip Furneaux embarked on his defence of nonconformity, he declared that it was part of his aim 'to promote amongst my readers in general just conceptions of the right of private judgment and of impartial liberty in matters of conscience, which of all human rights seems to me to be one of the most sacred and inalienable'.² Freedom, of course, is worthless without security, and the superiority of one form of government over another can be accurately assessed 'in proportion as it gives more of this security'.³

The inferences which the nonconformists drew from the primacy of liberty affected life at many points. The right to freedom made the traffic in human beings intolerable; therefore the dissenters joined in the attack on the slave trade.⁴ 'The right of private judgment' became an inseparable part of true religion; to deny it was 'destructive of the nature of Christianity in general' and of the witness of the reformed churches in particular.⁵

Even more characteristic was the emphasis which the dissenters laid on intellectual liberty. They admitted the dangers which lurked in 'the spirit of enquiry', but though it might 'lead some into error' it was the only way of deliverance from superstition. To restrict free investigation of Christianity was equivalent to denying its truth, and dissenters, above all others, should be committed to the view that 'truth will always have an infinite advantage over error if free scope be given to enquiry'.⁶ To exemplify the virtue of 'candour' was the aim of all rational dissenters, and they defined it as 'the disinterested pursuit of truth'.⁷ Intellectual honesty was the guiding principle of their various activities. It inspired Priestley's scientific researches, Price's investigation of the principles of public finance, and the theological studies of both men. To preserve an ordered liberality of mind, to 'form a fair and impartial judgment on questions and action'⁸—this was their ideal; it explains the curious blend of intensity and calm which marked their intellectual outlook.

This emphasis on liberty forms the background of the dissenters' reforming zeal. Because of it they intensified their opposition to subscription. They renewed their attacks on the principles of religious uniformity. They emphasised the injustice of their exclusion from the universities, and they detected, in the restrictive policies from which they suffered, the cause of the intellectual stagnation to which Oxford and Cambridge had succumbed.¹ They were grateful for toleration, but they did not hesitate to emphasise its limitations; 'to be exposed to civil penalties on account of . . . religious principles . . . is the precise definition of persecution'.² They believed that the scope of religious freedom should be greatly expanded. 'A full toleration of religious opinions and the protection of all parties in their respective modes of worship are the natural operations of a free government.'³ Under existing conditions, the nonconformists found themselves penalised at every point. 'We are a part of the community', wrote Priestley, 'which, in return for great merit, have received great injuries.'⁴ The immediate need was to restrain the civil power from usurping rights which belong to the Church alone: '. . . no human authority should be permitted to make that necessary to Christian communion which Christ has not made necessary'. All present corruptions in the Church come from 'the alliance of the Kingdom of Christ with the kingdoms of this world (an alliance which our Lord himself expressly disclaimed)'.⁵ The truth is clear; a religious establishment cannot form a part of the civil ordering of society, and the sooner existing anomalies are swept away, the better for all concerned.⁶

The dissenters were not content to ask for changes in the Church. They threw themselves into political controversy with a zeal to which there had been no parallel for over a hundred years. They had unique inducements to engage in politics; they suffered daily from disabilities which presupposed political remedies.⁷ They represented a common position, but they did not form a single party. Gilbert Wakefield insisted that they were 'a very numerous, heterogeneous and unconnected body'; Priestley declared that 'they had no peculiar principles of government at all'.⁸ Yet there was no question as to their essential agreement

The Authority of Tradition and the Demand for Reform

among themselves. Indeed, one of the conspicuous features of English public life in the generation before the French Revolution was the dramatic change in the political sympathies of the dissenters. No longer were they the docile camp-followers of the Whig party, the unquestioning supporters of the reigning house. To a large degree they controlled the organs of public opinion; through them they carried on their agitation to sever the link between Church and State. Politics, they felt, ought to be secularised; it should not be a branch of the establishment. But their dissent from the Church of England did not imply disaffection to the English constitution. History testified to their loyalty. They had not given the faintest excuse for accusing them of republican principles.[1] But they were perfectly within their rights, they felt, in keeping up a sustained agitation against the Test and Corporation Acts. They did so with such skill and pertinacity that their opponents watched their efforts with mounting dismay. This was quite unnecessary, said Priestley, yet in due course he admitted the need to teach the public 'not to fear where no fear is'.[2]

The fear, however, was quite enough to thwart every effort to remove disabilities which were increasingly anomalous as well as vexatious. The Test Act had been designed as a protection against Roman Catholics, not against dissenters; the Roman Catholics had now gained relief, but the dissenters had not.[3] The suggested strategy was simple. Let the nonconformists take unified action— as Englishmen, and as Christians. 'The voice of reason, of truth, and of right is sure to be heard and to prevail in the end.'[4] But the desired results did not materialise. In 1773 a bill for the relief of nonconformists was introduced into the House of Commons and was defeated. In 1778 a similar measure for relief of the Roman Catholics was passed. In the resulting reaction an Act for the Relief of Dissenters[5] exempted nonconformist ministers and schoolmasters from subscribing to the Articles. It left the restrictive Acts in force, but it encouraged the Protestant Dissenting Deputies to solicit support for a bill to remove the ancient grievances.[6]

In 1787, an attempt to pass a measure of relief was defeated by 178 votes to 100. Pitt professed his reluctance to oppose the bill and praised the private virtues of the dissenters, but he threw his weight against it. Two years later a similar motion failed by only 20 votes. But by 1790, when the question was re-introduced, it had been caught by the rising tide of emotional excitement engendered by the French Revolution. Fox argued for repeal in a speech of great courage and eloquence, but Pitt opposed it with fewer reservations than before and with far greater vigour. The dissenters, he claimed, already enjoyed toleration; they were now demanding equality, but to grant it would presage the destruction of the establishment and the overthrow of the constitution. Burke's contribution to the debate carried even greater weight. On previous occasions he had advocated toleration. Ten years earlier, he said, he would have supported the present motion. But on the other side of the Channel they were now witnessing a nation in dissolution and a church in ruins. By their pamphlets and sermons the English dissenters had proved that they were deeply infected by revolutionary impiety. Men inspired by such destructive principles could claim no concessions. The motion was lost by 294 to 105.[1] The numbers participating and the size of the majority reflect the mounting concern with the issues involved. Liberty and reform had come under the menacing shadow of the French Revolution.

For some years the nonconformists had been courting unpopularity. They had been vociferous champions of the American Revolution. They had acted as colonial agents; they had supported the colonial cause in pamphlets and sermons; they had consistently hailed it as a solemn manifestation of the philosophical virtue of liberty. Their theological position also aroused suspicion and their most conspicuous spokesmen were most clearly inclined to heresy. 'In no age', wrote an indignant journalist, 'did Socinianism prevail more in England than among the dissenters in the last thirty years',[2] and one who was himself infected with heresy ruefully remarked that 'a Socinian is still a sort of monster in the world'.[1] The vilification which they drew upon themselves can find a parallel only in the hatred inspired by Godwin and Paine. Theological error seldom arouses such violent fears. It was the skill and persistence with which the dissenters pursued their political aims which alarmed their foes. They had developed the art of agitation to a high pitch of effectiveness. They had refused to let their grievances against the penal acts subside into oblivion. In the pamphlet warfare they had scored repeated successes. Adroit and closely argued works like Robinson's *Arcana* and Furneaux's *Letters to The Hon. Mr Justice Blackstone* had related the dissenters' case to the law of nature and the principles of justice. Joseph Priestley had kept up a running commentary on developments, marked by good sense, by an unruffled temper, and by an assured belief that logic and enlightenment would inevitably prevail. Liberty had been their watchword, complete toleration their goal. To such men the French Revolution seemed like a glorious vindication of truth and justice. A note of millennial enthusiasm crept into their utterances. A new day was breaking. 'Error and superstition are falling everywhere abroad', wrote Priestley;[2] in England, too, they must at length give way. Robert Hall believed that the Revolution promised 'a firmer establishment to liberty than any [event] recorded in the annals of the world'. It seemed to him that 'a fatal lethargy has long been spreading amongst us, attended, as is natural, with a prevailing disposition . . . to treat plans of reform with contempt'. To this apathetic spirit, the Revolution was a standing challenge, and consequently Hall felt 'free to confess, the French Revolution has always appeared to me, and does still appear, the most splendid event recorded in the annals of history'.[3] Richard Price believed that he was witnessing a new revelation; he saw clear evidence that the hand of Providence had fashioned these great events.[4] When Priestley was informed of his election as a member of the French Revolutionary Society he replied in a letter which admirably reflected the feelings of many besides himself. 'Dear Sir, I beg you would make my acknowledgments in the most respectful manner to the committee of the Revolutionary Society for their grateful address to me. Our principles are entirely the same, and notwithstanding all opposition must prevail in this as well as in other countries. Violence is temporary but truth is eternal. I am, etc. . . .'[1] When men of such principles organised to give them effect, general alarm became panic. Nor were they always wise in the language they used; to describe their activities as placing gunpowder 'under the old building of error and superstition' was, in the fevered state of public feeling, to invite misunderstanding.[2] The Revolution Society, in which many dissenters were active, happened to commemorate a different revolution—that of 1688—but this fact was conveniently forgotten. It contained many Anglicans and a sprinkling of progressive peers. It was before this society that Richard Price preached the famous sermon which provoked Burke's yet more famous *Reflections*. But before considering this great diatribe and the view of tradition which it expounded, it is necessary to retrace our steps and observe how national feeling, in reaction to the claims of the nonconformists, had been hardening against reform of any kind.

The eighteenth-century mood was a strange combination of seemingly incongruous elements. On the one hand it contemplated, with an almost morbid despair, the corruptions of the age; on the other hand it regarded with complacent self-satisfaction the institutions of society. In their pessimism about the future a great bishop like Butler stood on common ground with a mediocre one like Newton. His concern for the public, said Newton, 'was not less than Lord Mansfield's, for we have very little to hope and very much to fear from the sad dismal prospect before us, from the gross immorality and irreligion of our people, from the want of spirit and resolution and steadiness in counsel, from the great attention to private interest and little regard to public welfare'. Newton was quite aware of the political servitude in which the king's ministers kept the bishops. He knew it at first hand, and described it in vivid terms, but he considered it a less formidable threat than the agitation for reform. He regarded the parliamentary opposition as a party of reckless men, pursuing wild and irresponsible policies. They had 'advanced and propagated such levelling notions as would not only be the total ruin of our happy constitution, but are subversive of all law, of all government, of all society whatever: that all men are born equals; that no man ought to pay taxes who is not represented; that every man at the age of twenty-one should have a vote; that the people have a right to call their governors to account, and to redress all grievances; that the king was made for the people and not the people for the king. . .'.[1] To men like Newton even the cautious reforms proposed by Watson threatened such elementary rights as the sanctity of property, and Watson himself took care to dissociate himself from democratic or republican notions. To this cautious age 'the visionary and dangerous schemes afloat for the reform of civil government' endangered a system hallowed by time.[2] Always in the background was the shadowy threat of popular violence. The mob, so ready to rabble the Methodist field preachers or to burn dissenting meeting houses, could easily be aroused to frenzied protest against religious innovation.

In a country where there was so little demand for reform and so much suspicion of change the French Revolution rapidly created a new mentality. During a brief spell of exultation, reformers and romantic poets hailed the dawning of a new day, but the enthusiasm was soon dampened by revolutionary excesses. A strong reaction set in. Men of liberal outlook succumbed to the pervasive atmosphere. Bishop Watson, indignant that the cause of reform was being fatally compromised, protested that 'this impious fever of the mind, this paralysis of human intellect' was spreading like a foul contagion; and he knew that 'when religion shall have lost its hold on men's conscience, government will lose its authority over their persons, and a state of barbarous anarchy will ensue'. As he considered the activities of the revolutionaries, 'I know not', he said, 'which most to admire and deplore, their wickedness as men or their weakness as statesmen.'¹ Gibbon, who had spent his life 'putting a polished surface on human turbulence', found himself suddenly jolted out of his customary pose of quizzical detachment from the political scene. His tolerant sympathies were swept away by a torrent of fears. He saw in the Revolution a 'total subversion of all rank, order and government'. 'The daemon of democracy' stood revealed as 'the blackest daemon of hell'. He regarded with horror any suggestion of change. Even in the attempt to abolish slavery he detected the 'leaven of new democratical principles', the 'wild ideas of the rights and natural equality of man'. He besought his friend Lord Sheffield not to countenance any movement for reform: 'if you admit the smallest and most specious change in our parliamentary system you are lost. You will be driven from one step to another, from principles just in theory to consequences most pernicious in practice'; 'the slightest innovation launches you without rudder or compass on a dark and dangerous ocean of theoretical experiment'.²

The effects of alarm appeared in a variety of ways. Hatred of revolutionary principles modified the traditional English antipathy to Roman Catholics. French *émigré* priests were received as martyrs for a common cause.³ Roman Catholic Relief Acts were passed in 1791 and 1793. In face of the formal abolition of Christianity in France, the Church of England achieved in many quarters a new status as a bulwark against anarchy and atheism.⁴ Its clergy were treated with greater respect. Even its abuses were invested with the dignity associated with the symbols of continuity. Fear of Jacobinism intensified suspicions of any source from which the revolutionary taint might spread. Methodists and dissenters were regarded with increased hostility; since they were active in promoting Sunday Schools, some Anglican bishops urged their clergy to withdraw their co-operation and to establish schools under their own control. Many believed that any form of education for the lower classes was dangerous. Pitt seriously weighed the desirability of suppressing Sunday Schools; in the

House of Lords Bishop Horsley denounced them as the refuge of Jacobinical propagandists.[1] Political wolves, it was felt, were disguising themselves in religious sheep's clothing; the prevalent fear found clear expression in the debate in the House of Commons on Fox's motion to grant Unitarians the legal status and protection enjoyed by the old Dissent. The move was inexpedient, said Pitt; at a time when the enemies of religion and morality were overrunning Europe it was foolish to grant any concession to a disaffected group. Burke's speech on this occasion was a serious re-examination of the principles on which a state can tolerate religious minorities. Nearly twenty years before, in supporting the Dissenters Relief Bill of 1773, he had claimed that the magistrate can restrict freedom only 'upon this ground—that the person dissenting does not dissent from the scruples of an ill-informed conscience, but from a party ground of dissension, in order to raise a faction in the state'. If a man 'abets diversity of opinions in religion in order to distract the state and destroy the peace of his country' he may be punished: 'this is the only plausible—for there is no true, ground of persecution'.[2] During the intervening years, his views had hardened. The Unitarians fulfilled in every respect what he had once regarded as an extreme and improbable eventuality. The magistrate should be specially vigilant when men begin to 'mingle a political system with their religious opinions, true or false, plausible or implausible'. This, he believed, was precisely what the Unitarians had done. 'This faction', he said, '. . . are not confined to a theological sect, but are also a political faction.' Their aim was proselytism; when they had gained enough adherents they would first 'by force and violence overturn the Church'; then they would subvert the State, and the model which they would follow had been provided by France. 'As a party they are infinitely mischievous', and for proof Burke appealed to 'the declarations of Priestley and Price'.[3]

This stampede to the security of tried and tested ways fixed the pattern of English life for more than a generation. 'In England', wrote Dicey, 'the French Revolution worked nothing but evil; it delayed salutary changes for forty years, and rendered reforms, when at last they came, less beneficial than they might have been if gradually carried out as the natural result of the undisturbed development of ideas suggested by English good sense and English love of justice.'[1] But fear alone cannot account for the magnitude of Burke's contribution to political thought. It gave to his work a stridency from which it had not previously suffered, and furnished him with a unique opportunity to exploit his gift of sustained declamation, but Burke did more than create a system out of the fears and prejudices of his age. He fashioned a political philosophy which dealt in a new way with the source and nature of authority and which by taking account of man's experience was able to do justice both to the past and to the future.

Burke could claim with reason that he was not opposed to change as such. He could appeal to his record: to the courage and wisdom of his speeches on America, to his consistent support of greater freedom and an enlarged toleration. At the end of his sustained philippic against revolutionary tendencies he could describe himself as 'one, almost the whole of whose public exertion has been a struggle for the liberty of others'.[2] He had always admitted that changing circumstances could render ancient institutions obsolete.[3] Even in the full tide of his reaction against innovations in France he conceded that reform was often legitimate and occasionally necessary. He was convinced, however, that change must take place within the proper framework. 'A sure principle of conservation and a sure principle of transmission' need not exclude 'a principle of improvement'.[4] 'I would not exclude alteration . . .,' he declared, 'but even when I changed, it should be to preserve.'[5] He reserved his indignation for doctrinaire enthusiasts. He felt that the radical dissenters were investing the French Revolution with a respectability which it could not rightly claim. Price's famous *Discourse on the Love of our Country* seemed to Burke a dangerous piece of special pleading, and the parallel it drew with the Revolution of 1688 was false and misleading. Price, it was clear, had failed to appreciate the distinctive genius of English constitutional change. He had ignored the need 'to call back our attention to the true principles of our domestic laws'.[1] As the excesses of the French Revolution became more pronounced, Burke's denunciations grew increasingly shrill and vehement, and his record as a moderate reformer was lost in his tirade against excessive change. The upheaval in France was demonstrating that a movement which began as a plea for necessary reform could sear and blight all the sanctities of human life.

The errors of the revolutionaries, said Burke, were not restricted to mistakes in practice. These men had been beguiled by theories which were basically false. They had tried to guide political life by an appeal to abstractions. Instead of submitting to wisdom guided by experience, they had relied on theories which were unrelated to real life. They had reduced the complexities of human society and the intricacies of human nature to an artificial simplicity; when Burke contemplated the result, he was 'at no loss to decide that the artificers [were] grossly ignorant of their trade, or totally negligent of their duty'. This is the nemesis which overtakes all abstractions. 'The pretended rights of these theorists are all extremes: and in proportion as they are metaphysically true, they are morally and politically false'.[2] The appeal to theory springs from an undue reliance on reason. Burke was not mounting an attack on reason as such, though he laid bare the consequences which follow from an exaggerated confidence in its powers. Theory rests on a critical and selective use of reason; it is valid within its proper sphere, but that sphere is limited. Once it oversteps its bounds it proves misleading; it may actually be dangerous.[3] It shatters the unity of human experience, the wholeness of human life. It tries to contemplate an object in unreal isolation, 'as it stands stripped of every relation, in all the nakedness and solitude of metaphysical abstraction'.[4]

Because abstract theories have misled us, we are not obliged to renounce reason altogether. Burke saw reason as one of the factors contributing to the proper equilibrium of life. It is neither sovereign nor independent; therefore it must acknowledge its proper place and its partial role. It must admit the authority of a higher reason, and acknowledge its dependence upon something it cannot fully comprehend. Beyond our limited reason there is the objective reason of the moral order. The reality and supremacy of this moral order embraces our lives; in our humble submission to it we find our fulfilment, in our arrogant flouting of it we court our own overthrow. Abstract reason, playing with abstractions, expresses itself in the bold assertion of will, and in doing so breaks through the fabric of the moral order. Passion and will, for Burke, are disruptive and unnatural forces; instinct, feeling, even prejudice, are sound and reliable, because they embody a wisdom deeper than any which intellect alone can achieve.[1] Two types of reason—the one abstract, the other concrete—face each other in the sharpest contrast. The one is analytical, the other synthetic. The one divides life into artificial compartments, the other unifies it in its wholeness. The one finds its political expression in the rash generalisations of Jacobinical schemes; the other has its counterpart in the balanced wisdom with which history has infused the British constitution.

For this reason Burke never wearied of stressing the importance of the things which he regarded as natural.[2] 'A constitutional policy', he said, should work 'after the pattern of nature', and its virtue lies in 'wisdom without reflection and above it. . . . Thus, by preserving the method of nature in the conduct of the state, in what we improve, we are never wholly new; in what we retain we are never wholly obsolete.'[3] He constantly returned to the unity which is achieved when man's whole nature is disciplined by all the factors which control his life. The distinctive fault of the revolutionaries was to be 'so taken up with their theories about the rights of man that they have totally forgotten his nature'.[4] This explains the contrast which Burke always drew between expediency and abstract right. This was one of the basic distinctions which he emphasised throughout his entire career. By expediency he meant those forces which contribute to the well-being of the whole community, not to the narrow advantage of the individual. It did not flout the precepts of an enlightened self-interest; rather it embraced them, but in such a way as to include 'reason, justice and humanity'.[1] Moreover, expediency should never be divorced from duty. Only in such a comprehensive setting are the exciting watchwords of political life saved from the perils of abstraction. To Burke 'that liberty [was] very equivocal in her appearance, which has not wisdom and justice for her companions; and does not lead prosperity and plenty in her train'.[2]

Burke emphasised the unity of man's nature and the comprehensiveness of his experience. As a natural consequence he also stressed the importance of history. The higher reason, the moral order which gave man's life its dignity were disclosed in and through the historical process. This is the stage on which the Providence of God is displayed.[3] In his attack on doctrinaire theorists, Burke always relied on an appeal to history. He believed that there was no possibility of reaching truth about human life and its proper ordering except through a searching study of man's experience in the past. It is easy to prove that in the strict sense Burke was no historian; he knew little about the past, whether in India or in France, but he had an unusually sensitive awareness of the influences which have moulded human institutions. His historical sense, therefore, profoundly affected his view of the State. In a day when enthusiasts oversimplified without shame, Burke recognised the full complexity of the political community. 'It is a partnership in all science; a partnership in all art; a partnership in every virtue and in all perfection. As the ends of such partnership cannot be obtained in many generations, it becomes a partnership not only between those who are living but between those who are living, those who are dead, and those who are to be born.'[4] He saw the way the individual was embraced by society and came to self-realisation within it. He understood the role of natural feelings, and the significance of a stable moral order. He realised that traditions develop in slow and subtle ways, but play an incalculable part in constructing man's spiritual environment. Historical insight, he believed, affected political policy. It was an 'old settled maxim' of British statecraft 'never entirely nor at once to depart from antiquity. We found these old institutions, on the whole, favourable to morality and discipline.'[1] This reverence for the past has always been a restraining force. Wisdom is reluctant to change: 'it is with infinite caution that any man ought to venture upon pulling down an edifice, which has answered in any tolerable degree for ages the common purposes of society, or on building it up again, without having models and patterns of approved utility before his eyes'.[2] The essence of Burke's conservatism is best defined in his own words: 'a politic caution, a guarded circumspection, a moral rather than a complexional timidity'.[3]

Burke was well aware of the dangers of an exaggerated reverence for the past. Its lessons should teach us prudence; they cannot always determine our policies. If we let the past control the present, its dead hand inhibits all advance. Burke's keen perception of the relation between history and the moral order normally saved him from blind adulation of the ancient ways. Unless we exercise proper care history 'may be used to vitiate our minds and to destroy our happiness. In history, a great volume is unrolled for our instruction, drawing the materials of future wisdom from the past errors and infirmities of mankind.'[4] Rightly used, history shows us that beneath the pattern of events there lies an abiding moral order. The lessons of the past must be appropriated in the present. We must respond in our own experience to the providential order which we can discern in history. Burke's emphasis on tradition is consequently not a pessimism which binds us to what has been. In each generation men must respond creatively to the moral order which undergirds their lives. 'It is ordained in the eternal constitution of things, that men of intemperate minds cannot be free.'[5] Liberty is for those who recognise the conditions which govern the gift of freedom; and it must be appropriated anew by every man who wishes to enjoy its blessings.

The Authority of Tradition and the Demand for Reform

An eternal moral order undergirds the fabric of our human life. This is only another way of saying that religious truth is the foundation of all human values. 'We know', said Burke, 'and what is better, we feel inwardly, that religion is the basis of civil society, and the source of all good and all comfort.' This follows of necessity from human nature itself. 'We know, and it is our pride to know, that man is by his constitution a religious animal; that atheism is against, not only our reason, but our instincts; and that it cannot prevail long.'¹ Religion provides the framework within which all the elements which Burke esteemed most highly naturally find their proper place. History and the moral order, expediency, instinct, feeling, concrete reason, the prejudices which are merely feelings built by time into familiar patterns—all are embraced and unified by religious insight. His fiercest denunciations of the French Revolution were inspired by its arrogant denial of man's creaturely status. Its doctrinaire idealism presupposed a moral autonomy in man which violated the simplest yet the most profound law of his life. Those who insist that human values are ultimate may pay lip-service to man's innate dignity but they end by treating him like a beast.

History convinced Burke of the importance of the institutions which preserve and transmit what man has learned from the past. His belief in the supreme importance of religion had its counterpart in his veneration for the Church. He resented any suggestion that those who were blind to religious truths were competent to reform religious institutions. Through the long course of many ages the Church had gradually assumed its recent form. The pattern, he said, may not be perfect, but it enshrines great values and satisfies fundamental human needs. It has its proper and necessary place in the structure of society; in the delicate balance of the State it plays an essential role. Indeed, the religious establishment provides the necessary consecration of the life of the whole community. 'We will have her mixed throughout the whole mass of life, and blended with all the classes of society.' To pursue the schemes of the champions of reform would be both wild and irresponsible. As far as the English people are concerned, 'Church and State are ideas inseparable in their minds, and scarcely is the one ever mentioned without mentioning the other'. A church establishment is consequently 'the first of our prejudices, not a prejudice destitute of reason, but involving in it profound and extensive wisdom'.[1]

Burke's political philosophy grew out of his active participation in political life. His most famous works were addressed to problems which excited intense emotions. He invited attack;[2] his involvement in partisan activities made him vulnerable to it. It is easy to detect his weaknesses. Priestley claimed that Burke so completely identified Church and State that reform in either became virtually impossible.[3] Mackintosh argued with great cogency that the Revolution was not the work of a few extremists (as Burke believed) but of a people tried beyond endurance and at last aroused to grapple with its problems.[4] Burke's ignorance of France—its history, its political life, its economic difficulties—betrayed him into a defence of indefensible abuses. 'I am no stranger', he claimed, 'to the faults and defects of the subverted government of France',[5] yet he revealed his blindness on every page and invited Paine's devastating retort: 'he pities the plumage and forgets the dying bird'.[6] He was guilty of inconsistencies which seriously weakened the force of his argument. He defended tradition because he cherished values which only a true conservatism can preserve; yet unquestionably he ministered comfort to blind reactionaries. He defended the role of the Church in consecrating the life of the State; he encouraged the disastrous tendency to treat religion as an adjunct to politics. As much as any man he was responsible for checking any possibility of reasonable reform; more than any man he inspired the reactionary temper which maintained its ascendancy for a whole generation. In this respect his *Reflections* was a manifesto as mischievous as it was successful. And even when he commended the values by which he set the greatest store, he seldom carried complete conviction.[7]

Yet there is no denying the power and persuasiveness of Burke's position. For the first time he broke through the shallow rationalism which marked so much of the political thought of the eighteenth century. Locke had worthily served his day; now, for the first time, his assumptions about man and society were boldly challenged. With the verve and passion of an incomparable master of rhetoric, Burke set forth an alternative view of the true nature of the State and of the fundamental character of man. He revealed the forces, half-perceived and often forgotten, by which human life has been shaped and moulded. He allowed for the power of the past and for the complexity of the present. He saw that man in his impotence must be supported by the forces which are rooted in his own nature and in the experience of the race. And he realised that the dignity of man's evanescent life can be maintained only by humble dependence upon that moral order which undergirds all human values. So

> bewildered men,
> Beginning to mistrust their boastful guides,
> And wise men willing to grow wiser,

responded to his teaching. So Wordsworth, recovering from the revolutionary fever, recalled with gratitude the part which Burke had played, and indicated the essential nature of his contribution:

> While he forewarns, denounces, launches forth,
> Against all systems built on abstract rights,
> Keen ridicule; the majesty proclaims
> Of Institutes and Laws, hallowed by time;
> Declares the vital power of social ties
> Endeared by custom; and with high disdain,
> Exploding upstart theory, insists
> Upon the allegiance to which men are born.[1]

CHAPTER X

CONCLUSION

At first glance the eighteenth century appears to be an age serenely self-assured in spirit and amazingly stable in the pattern of its outward life. Actually the thought of the period, like its literature, its politics, even its manners, underwent a subtle but continuous change, and the end of the century brought a reaction more violent than that in which the Age of Reason repudiated the preceeding Age of Revolution. Many of the characteristic features of the eighteenth century vanished as completely as the wigs which had been the symbols of gentility. Many of the cherished convictions of the period were repudiated with contempt. But other elements in its thought have persisted as permanent elements in the intellectual outlook of man; though often unacknowledged, they have shaped many of the presuppositions which govern modern life.

The place of reason was a matter of intense debate. As the eighteenth century began, men beguiled themselves with extravagant expectations: human intelligence would speedily accomplish what ardour and fanaticism had failed to achieve. This faith was not easily superseded. In 1743, when Hume had attacked its theoretical basis and Wesley had announced its practical insufficiency, Henry Dodwell the younger published his famous work, *Christianity Not Founded on Argument*. The popular reaction was vehement. Men were not prepared to abandon their favourite assumptions without a protest. But gradually it became apparent that a confident rationalism was not the natural and normal form of human thought whenever it is left free to go its own way.[1] Reluctantly men conceded that some subjects do not

276

Conclusion

admit of logical proof. The weight of Butler's arguments convinced them that in many instances we must be content with probability instead of certainty. Because Soame Jenyns was not a creative thinker, he reflected his age with the faithfulness which only a minor author can achieve. In his early works he affected a Deistic scepticism about religion and placed his entire confidence in reason. Gradually he veered towards a more orthodox position, and in his *View of the Internal Evidence of the Christian Religion* he boldly argued that the traditional faith must be divine because it was so totally at variance with the principles of human reason. The reaction against rationalism took many forms, from the visionary mysticism of Blake to the luminous supernaturalism of Coleridge. But faith in reason was never wholly displaced. At the end of the century the influence of Locke was still powerful and pervasive. Bishop Watson echoed the very words of Locke when he claimed that 'there may be doctrines above reason; but nothing, which is evidently contrary to reason, can ever be justly considered a part of the Christian dispensation'.[1]

The strength of much of eighteenth-century thought lay in its vigour, its directness and its clarity. Its weakness was a tendency to be satisfied with externals. This was not true of Berkeley or Butler or Hume; it was emphatically true of Warburton and of many of the secondary writers. They approached the profounder problems of human experience from the outside. They were not troubled by the mysteries of human life or by the inscrutability of human destiny; logic could resolve every difficulty into the neat pattern of a conclusive demonstration. Much of the thought of the age moved in the orbit of an unquestioning self-assurance. Sometimes, as with Tom Paine, the fault lay in a superficial analysis which over-simplified every problem. Sometimes it was an indirect consequence of the scientific movement. The precise exactitude of physics made men impatient of anything that was vague or indefinite. Doubtless this attitude was responsible for blunting many of the finer sensibilities, but it also helped to banish fear and to lift the incubus of superstition. It encouraged a reasonable attitude toward every problem and unquestionably extended the domain of toleration. Individualism was allowed a freer scope and love of liberty was recognised as a valid aspiration which could legitimately claim a wider fulfilment. But the balanced propriety of eighteenth-century life often made the age content with a surface elegance. This disguised the restricted nature of many of its vaunted achievements and hid from view the vast areas which its civilising influence left untouched.

Against both the rationalism and the externalism of the century a reaction was inevitable. It came in the Romantic movement. The Age of Reason, men complained, had treated nature as though it were static and inert. There had been no sympathetic feeling for beauty in its wilder forms. Emotion had been banished from human experience. Propriety had spread like a blight over every sphere of man's endeavour. Poetry had been frozen into formalism, artificiality was beginning to paralyse even the splendid vitality of English art and architecture. An age which placed its confidence in reason had failed to provide an adequate philosophy of life. The Romantic revival was a protest against the suppression of deep-seated human needs. Cravings which had not been satisfied demanded recognition. The reaction awakened hopes which it was easier to recognise than to satisfy; and while it encouraged the tendency to dismiss the eighteenth century with contempt, it scarcely affected the continuing vigour of many aspects of its thought. The Georgian period, for example, firmly established the rule of law. This rule unquestionably had its faults, but it attempted to bring all of life under its sway and increasingly it proved to be a law of freedom. The great popularity of Blackstone's *Commentaries* was an evidence of its growing authority. The eighteenth century was insufficiently concerned about social change, but it provided the necessary foundation on which the reforms of the next century could be effected. The rule of law guaranteed that necessary changes would be gradual and peaceful. The alternative would have been revolution by violence.[1]

Conclusion

Among the movements which powerfully influenced the future was philosophical radicalism. It was part of the legacy of the eighteenth century to the nineteenth. In England Utilitarianism had a twofold source. It was developed by a succession of writers whose interests were theological and ethical; it was given the widest possible currency by Bentham and the Mills, whose concerns were ethical and political. The first explicit statement of the Utilitarian position occurs in the anonymous preface to a translation of a minor work, originally written in Latin, on the perennial problem of evil.[1] Gay, the author of this brief but very influential dissertation, provided the essential outlines of a theory which his successors merely amplified. The psychological foundation of his ethics he found in the theory of association. The 'immediate criterion' of virtue was the will of God, but since God desires the happiness of men it is towards such happiness that his will is always directed. Happiness, of course, means the gratification of the desire for pleasure, and hence the moral agent is always prompted by egotistic motives. But how can we be sure that the happiness of the individual will coincide with the well-being of society? This was the problem which perplexed all the Utilitarians from Gay to John Stuart Mill. Gay's solution was contained in his theory of sanctions. These are four in number—natural, social, legal, and religious—and he laid the heaviest stress on the last of them. Only a supernatural sanction can guarantee that the pleasure of the individual will coincide with the pleasure of society. Here, too, Gay detected the source of all effective obligation. He believed that the moral imperative is conditional on the required action promoting the happiness of the individual. Consequently absolute obligation can come only from God, since he alone can make 'my happiness' identical with the 'general happiness'. 'Thus those who either expressly exclude or don't mention the will of God . . . must either allow that virtue is not in all cases obligatory . . . or they must say that the good of mankind is no sufficient obligation. . . . But how can the good of mankind be any obligation to *me*, when perhaps in particular cases,

279

such as laying down my life, or the like, it is contrary to my happiness?'[1]

In this brief treatise of thirty pages we have the essentials of Utilitarianism as it persisted for a whole century. Only with John Stuart Mill did any significant modifications appear in the theory. But lack of development was certainly not due to any lack of exposition. Abraham Tucker's *The Light of Nature Pursued* extended to seven volumes. With Brown and Paley, he maintained the emphasis on the supernatural sanction. All three began with a selfish theory of moral motive; only by an appeal to God's will were they able to maintain the unity and consistency of their position. Brown claimed that common sense should convince us that virtue can be equated with what promotes happiness. He defined the goal of good conduct as 'the voluntary production of the greatest happiness'.[2] But the individual's motive is selfish. The end and the motive thus seem incompatible: they can be reconciled only by 'the lively and active belief of an all-seeing and all-powerful God . . . who will hereafter make them happy or miserable, according as they designedly promote or violate the happiness of their fellow-creatures'.[3] In his singularly prolix work, Tucker maintained the same general theory, but sharpened certain points. He developed the psychological strain present in Gay's work. He emphasised the strength of the egotistic motive. He introduced a larger measure of determinism. He denied that there are qualitative differences among pleasures, and he was critical of any attempt to elaborate a hedonistic calculus. It is better, he said, to rely on general rules of expediency than to try to estimate the degree to which various actions will promote happiness.[4]

Bentham seldom acknowledged his indebtedness to others, but relatively little in his system was original. He accepted egotistic motivation in a particularly unmitigated form. He took for granted that pleasure is the chief end of conduct, and in terse and dogmatic form he expressed it as a principle: 'the greatest happiness of the greatest number'. Like Gay, he enumerated four

Conclusion

types of sanction—physical, political, moral, and religious—but he placed less emphasis than Gay on the last of these. 'As to such of the pleasures and pains belonging to the religious sanction, as regards a future life, of what kind these may be, we cannot know. These lie not open to our observation.'[1] In his treatment of the hedonistic calculus, Bentham admittedly showed greater originality. But it was not to the quality of his thought that he owed his influence in the new age. He applied the principle of utility to the spheres of economics, jurisprudence and politics, and he did so with great thoroughness and consistency. Moreover, he gathered about him a band of followers who erected his principle into the doctrines of a school and who made certain that Bentham's name would permanently be associated with Utilitarianism.

William Paley's *Moral and Political Philosophy* appeared in 1785 —five years after Bentham printed *The Principles of Morals and Legislation*, four years before he published it. Thus neither man influenced the other; yet both, though in different ways, re-capitulated previous thought and transmitted it to the future. Paley is representative of much besides a certain type of Utilitarianism. With unusual accuracy he represented an outlook which had considerable influence in the opening years of the new century. He was a leading exponent of the liberalism represented by a distinguished group of Cambridge divines. Edmund Law had advanced with sober learning a position which relied on Locke and proposed to work out the implications of his thought. Paley, a protégé of Law, was the most influential religious writer of the closing years of the eighteenth century. His mind was as devoid of originality as his soul was of poetry, but he had unrivalled facility in ordering and expounding the thoughts of others. With rare vigour and clarity he reduced to systematic form the views which had emerged from the debates of the eighteenth century. The general position of this school is represented even more exactly by John Hey and Richard Watson. Hey's lectures were famous, and bishops required ordinands at Cambridge to attend them.[2] In their published form they impressed Beilby Porteus as

281

'one of the ablest and most compendious systems of divinity of which [the world] is at present in possession'.[1] Watson's lectures have gained a modest celebrity for rather different reasons. In his autobiography he described with engaging naïveté the way in which a man with few obvious qualifications equipped himself for the duties of the Regius Professorship of Divinity. He also indicated the aims he set before himself and the kind of instruction he offered.[2] Both Hey and Watson reflect the prevailing disposition to minimise doctrinal differences. 'Articles of the Church', said Watson, 'are not of divine authority; have done with them.'[3] Hey advocated dropping controversial words and phrases from the theological vocabulary. 'Though Christ seems to us to be *called* God in several places, yet there is some *dispute* on that head; and, for the sake of *Unity*, we would pay all possible *respect* to the opinions of our adversaries. I should imagine that such an omission would tend, almost as much as anything, to mollify and conciliate.'[4] Watson described this approach to theological problems as 'honest' and 'liberal'. It caused some uneasiness among the bishops and aroused a good deal of opposition among some of the clergy. But it awakened a ready response in lay circles. In the brief interval before the reaction inspired by the French Revolution discredited every form of liberalism, Hey and Watson represented an outlook which commanded considerable respect.

The tide of the future, however, was moving in a different direction. The turn of the century roughly coincided with the beginning of a far-reaching change. In the new day credal and confessional theology would enjoy such a renaissance as the men of the eighteenth century could never have foreseen. In another and different respect, the nineteenth century saw a complementary change. Law and Paley and Watson knew the precise meaning of the terms they used. They had little patience with theological niceties, but they stood in a tradition which understood exactly what it meant by the technical language it chose to employ. The days of theological relativity still lay ahead, but the eighteenth century helped to prepare the reaction which destroyed the precision which it had maintained.

The French Revolution swept away many of the assumptions which had served the Age of Reason, but it did not overthrow one of the favourite convictions of the recent past: the belief in progress. The method and the means of human advance might be altered, but the perfectibility of man could not be challenged. This anticipation of unlimited progress ahead was distinctively an eighteenth-century development. Hitherto men had located the golden age in some distant past. But Bacon, Boyle, Locke and Newton had eclipsed anything that the ancients had achieved. Edward Gibbon confidently assumed that progress was continuous and automatic. 'We may therefore acquiesce', he wrote, 'in the pleasing conclusion that every age of the world has increased, and still increases, the real wealth, the happiness, the knowledge, and perhaps the virtue, of the human race.'[1] This was an assurance in which Gibbon was doubtless confirmed by the French *philosophes*, and their secular faith was specially congenial to him. But this belief appeared in a religious form as well; progress was accepted as a confirmation of providence and as an incitement to religious advance. 'We live in an enlightened age', said Lowth, 'in which knowledge is still increasing . . . may we not hope that these improvements will have their proper effects though we do not yet perceive it, in introducing a reformation of another nature. . . ?'[2] The optimism of the Victorian Age was the culmination of the eighteenth-century belief in progress.

'A reformation of another nature' was already at the door. Changes which the Age of Reason could not have anticipated and would not have approved affected every area of life. Yet the legacy of the eighteenth century has proved singularly resilient. In subtle and often imperceptible ways it has shaped the thought of subsequent generations. Even those who reacted against its outlook unconsciously applied its standards. William Wordsworth was a persuasive interpreter of the spirit of the new day, yet in explaining his aim and purpose to a friend he used words which the Age of Reason would willingly have applied to its own endeavour: his poems, he said, 'will co-operate with the benign tendencies in human nature and society, and will, in their degree, be efficacious in making men wiser, better, and happier'.

BIBLIOGRAPHY

This is not a complete bibliography of the subject; it is merely a list of the works to which direct reference is made in the course of this book. Unless otherwise stated, the place of publication is London.

I. PRIMARY WORKS

Aikin, John. *Letters of a Father to his Son.* 2 vols. 1796.
Annet, Peter. *The Resurrection of Jesus Examined by a Moral Philosopher* (3rd edition). 1744.
—— *The History of St Paul Examined.* 1747.
—— *The History of the Man after God's Own Heart.* 1761.
—— *A Collection of the Tracts of a Certain Free Enquirer.* V.d.
(Atterbury.) *A Letter to a Convocation Man.* 1697.
Atterbury, Francis. *The Rights, Powers and Privileges of an English Convocation.* 1700.
—— *The Power of the Lower House of Convocation to Adjourn Itself.* 1701.
—— *The Mitre and the Crown.* 1711.
—— *Sermons and Discourses on Several Subjects and Occasions.* 4 vols. 1735.

Balguy, John. *A Collection of Tracts,* 1734.
Bentham, J. *The Works of Jeremy Bentham.* 11 vols. Edinburgh, 1843.
Bentley, Richard. *The Folly and Unreasonableness of Atheism* (4th edition). 1699.
—— *Remarks upon a Late Discourse of Free Thinking.* 1713.
Berkeley, George. *The Works of George Berkeley.* Edited by A. A. Luce and T. E. Jessop. 9 vols. 1948–57.
Berriman, William. *The Gradual Revelation of the Gospel.* 2 vols. 1733.
Blackburne, Francis. *The Confessional.* 1766.
Blount, Charles. *Anima Mundi.* 1679.
—— *Philostratus.* 1680.
—— *Miracles No Violations of the Laws of Nature.* 1683.
—— *Religio Laici.* 1683.
—— *A Just Vindication of Learning and the Liberty of the Press.* 1695.
—— *Great is Diana of the Ephesians.* 1695.
Bolingbroke. *The Works of Henry St John, Viscount Bolingbroke.* 5 vols. 1754.
(Boyle Lectures.) *A Defence of Natural and Revealed Religion.* 3 vols. 1739.
Bradford, Samuel. *The Credibility of the Christian Revelation.* 1700.
Brine, J. *Animadversions upon the Letters of Theron and Aspasio.* 1758.

Brooke, Z. *An Examination of Dr Middleton's Free Inquiry into the Miraculous Powers.* . . . Cambridge, 1753.

Brown, John. *Essays on the Characteristics.* 1751.

Browne, Simon. *A Defence of the Religion of Nature and the Christian Revelation.* 1732.

Burke, E. *The Works of the Rt. Hon. Edmund Burke.* 3 vols. 1792; also 12 vols. 1887.

Burnet, Gilbert. *Reflections on a Book entitled the Rights, Powers and Privileges of an English Convocation.* 1700.

Burnet, Gilbert, jun. (ed.). *A Defence of Natural and Revealed Religion* (Boyle Lectures abridged) (3rd edition). 4 vols. 1765.

Burnet, Thomas. *The Demonstration of the True Religion* (in Boyle Lectures, vol. III).

Butler, J. *The Works of Joseph Butler.* Edited by W. E. Gladstone. 2 vols. Oxford, 1896.

Butler, Lilly. *A Discourse Proving that the Faith and Practice of True Christians are no just matter of Shame or Reproach.* 1711.

Campbell, George. *A Dissertation on Miracles.* 1763.

Chandler, Edward. *A Defence of Christianity from the Prophecies of the Old Testament.* 1725.

—— *A Vindication of the Defence of Christianity.* 1728.

Chandler, S. *A Vindication of the Christian Religion.* 1725.

—— *A Second Letter to the Rev. Mr John Guyse.* 1730.

—— *The Case of Subscription.* 1748.

—— *The History of Persecution (1736).* Hull, 1813.

Chapman, John (Philobiblicus Cantabrigiensis). *Remarks on a Letter to Dr Waterland.* Cambridge, 1731.

—— *Eusebius, or the true Christian Defence.* Cambridge, 1739.

Christianity No Creature of the State. 1717.

Chubb, Thomas. *A Collection of Tracts.* 1730.

—— *The Posthumous Works of Thomas Chubb.* 2 vols. 1748.

Clarke, J. *An Enquiry into the Cause and Origin of Evil.* 1720.

Clarke, S. *A Demonstration of the Being and Attributes of God* (2nd edition). 1706.

—— *A Discourse Concerning the Unchangeable Obligations of Natural Religion and the Truth and Certainty of the Christian Revelation.* 1706.

—— *The Scripture Doctrine of the Trinity* (2nd edition). 1712.

—— *One Hundred and Seventy-Three Sermons on Several Subjects* (8th edition). 5 vols. Dublin, 1717.

—— *Evidences of Natural and Revealed Religion* (in R. Watson, *A Collection of Theological Tracts.* 6 vols.). 1785.

Collins, A. *An Essay Concerning the Use of Reason in Propositions.* 1707.

—— *Priestcraft in Perfection.* 1710.

Bibliography

Collins, A. *A Discourse of Free-Thinking*. 1713.
—— *A Discourse of the Grounds and Reasons of the Christian Religion*. 1724.
—— *The Scheme of Literal Prophecy Considered*. 1726.
Conybeare, John. *A Defence of Revealed Religion*. 1732.
Cowper, W. *The Poetical Works of William Cowper*. Oxford, 1911.

Denne, J. *Want of Universality No Just Objection to the Truth of the Christian Religion*. 1730.
Derham, W. *Physio-Theology, or a Demonstration of the Being and Attributes of God from his Works of Creation* (5th edition). 1720.
Disney, J. *Memoirs of the Life and Writings of Arthur Ashley Sykes*. 1785.
Doddridge, Philip. *A Course of Lectures* (2nd edition). 1776.
—— *Correspondence and Diary*. 5 vols. 1829–31.
—— *Letters to and from the Rev. Philip Doddridge*. Shrewsbury, 1790.

Evans, J. *An Attempt to Account for the Infidelity of the late Edward Gibbon*. 1797.

Foster, James. *The Usefulness, Truth, and Excellency of the Christian Religion*. 1731.
—— *Sermons*, vol. III. 1744.
—— *Discourses on all the Principal Branches of Natural Religion and Social Virtue*. 2 vols. 1749.
Foster, Michael. *An Examination of the Scheme of Church-Power laid down by the Codex Juris Ecclesiastici Anglicani*. 1735.
Furneaux, Philip. *Letters to the Hon. Mr Justice Blackstone* (2nd edition). 1771.

Gastrell, Francis. *The Certainty and Necessity of Religion in General*. 1703.
—— *Some Considerations Concerning the Trinity* (3rd edition). 1707.
—— *A Defence of some Considerations concerning the Trinity*. 1709.
(Gay, J.) *Preliminary Dissertation: Concerning the Fundamental Principle of Virtue or Morality* (prefaced to E. Law's translation of King, *The Origin of Evil*, 1731).
Gibbon, Edward. *A Vindication of some Passages in the Fifteenth and Sixteenth Chapters of the History*. 1779.
—— *The Autobiographies of Edward Gibbon*. Edited by J. Murray. 1896.
—— *The History of the Decline and Fall of the Roman Empire*. Edited by J. B. Bury. 7 vols. 1900.
—— *The Letters of Edward Gibbon*. Edited by J. E. Norton. 3 vols. 1956.
Gibson, Edmund. *The Right of the Archbishop to continue or prorogue the whole Convocation*. 1701.
—— *The Schedule Reviewed*. 1702.
—— *Codex Juris Ecclesiastici Anglicani*. 1713.
—— *The Bishop of London's Three Pastoral Letters*. 1732.

Gibson, Edmund. *The Dispute Adjusted about the Proper Time of Applying for a Repeal of the Corporation and Test Acts.* Dublin, 1733.

Gildon, C. *Miscellaneous Works.* 1695.

Godwin, William. *Enquiry Concerning Political Justice* (3rd edition). 2 vols. 1798.

—— *Thoughts Occasioned by the Perusal of Dr Parr's Sermon.* 1801.

Gurdon, Brampton. *The Pretended Difficulties in Natural or Revealed Religion No Excuse for Infidelity.* (In Boyle Lectures, vol. III.) 1739.

Hall, R. *The Works of Robert Hall* (7th edition). 5 vols. 1841.

Halyburton, Thomas. *Natural Religion Insufficient and Revealed Necessary to Man's Happiness in His Present State.* Edinburgh, 1714.

—— *An Essay Concerning the Reason of Faith.* Edinburgh, 1714.

Hancock, John. *Arguments to Prove the Being of God.* 1707.

Hare, Francis. *The Works of the Rt. Rev. Francis Hare* (2nd edition). 4 vols. 1775.

Harris, John. *Refutation of the Atheistical Objections Against the Being and Attributes of a God.* 1698.

Hartley, David. *Observations on Man* (4th edition). 3 vols. 1801.

Herring, T. *Letters of Archbishop Herring to William Duncombe, Esq.* 1777.

Hervey, James. *Theron and Aspasio.* 3 vols. 1755.

—— *Meditation and Contemplations.* 1862.

Hey, J. *Lectures in Divinity.* 4 vols. Cambridge, 1796.

Hickes, George. *The Constitution of the Catholic Church.* 1716.

Hill, Rowland. *Apology for Sunday Schools.* 1801.

Hoadly, B. *A Preservative against the Principles and Practices of the Non-Jurors* (2nd edition). 1716.

—— *The Nature of the Kingdom, or Church, of Christ.* 1717.

—— *An Answer to a Calumny Cast upon the Bishop of Bangor.* 1718.

—— *An Answer to a late Book, Written by the Rev. Dr Sherlock.* 1718.

—— *The Common Rights of Subjects Defended.* 1719.

—— *The Works of the Rt. Rev. Benjamin Hoadly.* Edited by J. Hoadly. 3 vols. 1773.

Hobbes, T. *The English Works of Thomas Hobbes.* Edited by Sir William Molesworth. 11 vols. 1839–45.

—— *Leviathan* (Everyman edition).

Horsley, S. *Tracts in Controversy with Dr Priestley.* 1789.

—— *A Review of the Case of the Protestant Dissenters.* 1790.

Hume, David. *The History of England.* 8 vols. Oxford, 1826.

—— *A Treatise of Human Nature.* Edited by L. A. Selby-Bigge. Oxford, 1888.

—— *Essays, Moral, Political and Literary.* Edited by T. H. Green and T. H. Grose. 2 vols. 1898.

Bibliography

Hume, David. *Enquiries Concerning the Human Understanding and Concerning the Principles of Morals.* Edited by L. A. Selby-Bigge. (2nd edition.) Oxford, 1902.

—— *The Letters of David Hume.* Edited by J. Y. T. Grieg. 2 vols. Oxford, 1932.

—— *Dialogues Concerning Natural Religion.* Edited by N. Kemp Smith. Oxford, 1935.

Hurd, R. *Sermons Preached at Lincoln's Inn* (3rd edition). 4 vols. 1785.

—— *The Correspondence of Richard Hurd and William Mason.* Cambridge, 1932.

Hutcheson, Francis. *A System of Moral Philosophy.* 2 vols. 1755.

—— *An Essay on the Nature and Conduct of the Passions and Affections, with Illustrations upon the Moral Sense* (3rd edition). Glasgow, 1769.

—— *Inquiry Concerning Beauty, Order, Harmony, Design* and *Inquiry Concerning Moral Good and Evil* (3rd edition). 1729.

Ibbot, Benjamin. *The True Notion of the Exercise of Private Judgment.* 2 vols. 1727.

Jackson, John. *Three Letters to Dr Clarke.* 1714.

—— *The Grounds of Civil and Ecclesiastical Government.* 1718.

—— *A Plea for Humane Reason.* 1730.

—— *The Existence and Unity of God Proved from his Nature and Attributes.* 1734.

—— *A Confutation of the Fifth of Mr Moore's Propositions of Natural and Revealed Religion.* 1738.

—— *An Address to the Deists, being a Proof of Revealed Religion from Miracles and Prophecies.* 1744.

—— *Remarks on Dr Middleton's Free Inquiry.* 1749.

Jenkin, R. *A Brief Confutation of the Pretences against Natural and Revealed Religion.* 1702.

—— *The Reasonableness and Certainty of the Christian Religion* (5th edition). 2 vols. 1721.

Jennings, Joseph. *Memoirs of Dr Lardner.* 1769.

Jenyns, S. *The Works of Soame Jenyns.* 4 vols. 1790.

Kennett, White. *Ecclesiastical Synods and Parliamentary Convocations in the Church of England.* 1701.

—— *An Occasional Letter on the Subject of English Convocations.* 1701.

—— *A Second Letter to the Lord Bishop of Carlisle.* 1716.

Kilvert, F. *Memoirs of the Life and Writings of the Rt. Rev. Richard Hurd.* 1860.

Lardner, N. *The Credibility of the Gospel History* (in *Works*, 10 vols.). 1829.

Lardner, *Memoirs of. See* Jennings, Joseph.

Law, Edmund. *Considerations on the Theory of Religion* (new edition). 1820.

Law, W. *The Case of Reason.* 1731.
—— *Three Letters to the Bishop of Bangor.* Edited by J. O. Nash and C. Gore. Edinburgh, 1909.
—— *A Serious Call to a Devout and Holy Life.* 1728.
—— *Remarks upon . . . the Fable of the Bees.* 1723.
Leland, J. *A View of the Principal Deistical Writers* (5th edition). 2 vols. 1798.
—— *The Divine Authority of the Old and New Testaments Asserted.* 1837.
Leng, John. *Natural Obligations to Believe the Principles of Religion and Divine Revelation* (2nd edition). 1730.
Leslie, C. *The New Association of those called Moderate Churchmen with the Modern-Whigs and Fanaticks.* 1702.
—— *The Case of the Regale and the Pontificat Stated.* 1710.
—— *A Letter to the Rev. Mr Law.* 1719.
The Lives of Dr Edward Pocock, by Dr Twell; of Dr Zachary Pearce and of Dr Thomas Newton, by themselves; and of the Rev. Philip Skelton by Mr Burdy. 2 vols. 1816.
Locke, John. *The Reasonableness of Christianity.* 1695.
—— *The Works of John Locke.* 10 vols. 1823.
Lofft, Capel. *An History of the Corporation and Test Acts.* Bury, 1790.
Lowman, Moses. *The Argument from Prophecy Vindicated.* 1733.
Lowth, Robert. *A Letter to the Right Reverend Author of the Divine Legation* (2nd edition). 1766.
—— *Sermons and other Remains.* Edited by Peter Hall. 1834.

Mackintosh, J. *Vindiciae Gallicae.* 1791.
Mandeville, B. *The Fable of the Bees* (1714). Edited by F. B. Kaye. 2 vols. Oxford, 1924.
—— *Letter to Dion.* 1732.
Middleton, Conyers. *Letter from Rome.* 1729.
—— *A Letter to Dr Waterland.* 1731.
—— *A Defence of a Letter to Dr Waterland.* 1732.
—— *Some Remarks on a Reply to the Defence of the Letter to Dr Waterland.* 1732.
—— *A Free Inquiry into the Miraculous Powers which are Supposed to have subsisted in the Christian Church.* 1749.
More, Hannah. *Thoughts on the Importance of the Manners of the Great to General Society.* 1788.
—— *An Estimate of the Religion of the Fashionable World.* 1790.
Morgan, Thomas. *The Moral Philosopher.* 1737; 1739; 1740.
—— *Physico-Theology.* 1741.

Newton, Isaac. *Opticks* (4th edition). 1730.
—— *Theological Manuscripts.* Edited by H. McLachlan. Liverpool, 1950.
Newton, Thomas, *The Life of,* by himself. (See under *Lives of Dr Edward Pocock,* etc.) 1816.

Bibliography

Paine, Thomas. *The Rights of Man* (3rd edition). 1791.
—— *The Age of Reason.* 1794.
Paley, W. *The Works of William Paley.* 6 vols. Cambridge, Mass., 1830.
Parker, William. *The Expedience of some Divine Interpositions.* Oxford, 1749.
—— *The Supposal of the Continuance of Divine Interpositions.* Oxford, 1749.
—— *The Miracles of Jesus Vindicated.* 1729.
Pearce, Zachary. *A Reply to the Letter to Dr Waterland* (2nd edition). 1732.
—— *A Reply to the Defence of the Letter to Dr Waterland.* 1732.
—— *The Life of,* by himself. (See under *Lives of Dr Edward Pocock,* etc.) 1816.
Phileleutherus Cantabrigiensis. *An Essay on Imposing and Subscribing Articles of Religion.* 1719.
Pope, A. *The Works of Alexander Pope.* Edited by William Roscoe. 8 vols. 1847.
Porson, R. *Letters to Mr Archdeacon Travis.* 1790.
Porteus, B. *The Works of the Right Reverend Beilby Porteus.* 6 vols. 1823.
Potter, John. *A Discourse of Church Government.* 1707.
Price, R. *Observations on the Nature of Civil Liberty, the Principles of Government, and the Justice and Policy of the War with America.* 1776.
—— *Additional Observations on the importance of the American Revolution.* 1784.
—— *A Review of the Principal Questions in Morals* (3rd edition). 1787.
—— *Discourse on the Love of our Country.* 1790.
Priestley, J. *View of the Principles and Conduct of Protestant Dissenters.* 1767.
—— *Essays on the Principles of Civil Government.* 1771.
—— *Hartley's Theory of the Human Mind on the Principles of the Association of Ideas.* Birmingham, 1775.
—— *The Doctrine of Philosophical Necessity Illustrated.* Birmingham, 1777.
—— *A Free Discussion of the Doctrines of Materialism and Philosophical Necessity.* 1778.
—— *Letters to a Philosophical Unbeliever.* 2 vols. 1780; 1787.
—— *Disquisitions relating to Matter and Spirit* (2nd edition). 2 vols. Birmingham, 1782.
—— *The Importance and the Extent of Free Inquiry in Matters of Religion.* Birmingham, 1785.
—— *A History of Early Opinions concerning Jesus Christ.* Birmingham, 1786.
—— *A Letter to the Rt. Hon. William Pitt . . . on Toleration and Church Establishment.* Birmingham, 1787.
—— *A Sermon on the Subject on the Slave Trade.* Birmingham, 1788.
—— *Familiar Letters Addressed to the Inhabitants of Birmingham.* Birmingham, 1790.
—— *The Evidence of the Resurrection of Jesus Considered.* Birmingham, 1791.
—— *Letters to the Rt. Hon. Edmund Burke.* Birmingham, 1791.
—— *An Appeal to the Candid and Earnest Professors of Christianity* (1771). American edition. Philadelphia, 1794.

Reason and Authority

Priestley, J. *A History of the Corruptions of Christianity* (3rd edition). 2 vols. Boston, 1797.
—— *Memoirs of the Rev. Dr Joseph Priestley*, written by himself. 1809.
—— *The Theological and Miscellaneous Works of Joseph Priestley*. Edited by J. T. Rutt. 25 vols. 1821.
Pyle, E. *Memoirs of a Royal Chaplain, 1729–63.* 1905.

Reflections on the Letter to Dr Waterland and the Defence of it. 1732.
Reid, Thomas. *An Inquiry into the Human Mind on the Principles of Common Sense.* 1819.
Robinson, John. *A Letter to the Incumbents of all Churches and Chapels.* 1718.
Robinson, Robert. *Arcana; or Principles of the late Petitions to Parliament for Relief.* 1773.
—— *A Plan of Lectures on the Principles of Nonconformity* (6th edition). Nottingham, 1797.
—— *Reflections on Christian Liberty.* (Cf. Jared Sparks, vol. III.)
Rogers, John. *A Discourse of the Visible and Invisible Church of Christ.* 1719.
—— *A Vindication of the Civil Establishment and of Religion.* 1728.
—— *A Persuasive to Conformity Addressed to the Dissenters.* 1736.

The Scandal and Folly of the Cross Removed. 1699.
Scott, Thomas. *Theological Works* (1st American edition). 8 vols. Philadelphia, 1810.
Secker, T. *An Answer to Dr Mayhew's Observations.* 1764.
—— *The Works of Thomas Secker.* Edited by Beilby Porteus. 6 vols. 1811.
Shaftesbury, Anthony, Earl of. *Characteristicks.* 3 vols. 1733.
Sharp, John. *Fifteen Sermons Preached on Several Occasions.* 1700.
Sherlock, Thomas. *The Use and Intent of Prophecy.* 1725.
—— *The Tryal of the Witnesses of the Resurrection.* 1729.
—— *Several Discourses Preached at the Temple Church.* 4 vols. 1764.
—— *Discourses Preached on Several Occasions.* 5 vols. Oxford, 1797.
—— *The Works of Bishop Sherlock.* Edited by T. S. Hughes. 5 vols. 1830.
Smalbrook, R. *A Vindication of Our Saviour's Miracles.* 2 vols. 1729.
Sparks, Jared. *A Collection of Essays and Tracts.* 6 vols. 1824.
Stackhouse, Thomas. *A Fair State of the Controversy between Mr Woolston and his Adversaries.* 1730.
Stanhope, George. *The Christian Religion No just Offence to the Jews.* 1702.
Stephens, William. *An Account of the Growth of Deism in England.* 1696.
Sykes, A. A. *The External Peace of the Church.* 1716.
—— *An Answer to the Non-Jurors' Charge of Schism upon the Church of England.* 1716.
—— *A Letter to the Reverend Dr Sherlock.* 1717.
—— *A Second Letter to the Reverend Dr Sherlock.* 1717.

Bibliography

Sykes, A. A. *The Authority of the Clergy and the Liberties of the Laity Stated and Vindicated.* 1720.

—— *The Case of Subscription.* 1721.

—— *The Consequences of the Present Conspiracy to the Church and State Considered.* 1722.

—— *An Essay Upon the Truth of the Christian Religion.* 1725.

—— *The True Foundations of Natural and Revealed Religion Asserted.* 1730.

—— *The Reasonableness of Applying for the Repeal or Explanation of the Corporation and Test Acts Impartially Considered.* 1736.

—— *The Corporation and Test Acts Shewn to be of No Importance to the Church of England.* 1736.

—— *The Principles and Connexion of Natural and Revealed Religion.* 1740.

—— *A Brief Discussion touching the Credibility of Miracles and Revelation.* 1742.

Swift, J. *The Works of Jonathan Swift.* Edited by Walter Scott. 19 vols. Edinburgh, 1814.

Thomson, J. *The Complete Poetical Works of James Thomson.* Edited by J. Logie Robertson. Oxford, 1908.

Tillotson, J. *The Works of the Most Reverend Dr John Tillotson.* 3 vols. (vol. I, 10th edition; vols. II and III, 5th edition). 1735.

Tindal, M. *Essay of Obedience to the Supreme Power.* 1694.

—— *Essay on the Power of the Magistrate and the Rights of Mankind in Matters of Religion.* 1697.

—— *New High Church Turned Old Presbyterian.* 1706.

—— *The Rights of the Christian Church Asserted* (3rd edition). 1707.

—— *A Defence of the Rights of the Christian Church.* 1709.

—— *An Address to the Inhabitants . . . of London and Westminster* (2nd edition). 1730.

—— *A Second Address to the Inhabitants . . . of London and Westminster* (2nd edition). 1730.

—— *Christianity as Old as the Creation.* 1730.

Toland, John. *Christianity Not Mysterious.* 1696.

—— *Amyntor.* 1699.

—— *Nazarenus.* 1718.

Toplady, A. M. *The Works of the Rev. A. M. Toplady.* 6 vols. 1828.

Towgood, Michaijah. *Serious and Free Thoughts on the Present State of the Church and of Religion.* 1755.

—— *A Dissent from the Church of England fully Justified, Being the Dissenting Gentleman's Letters . . . in answer to the Letters of the Rev. Mr White* (11th edition). Harlow, 1809.

Tucker, Abraham. *The Light of Nature Pursued.* 7 vols. 1768.

Turner, John. *The Wisdom of God in the Redemption of Man.* 1709.

Venn, Henry. *The Complete Duty of Man* (7th edition). Bath, 1803.
Voltaire. *Œuvres Complètes de Voltaire*. 75 tomes. Paris, 1825–8.

Wake, William. *The Authority of Christian Princes over their Ecclesiastical Synods Asserted*. 1697.
—— *The State of the Church and Clergy of England*. 1703.
—— *The Danger and Mischief of a Misguided Zeal*. 1710.
Wakefield, Gilbert. *Memoirs*, vol. i. 1792.
Walpole. *The Letters of Horace Walpole*. Edited by Mrs Paget Toynbee. 16 vols. Oxford, 1903–5.
Warburton, W. *The Alliance between Church and State* (3rd edition). 1748.
—— *The Divine Legation of Moses*. 1738, etc.
—— *A Vindication of Mr Pope's Essay on Man*. 1739.
—— *The Works of William Warburton*. 7 vols. 1788.
—— *Letters from a Late Eminent Prelate*. New York, 1809.
Waterland, D. *Scripture Vindicated* (3rd edition). 1734.
—— *The Case of Arian Subscription*.
—— *The Importance of the Doctrine of the Holy Trinity Asserted*. 1734.
Watson, Richard. *Miscellaneous Tracts*. 2 vols. 1815.
—— *Anecdotes of the Life of Richard Watson, Bishop of Llandaff, written by himself*. 1819.
—— *An Apology for Christianity* (9th edition). 1820.
—— *An Apology for the Bible* (12th edition). 1820.
—— *A Defence of Revealed Religion* (6th edition). 1820.
Watts. *The Works of the Rev. Isaac Watts*. 9 vols. Leeds and London, 1813.
Wesley, J. *A Christian Library*. 30 vols. 1750.
—— *Explanatory Notes upon the New Testament*. 1818.
—— *The Works of the Rev. John Wesley*. 14 vols. 1872.
—— *The Journal of John Wesley*. Standard Edition. Edited by N. Curnock. 8 vols. 1906–16.
—— *The Standard Sermons*. Edited by E. H. Sugden. 2 vols. 1921.
—— *The Letters of John Wesley*. Standard Edition. Edited by J. Telford. 8 vols. 1931.
Whiston, W. *The Accomplishment of Scripture Prophecies*. 1708.
—— *Primitive Christianity Revived*. 4 vols. 1711.
—— *An Account of the Convocation Proceedings*. 1711.
—— *Reflections on an Anonymous Pamphlet, Entitled a Discourse of Free Thinking* (2nd edition). 1713.
—— *Astronomical Principles of Religion, Natural and Revealed*. 1725.
—— *Memoirs of the Life and Writings of Mr William Whiston, by himself*. 3 vols. 1749.
White, John. *Three Letters to a Gentleman Dissenting from the Church of England*.
Whitefield, George. *Of Justification by Christ*. 1738.

Bibliography

Whitefield, George. *The Works of the Rev. George Whitefield*. 7 vols. 1771–2.
—— *A Letter to the Rev. Mr John Wesley*. 1791.
—— *Select Sermons*. 1959.
Wilberforce, William. *A Practical View of the Prevailing Religious System of Professed Christians* (1st American edition). Philadelphia, 1798.
Wilkins, J. *Of the Principles and Duties of Natural Religion* (6th edition). 1710.
Williams, John. *On Revelation* (in Boyle Lectures, vol. I). 1739.
Wollaston, W. *The Religion of Nature Delineated* (1725). 1726.
Woodward, J. *The Divine Original and Incomparable Excellence of the Christian Religion* (in Boyle Lectures, vol. II). 1739.
Woolston, T. *Free Gifts to the Clergy*. 1722.
—— *Six Discourses on the Miracles of Our Saviour*. 1727–9.
—— *A Defence of the Discourses on Miracles, etc.* 1729, 1730.
Wordsworth, W. *The Complete Poetical Works of William Wordsworth*. 1893.

II. SECONDARY WORKS

Aaron, R. I. *John Locke*. 1937.

Bagehot, Walter. *Works*. Edited by Mrs Barrington. 9 vols. 1915.
Basson, A. H. *David Hume*. 1958.
Becker, C. L. *The Heavenly City of the Eighteenth Century Philosophers*. New Haven, 1932.
Beeching, H. C. *Francis Atterbury*. 1909.
Bennett, G. V. *White Kennett, 1660–1728*. 1957.
Black, J. B. *The Art of History*. 1926.
Brett, G. S. *A History of Psychology*, vol. II. 1921.
Broad, C. D. *Fives Types of Ethical Theory*. 1930.
Brown, Ford K. *The Life of William Godwin*. 1926.

Cambridge History of English Literature (new edition). Cambridge, 1932.
Carpenter, E. F. *Thomas Sherlock, 1678–1761*. 1936.
Colligan, J. H. *The Arian Movement in England*. Manchester, 1913.
Copleston, F. *A History of Philosophy*, vol. V. 1959.
Coupland, R. *Wilberforce*. Oxford, 1923.
Crane, R. S. *Anglican Apologetics and the Idea of Progress, 1699–1745* (*Modern Philology*, vol. XXXI). Chicago, 1934.
Creed, J. M. and Boys Smith, J. S. *Religious Thought in the Eighteenth Century*. Cambridge, 1934.

Dawson, C. *Edward Gibbon*. 1934.
Dicey, A. V. *Lectures on the Relation between Law and Public Opinion in England during the Nineteenth Century*. 1905.

Reason and Authority

Evans, A. W. *Warburton and the Warburtonians.* Oxford, 1932.

Fleisher, D. *William Godwin: A Study in Liberalism.* 1951.
Flew, R. N. *The Idea of Perfection in Christian Theology.* 1934.
Frost, S. B. *Die Autoritätslehre in den Werken John Wesleys.* Munich, 1938.

Griffiths, O. M. *Religion and Learning.* Cambridge, 1935.

Hawkins, L. M. *Allegiance in Church and State.* 1928.
Hazard, P. *The European Mind.* (Eng. trans.) 1953.
—— *European Thought in the Eighteenth Century.* (Eng. trans.) 1954.
Hazlitt, W. *The Spirit of the Age.* 2 vols. Paris, 1825.
Hefelbower, S. G. *The Relation of John Locke to English Deism.* Chicago, 1918.
Hendel, C. W. *Studies in the Philosophy of David Hume.* Princeton, 1925.
Hone, J. M. and Rossi, M. M. *Bishop Berkeley, His Life, Writings and Philosophy.* 1931.

Jones, M. G. *The Charity School Movement.* Cambridge, 1938.

Laing, B. M. *David Hume.* 1932.
Laird, J. *Philosophical Incursions into English Literature.* Cambridge, 1946.
Lincoln, Anthony. *Some Political and Social Ideas of English Dissent, 1763–1800.* Cambridge, 1938.
Lindström, H. *Wesley and Sanctification.* Stockholm, 1946.
Low, D. M. *Edward Gibbon, 1737–1794.* 1937.

Manning, B. L. *The Protestant Dissenting Deputies.* Cambridge, 1952.
Mossner, E. C. *Bishop Butler and the Age of Reason.* New York, 1936.
Munroe, D. H. *Godwin's Moral Philosophy.* 1953.

Parkin, C. W. *The Moral Basis of Burke's Political Thought.* Cambridge, 1956.
Pattison, Mark. *Essays.* 2 vols. Oxford, 1889.

Raphael, D. D. *The Moral Sense.* 1947.
Rodgers, B. *The Cloak of Charity.* 1949.
Rodway, A. F. *Godwin and the Age of Transition.* 1952.

Sainte-Beuve, C. A. *Causeries du lundi.* t. viii, 2me éd. Paris, 1855.
Schenk, H. G. *The Aftermath of the Napoleonic Wars.* 1947.
Stephen, L. *History of English Thought in the Eighteenth Century* (3rd edition). 2 vols. New York, 1902.
Stromberg, R. L. *Religious Liberalism in Eighteenth Century England.* Oxford, 1954.

Bibliography

Sykes, N. *Edmund Gibson.* Oxford, 1926.
—— *Church and State in England in the Eighteenth Century.* Cambridge, 1934.
—— *William Wake.* 2 vols. Cambridge, 1957.
—— *From Sheldon to Secker.* Cambridge, 1959.

Talon, H. *William Law.* 1948.
Taylor, A. E. *David Hume and the Miraculous.* Cambridge, 1927.
Thomas, R. *Richard Price.* 1924.
Tinker, C. B. *Nature's Simple Plan.* Princeton, 1922.
Torrey, N. L. *Voltaire and the English Deists.* New Haven, 1930.
Trevelyan, G. M. *English Social History* (illustrated edition). 4 vols. 1949–52.
Trevelyan, G. O. *The Early History of Charles James Fox* (edition of 1928).
Troeltsch, E. *Gesammelte Werke.* 4 vols. Tübingen, 1912–25.

Vaughan, C. E. *Studies in the History of Political Philosophy.* 2 vols. Manchester, 1925.
Vidler, A. C. *The Orb and the Cross.* 1945.

Wedgwood, C. V. *Gibbon.* 1955.
Westfall, R. S. *Science and Religion in the Seventeenth Century.* New Haven, 1955.
Willey, B. *The Eighteenth Century Background.* 1940.
—— *Christianity Past and Present.* Cambridge, 1952.
—— *The Religion of Nature.* 1957.
Williams, C. W. *John Wesley's Theology Today.* New York, 1960.

Yolton, J. W. *John Locke and the Way of Ideas.* Oxford, 1956.
Young, G. M. *Gibbon.* 1933.
—— *Burke.* 1943.

NOTES

PAGE 1

1 Hume, *A Treatise of Human Nature*, p. xxi.

PAGE 3

1 Locke, *Essay Concerning Human Understanding*, Book I, chapter 4, section 23.
2 *Ibid.* I, 4, 24.

PAGE 4

1 R. Lowth, *Sermons and Other Remains*, pp. 82–3.

PAGE 6

1 *Letters from a Late Eminent Prelate*, p. 207; Voltaire, *Œuvres Complètes*, vol. LXX, p. 250.
2 Cf. Mark Pattison, *Essays*, vol. II, pp. 142–3.
3 Bolingbroke, *Works*, vol. III, p. 329.
4 Locke, *Essay*, Epistle to the Reader.

PAGE 7

1 *Ibid.* I, 1, 4.   2 *Ibid.* I, 1, 5.

PAGE 8

1 *Ibid.* IV, 19, 14.   2 *Ibid.* IV, 17, 2.

PAGE 9

1 Newton, *Opticks*, p. 381.

PAGE 10

1 Locke, *Essay*, Bk. IV, ch. 19, sect. 3.
2 S. Clarke, *A Discourse Concerning the Unchangeable Obligations of Natural Religion and the Truth and Certainty of the Christian Revelation*, p. 348.

PAGE 11

1 Hartley, *Observations on Man*, vol. I, pp. 490–1.
2 Hume, *Dialogues Concerning Natural Religion*, p. 171.
3 Locke, *Essay*, Bk. IV, chap. 16, sect. 14.
4 *Ibid.* IV, 16, 24.
5 Locke, *Essay*, IV, 18, 2.

Notes

PAGE 12

1 *Ibid.* IV, 19, 4.   2 *Ibid.* IV, 19, 14.   3 R. I. Aaron, *John Locke*, p. 304.

PAGE 13

1 Newton, *Irenicum*: in *Theological Manuscripts*, p. 52.

PAGE 14

1 Locke, *The Reasonableness of Christianity*, p. 2.
2 *Ibid.* p. 43.   3 *Ibid.* p. 199.

PAGE 15

1 Dr Yolton, in *John Locke and the Way of Ideas*, gives detailed evidence of the consternation which Locke caused in certain quarters. He also indicates the sceptical implications of Locke's thought (pp. 72–166).

PAGE 16

1 James Thomson, *A Poem Sacred to the Memory of Sir Isaac Newton*, ll. 68–75.
2 S. Clarke, *A Demonstration of the Being and Attributes of God*, p. 40; Hume, *A History of England*, vol. VIII, p. 293; Voltaire, *Œuvres Complètes*, vol. XXXV, pp. 114, 135.

PAGE 17

1 Jackson, *An Address to the Deists*, p. 73.

PAGE 18

1 Newton, *Opticks*, p. 378.
2 R. S. Westfall, *Science and Religion in Seventeenth Century England*, p. 199.

PAGE 19

1 James Thomson, *The Seasons*, ll. 1560–2.

PAGE 20

1 Tillotson, *Works*, vol. II, pp. 304 ff.
2 *Ibid.* II, 490–570.
3 *Ibid*, II, 459 ff.

PAGE 21

1 *Ibid.* I, 5.   2 *Ibid.* I, 42.
3 *Ibid.* I, 46.
4 J. Sharp, *Fifteen Sermons Preached on Several Occasions*, p. 48.
5 *Ibid.* p. 57.   6 *Ibid.* pp. 88 f., 243 ff.
7 Tillotson, *Works*, II, 593 ff.
8 *Ibid.* II, 295 ff.

Reason and Authority

PAGE 22

1 Tillotson, *Works*, II, 571. 2 *Ibid.* I, 5.

PAGE 23

1 Pattison, *Essays*, vol. II, p. 161.
2 T. Secker. 'Charges to the Clergy of the Diocese of Canterbury', *Works*, vol. V, pp. 464, 469–70.
3 *Memoirs of Dr Lardner*, p. 98.

PAGE 24

1 R. Lowth, *Sermons and Other Remains*, p. 152.
2 B. Porteus, *Works*, vol. VI, p. 97.

PAGE 25

1 E. Pyle, *Memoirs of a Royal Chaplain*, p. 13.
2 A. A. Sykes, *The Principles and Connexion of Natural and Revealed Religion*, p. 1.
3 J. Swift, *A Project for the Advancement of Religion and the Reformation of Manners*: *Works*, vol. VIII, p. 205.
4 Butler, *A Charge to the Clergy of the Diocese of Durham*: *Works*, vol. II, p. 397.

PAGE 26

1 J. Addison, *The Spectator*, Nos. 381 and 387.

PAGE 27

1 B. Porteus, *Works*, vol. II, pp. 24–5.

PAGE 28

1 Mark Pattison, *Essays*, vol. II, pp. 45, 55.

PAGE 29

1 S. Clarke, *A Demonstration*, pp. 74–5. Cf. Jackson, who concludes an intricate argument about the metaphysical nature of God with the triumphant assertion, 'Thus, I hope, it is proved that there is an absolute and positive internal cause, ground or reason of the existence of God, which demonstrates his existence *a priori*'. (*The Existence and Unity of God*, p. 36).
2 Locke, *Essay*, IV, 10, 1.
3 Whiston, *Astronomical Principles of Religion, Natural and Revealed*, pp. 98 ff., 241–59.
4 Clarke, *op. cit.*, Preface, p. 112.
5 Warburton, *Works*, vol. I, p. 50.

Notes

PAGE 30

1 A. A. Sykes, *The True Foundation of Natural and Revealed Religion Asserted*, p. 59, and *An Essay Upon the Truth of the Christian Religion*, p. 84.
2 Hume is characteristic in the hostility to enthusiasm which appears in all his writings, cf. his essay, *Of Superstition and Enthusiasm*.
3 W. Wake, *The Danger and Mischief of Misguided Zeal*, p. 3.
4 Butler's words were: 'Sir, the pretending to extraordinary revelations and gifts of the Holy Ghost is a horrid thing—a very horrid thing.'
5 *Letters from a Late Eminent Prelate*, p. 205. For a cautious estimate of 'enthusiasm' by a dissenter see J. Foster, *Sermons*, vol. III, pp. 281–4. He finds that the danger of enthusiasm lies in its irrational impulsiveness.
6 *The Letters of Horace Walpole*, vol. VII, p. 50.
7 J. Wilkins, *Of the Principles and Duties of Natural Religion*, p. 410.
8 S. Clarke, *One Hundred and Seventy-Three Sermons*, vol. I, Preface.

PAGE 31

1 Clarke, *A Demonstration*, p. 121.
2 Sykes, *An Essay*, pp. vii–viii.

PAGE 32

1 M. Pattison, *Essays*, vol. II, p. 46.
2 Wollaston, *The Religion of Nature Delineated*, p. 26.

PAGE 33

1 Gibbon, *A Vindication of some Passages in the Fifteenth and Sixteenth Chapters of the History*, p. 83.
2 Cf. his letters in controversy with Waterland. In effect he insisted that the issue concerned questions of historical criticism, not of theological opinion. Christian testimony must be treated like any other evidence.
3 *Letters of Archbishop Herring to William Duncombe, Esq.*, p. 134.
4 *Three Letters to Dr Clarke*, from a Clergyman of the Church of England (John Jackson), p. 14.

PAGE 34

1 Whiston, *Primitive Christianity Revived*, Historical Preface, pp. lxvii, lv, xxi.
2 *Letters of a Late Eminent Prelate*, p. 35.

PAGE 35

1 Clarke, *One Hundred and Seventy-Three Sermons*, vol. I, Preface, p. xxxvi.
2 J. Robinson, *A Letter to the Incumbents of all Churches and Chapels*, p. 3.
3 Jackson, *The Existence and Unity of God*, pp. 3, 27.

PAGE 36

1 Jackson, *A Confutation of the Fifth of Mr Moore's Propositions*, p. 6, and *The Existence and Unity of God*, To the Reader.

Reason and Authority

PAGE 39

1 Watts, *The Arian Invited to Orthodox Faith*: *Works*, vol. VI, p. 372.

PAGE 40

1 P. Doddridge, *Correspondence and Diary*, vol. V, p. 222.

PAGE 41

1 Sherlock, *The Use and Intent of Prophecy*, p. 274.
2 Warburton, *Works*, I, 50.

PAGE 42

1 R. Lowth, *A Letter to the Right Reverend Author of the Divine Legation of Moses*, p. 18.
2 Warburton, *Works*, vol. III, p. 466.

PAGE 43

1 Lowth, *op. cit.* p. 9.
2 Nichols, *Literary Anecdotes*, vol. V, p. 548.
3 L. Butler, *A Discourse Proving that the Faith and Practice of True Christians are No Just Matter of Shame or Reproach*, pp. 97–117.

PAGE 44

1 Hancock, *Arguments to Prove the Being of God*, p. 34.
2 Gurdon, *The Pretended Difficulties in Natural or Revealed Religion No Excuse for Infidelity*: Boyle Lectures, vol. III, p. 343.
3 Gastrell, *The Certainty and Necessity of Religion in General*, pp. 17–37.
4 Harris, *Refutation of the Atheistical Objections against the Being and Attributes of a God*, Sermon II, p. 26.
5 Leng, *Natural Obligations to believe the Principles of Religion and Divine Revelation*, p. 67.
6 T. Burnet, *The Demonstration of the True Religion*, vol. III, p. 421.

PAGE 45

1 J. Clarke, *An Enquiry into the Cause and Origin of Moral Evil*, *passim*.
2 S. Clarke, *A Demonstration*, pp. 204–5. The general position of the paragraph could be supported, clause by clause, from all the writers thus far cited.

PAGE 46

1 N. Sykes, *Church and State in England in the Eighteenth Century*, p. 345.
2 W. Derham, *Physico-Theology, or A Demonstration of the Being and Attributes of God*, pp. 261–6. Cf. Woodward, *The Divine Original and Incomparable Excellence of the Christian Religion*, vol. II, pp. 435–7.

Notes

3 Burnet, *True Religion*, vol. III, pp. 442–5.
4 Bradford, *The Credibility of the Christian Revelation*, Sermon 2, pp. 19–30; Turner, *The Wisdom of God in the Redemption of Man*, pp. 37–40.

1 Hancock, *Arguments to Prove the Being of God*, vol. III, p. 416.
2 Ibbot, *The True Notion of the Exercise of Private Judgment*, vol. I, p. 247.
3 A. A. Sykes, *The Principles and Connexion*, pp. 50 ff.
4 Burnet, *True Religion*, vol. III, p. 416.
5 Jackson, *A Plea for Human Reason*, p. 61.
6 Warburton, *Works*, vol. III, p. 620.
7 Leng, *Natural Obligations*, p. 240; Burnet, *True Religion*, vol. III, pp. 451–2.
8 Jackson, *The Existence and Unity of God*, p. 65.

1 Harris, *Refutation*, Sermon VI, p. 18; Burnet, *op. cit.* vol. III, p. 414.
2 Gastrell, *The Certainty and Necessity of Religion in General*, p. 120.
3 Sherlock, *Works*, vol. III, p. 299.
4 Burnet, *True Religion*, vol. III, p. 406.
5 Wollaston, *The Religion of Nature Delineated*, p. 52.
6 Sykes, *The Principles and Connexion*, pp. 86–7, 93.

1 Sykes, *The True Foundations*, p. 91.
2 Wilkins, *Of the Principles and Duties of Natural Religion*, p. 1.
3 Sykes, *The Principles and Connexion*, p. 3.
4 Stanhope, *The Christian Religion No Just Offence*, passim.
5 Sherlock, *Discourses Preached on Several Occasions*, vol. V, pp. 134, 142–3; S. Clarke, *The Unchangeable Obligations*, p. 292; B. Porteus, *Works*, vol. II, p. 242.
6 Jackson, *A Confutation of the Fifth of Mr Moores' Propositions*, p. 3.
7 Sherlock, *Several Discourses Preached in the Temple Church*, vol. I, p. 3; Bentley, *The Folly and Unreasonableness of Atheism*, pp. 22–35.

1 Sykes, *The True Foundation*, p. 81; cf. Jackson, *A Confutation*, p. 66.
2 Jackson, *A Plea for Humane Reason*, pp. 7, 19.
3 R. Hurd, *Sermons at Lincoln's Inn*, vol. I, p. 83.
4 Gibson, *Three Pastoral Letters*, p. 93.
5 Berriman, *The Gradual Revelation of the Gospel*, vol. I, pp. 12–37.

1 Sherlock, *Several Discourses*, vol. I, p. 5; vol. IV, p. 107.
2 Sykes, *The Principles and Connexion*, p. 505.

PAGE 52

1 *Ibid.* p. iii; Gibson, *Three Pastoral Letters*, p. 89; Sherlock, *Discourses Preached on Several Occasions*, vol. II, p. 422; Lowth, *Sermons*, p. 48; Balguy, *A Collection of Tracts*, Ded.

2 Leng, *Natural Obligations*, pp. 298 ff.

3 Williams, *On Revelation*, vol. I, pp. 164 ff.

4 Sykes, *The External Peace of the Church*, pp. 10, 14.

PAGE 53

1 Williams, *op. cit.* I, 196.

2 S. Clarke, *The Unchangeable Obligations*, p. 241.

3 Sykes, *The Principles and Connexion*, pp. 100, 244.

4 Jackson, *A Plea for Humane Reason*, p. 65; Sykes, *op. cit.* pp. 352–4, 242; S. Clarke, *One Hundred and Seventy-Three Sermons*, vol. I, pp. 409–10; Conybeare, *A Defence of Revealed Religion*, ch. VIII; Sherlock, *Discourses Preached on Several Occasions*, I, p. 255.

PAGE 54

1 J. Denne, *Want of Universality No Just Objection to the Truth of the Christian Religion*, pp. 18, 42; J. Foster, *The Usefulness, Truth and Excellency of the Christian Revelation*, ch. II; S. Clarke, *The Unchangeable Obligations*, p. 261; Gurdon, *The Pretended Difficulties*, III, 373–4.

2 Jackson, *Address to the Deists*, p. 25.

PAGE 55

1 Sykes, *The Principles and Connexion*, p. 150. Cf. Williams, *On Revelation*, vol. I, pp. 218 ff.

2 Stanhope, *The Christian Religion No Just Offence*, Sermon 7, p. 24; Sherlock, *The Use and Intent of Prophecy*, p. 55.

3 Jackson, *Address to the Deists*, pp. 28–109; cf. E. Chandler, *A Defence of Christianity from the Prophecies of the Old Testament*; Whiston, *The Accomplishment of Scripture Prophecies*; Sykes, *An Essay*; M. Lowman, *The Argument from Prophecy Vindicated*; Berriman, *The Gradual Revelation of the Gospel*.

PAGE 56

1 Sherlock, *The Use and Intent of Prophecy*, To the Reader.

2 *Ibid.* pp. 21–4.   3 *Ibid.* pp. 21–4.   4 *Ibid.* pp. 44–6.

5 *Ibid.* p. 55.   6 *Ibid.* p. 56.   7 *Ibid.* pp. 83, 120, 123.

8 Jackson, *Address to the Deists*, p. 113; cf. Sykes, *The Principles and Connexion*, pp. 202–3.

9 Clarke, *The Unchangeable Obligations*, p. 367.

PAGE 57

1 Gurdon, *The Pretended Difficulties*, vol. III, pp. 350–1.

Notes

2 Clarke, *op. cit.* pp. 360–6; Gurdon, *op. cit.* p. 395; Leng, *Natural Obligations,*
p. 463.
3 Sykes, *An Essay,* p. 137.
4 Ibbot, *The True Notion,* II, 212–17; cf. Sherlock's exposition of miracles in
The Trial of the Witnesses.
5 Jackson, *op. cit.* p. 27.
6 Sherlock, *Works,* vol. I, pp. 170–87.

PAGE 58

1 S. Clarke, *One Hundred and Seventy-Three Sermons,* vol. I, p. 194.
2 Leng, *Natural Obligations,* p. 73; cf. S. Clarke, *The Unchangeable Obligations,*
p. 193.
3 Denne, *Want of Universality,* p. 7.
4 Leng, *op. cit.* p. 79; cf. B. Porteus, *Works,* vol. II, p. 86.

PAGE 59

1 Jackson, *Address to the Deists,* pp. 18–19; Sykes, *The Principles and Connexion,*
p. 434; S. Clarke, *The Unchangeable Obligations,* p. 337.
2 Pattison, *Essays,* vol. II, pp. 114–15.

PAGE 60

1 Disney, *Sykes,* p. 329.
2 Secker, *An Answer to Dr Mayhew's Observations,* p. 68.

PAGE 61

1 *Letters to and from the Rev. Philip Doddridge,* pp. 457–8.
2 *Letters from a Late Eminent Prelate,* p. 168.

PAGE 62

1 John Balguy, *A Collection of Tracts,* p. xxvii.

PAGE 63

1 Dr Harris' Preface to Simon Browne, *A Defence of the Religion of Nature and
the Christian Revelation,* p. iii.
2 Atterbury, *Sermons,* vol. II, p. 78; vol. III, p. 4.

PAGE 64

1 S. Clarke, *The Unchangeable Obligations,* pp. 17–39.
2 Collins, *A Discourse of Free Thinking,* p. 69; Tindal, *Christianity as Old as the
Creation,* p. 199; also pp. 69–71, 323 ff.
3 Tindal, *Second Address,* pp. 55–6.
4 *The Scandal and Folly of the Cross Removed,* p. 54.

PAGE 65

1 Blount, *Anima Mundi*, p. 116.
2 T. Sprat, *History of the Royal Society*, p. 346.
3 Cf. Robert Jenkin, *A Brief Confutation of the Pretences against Natural and Revealed Religion*, vol. I, pp. iii, v, viii.

PAGE 68

1 *The Lives of Dr Edward Pocock, of Dr Zachary Pearce and of Dr Thomas Newton, and of the Rev. Philip Skelton*, vol. I, p. 419.

PAGE 69

1 Tindal, *Christianity as Old as the Creation*, p. 19.

PAGE 70

1 *Ibid.* p. 220.
2 E. Gibbon, *The Autobiographies*, p. 119; J. Leland, *A View of the Principal Deistical Writers*, vol. I, pp. 54–93.

PAGE 71

1 Boswell, *Life of Samuel Johnson*, vol. I, p. 158.
2 Cf. M. Pattison, *Essays*, vol. II, pp. 384–90.
3 Warburton, *Works* (ed. 1841), vol. XI, p. 141.

PAGE 72

1 *Ibid.* XII, 336.
2 Johnson, *Lives of the Poets*.
3 Cf. the markedly Deistic character of Pope's *Universal Prayer*.
4 (Conyers Middleton), *Some Remarks on a Reply to the Defence of the Letter to Dr Waterland*, p. 25.

PAGE 73

1 Cf. Collins, *A Discourse of Free Thinking*, pp. 61 ff.
2 Cf. R. L. Stromberg, *Religious Liberalism in Eighteenth Century England*, p. 98.
3 Cf. Tindal, *Second Address to the Inhabitants . . . of London and Westminster*, pp. 67, 83 ff.
4 *Ibid.* p. 25.
5 Gibson, *Three Pastoral Letters*, p. 12. Cf. Jackson, *An Address to the Deists*, p. 161.
6 Tindal, *An Address to the Inhabitants of . . . London and Westminster*, p. 33.

PAGE 74

1 Whiston, *Reflections on an Anonymous Pamphlet Entitled a Discourse of Free Thinking*, pp. 3–6.

Notes

2 *The Scandal and Folly of the Cross Removed,* Preface and p. 1. Yet the attempt to appear clever often produced a very prosaic type of writing. For an example, cf. Blount, *Miracles No Violations of the Law of Nature,* p. 25.
3 Shaftesbury, *Characteristicks,* vol. I, p. 63; also vol. III, p. 225.
4 Clarke, *Evidences of Natural and Revealed Religion,* p. 31.

PAGE 75

1 (Bentley), *Remarks upon a late Discourse,* pt. II, p. 71. Whiston was equally severe on Collins' slipshod scholarship, *Reflections,* pp. 20, 37–9.
2 Balguy, *A Second Letter to a Deist,* pp. 276, 282 ff.
3 Woolston, *Fifth Discourse,* pp. 65–6.
4 Bolingbroke (A Letter Occasioned by one of Archbishop Tillotson's Sermons), *Works,* vol. III, p. 255.
5 Blount, *Great is Diana of the Ephesians,* pp. 3, 12.

PAGE 76

1 Tindal, *An Address,* pp. 48, 61–2; cf. *A Second Address,* pp. 68, 21–3, 29–30; also *Christianity as Old as the Creation, passim.*
2 Cf. Woolston, *Free Gifts to the Clergy, passim; Sixth Discourse,* p. 94.
3 Pope, *The Dunciad,* vol. II, line 399.
4 Whiston, *Reflections,* pp. 46–7.
5 Clarke, *Evidences of Natural and Revealed Religion,* p. 4; cf. pp. 29, 31.
6 Collins, *A Discourse of Free Thinking,* pp. 15, 5.
7 Collins, *The Scheme of Literal Prophecy Considered,* p. v.

PAGE 77

1 N. Sykes, *Edmund Gibson,* pp. 259 ff.
2 Tindal, *An Address,* pp. 4, 12–19, 68 ff.
3 S. Chandler, *A Vindication of the Christian Religion,* pp. xxi–xxiii, 154, 373.
4 Bentley, *Remarks upon a Late Discourse of Free Thinking,* pt. I, pp. 18 ff; pt. II, p. 13.
5 A. A. Sykes, *A Brief Discourse Touching the Credibility of Miracles and Revelation,* p. 81.

PAGE 78

1 S. Chandler, *op. cit.* pp. 402–4.
2 *Philostratus,* Bk. I, ch. v, illus. 6.
3 *Works,* vol. III, p. 329.

PAGE 79

1 A. Collins, *An Essay Concerning the Use of Reason in Propositions,* p. 3.
2 Tindal, *Christianity as Old,* p. 116.
3 Collins, *op. cit.* p. 16.

4 Tindal, *op. cit.* pp. 315, 171; cf. p. 238.
5 *Ibid.* pp. 5, 198.
6 Collins, *A Discourse of Free Thinking*, p. 124.
7 Tindal, *An Address*, p. 64.
8 Tindal, *A Second Address*, p. 41.

PAGE 80

1 Collins, *The Use of Reason*, p. 44.
2 Blount, *Religio Laici*, p. 94; *Miracles No Violation*, p. 11.
3 Tindal, *Christianity as Old*, pp. 273, 8.

PAGE 81

1 *Ibid.* p. 218.　　2 *Ibid.* pp. 3 ff. and *passim.*
3 *Ibid.* p. 11.　　4 *Ibid.* pp. 44–5.　　5 *Ibid.* pp. 68, 91.

PAGE 82

1 *Ibid.* p. 257. Cf. *Second Address*, p. 13.
2 Sherlock, *Discourses Preached on Several Occasions*, vol. I, p. 256.
3 Chubb, *The True Gospel of Jesus Christ Asserted*, p. 47.
4 Tindal, *Christianity as Old*, p. 184.
5 *Ibid.* p. 27.　　6 *Ibid.* p. 322.　　7 *Ibid.* p. 180.

PAGE 83

1 Collins, *A Discourse of Free Thinking*, p. 39.
2 *Ibid.* p. 40; Tindal, *Christianity as Old*, p. 94.
3 Toland, *Christianity Not Mysterious*, pp. 18, 36, 65. Toland's attitude was equivocal, as can be seen in *Nazarenus* and *Amyntor.*
4 Collins, *A Discourse of Free Thinking*, pp. 10, 174.
5 Whiston, *Reflections*, p. 14. This was the more remarkable since Collins had championed Whiston's right to modify biblical texts.
6 Tindal, *Christianity as Old*, pp. 296, 303; also 242, 262; *Second Address*, pp. 81–2.
7 Cf. Annet's three works on the Resurrection.
8 Collins, *A Discourse of the Grounds and Reasons of the Christian Religion*, p. 101.

PAGE 84

1 Tindal, *op. cit.* p. 46; Collins, *The Scheme of Historical Prophecy Considered*, pp. 71–2.
2 C. Middleton, *A Letter to Dr Waterland*, pp. 17–45; *A Defence of the Letter*, etc., pp. 14 ff.; *Some Remarks on a Reply to the Defence*, etc., pp. 70–80.
3 Tindal, *Christianity as Old*, p. 240.
4 Annet, *A Collection of Tracts*, p. 42.

Notes

1 Collins, *The Scheme of Literal Prophecy Considered*, pp. 25 ff.
2 Blount, *Miracles No Violation*, Preface.
3 *Ibid.* p. 13. Cf. 5–8.
4 Blount, *Life of Apollonius Tyanaeus*, Preface.

1 Woolston, *First Discourse*, p. 4; *Fourth Discourse*, p. 52; *Sixth Discourse*, p. 27.
2 Annet, *The Resurrection of Jesus* (1744); *The Resurrection Reconsidered* (1744); *The Resurrection Stript of All Defence* (1747).
3 Tindal, *Christianity as Old*, pp. 148–9.

1 Wollaston, *The Religion of Nature Delineated*, p. 4.
2 Clarke, *The Unchangeable Obligations*, p. 27.
3 Tindal, *Christianity as Old*, p. 27.
4 *Ibid.* p. 192.
5 Collins, *A Discourse of Free Thinking*, p. 12.
6 Morgan, *The Moral Philosopher*, vol. I, p. 94.
7 Tindal, *A Second Address*, p. 69.

1 Tindal, *Christianity as Old*, p. 14.
2 *Ibid.* pp. 44–50.
3 Tindal, *An Address*, p. 44.
4 Gibson, *Pastoral Letter*, p. 7.
5 Tindal, *Christianity as Old*, pp. 51–2.

1 Burke, *Reflections: Works* (1792 ed.), vol. III, p. 127.

1 The beginnings of such a sense can be detected in Warburton and in Conyers Middleton (*Miscellaneous Works*, vol. III, pp. 50–1).
2 F. Atterbury, *Sermons*, vol. III, pp. 272–3.

1 W. Harris in S. Browne, *A Defence of the Religion of Nature*, Preface, p. vi.

1 F. B. Kaye claims that Mandeville was misunderstood by Law and all his other critics. Cf. *Fable of the Bees* (Oxford, 1924), 2 vols. Mandeville himself made this point against Berkeley in his *Letter to Dion*.

2 Law, *The Case of Reason*, p. ii.
3 *Ibid.* p. 2.
4 *Ibid.* pp. 4–6.

PAGE 95

1 *Ibid.* p. 10.
2 *Ibid.* pp. 22–8.   3 *Ibid.* p. 32.

PAGE 96

1 *Ibid.* p. 56.
2 *Ibid.* p. 101.

PAGE 97

1 *Ibid.* p. 124.
2 *Ibid.* pp. 140–1.   3 *Ibid.* p. 148.   4 *Ibid.* p. 155.
5 *Ibid.* p. 158.

PAGE 98

1 Cf. H. Talon, *William Law*, pp. 36–7.

PAGE 99

1 Berkeley, *Alciphron*: in *Works*, vol. III, p. 48.
2 Berkeley, *Philosophical Commentaries*: § 493: *Works*, vol. I.

PAGE 100

1 Berkeley, *An Essay Towards a New Theory of Vision*, § 147.

PAGE 101

1 Berkeley, *A Treatise Concerning the Principles of Human Knowledge*, Introduction, § 3. Berkeley numbered the paragraphs in most of his works.
Henceforth I shall indicate *Principles* and the introduction to *The Principles*
(separately numbered) by *Introduction*.

PAGE 102

1 *Introduction*, § 21.
2 *Ibid.* § 1.

PAGE 103

1 *Ibid.* § 10.   2 *Ibid.* § 13.
3 *Principles*, § 11.

Notes

1 *Introduction,* § 12.
2 *Principles,* § 97.
3 *Ibid.* § 4.

PAGE 105

1 *Ibid.* § 3.
2 *Ibid.* §§ 25–6.   3 *Ibid.* § 6.

PAGE 106

1 *Ibid.* § 6.

PAGE 107

1 Berkeley, *Alciphron: Works,* vol. III, p. 73.
2 *Ibid.* p. 87.

PAGE 108

1 *Ibid.* p. 182.

PAGE 109,

1 Berkeley, *Alciphron: Works,* vol. III, p. 209.
2 *Ibid.* p. 178.   3 *Ibid.* p. 178.
4 *Ibid.* p. 218.

PAGE 110

1 *Ibid.* p. 241.   2 *Ibid.* p. 280.   3 *Ibid.* p. 280.
4 *Ibid.* p. 281–2.

PAGE 111

1 *Ibid.* p. 328.
2 *Ibid.* pp. 283–4.

PAGE 112

1 Butler, *Works,* I, 75. My references are by volume and page to Gladstone's edition; volume I contains the *Analogy,* and volume II the *Sermons.*

PAGE 113

1 *Ibid.* vol. I, p. 16.   2 *Ibid.* I, 130.   3 *Ibid.* I, 92.
4 *Ibid.* I, 130.
5 *Ibid.* I, 60–1.

PAGE 114

1 *Ibid.* I, I.   2 *Ibid.* I, 89.   3 *Ibid.* I, 52–3.
4 *Ibid.* I, 131.

PAGE 115

1 Walter Bagehot, *Works*, I, pp. 291–2.
2 Butler, *Works*, vol. I, p. 5.
3 *Ibid.* I, 8–9.   4 *Ibid.* I, 10.

PAGE 116

1 *Ibid.* I, 18.   2 *Ibid.* I, 47.

PAGE 117

1 *Ibid.* I, 55.   2 *Ibid.* I, 104.   3 Cf. *ibid.* I, 119–26.
4 *Ibid.* I, 145.   5 *Ibid.* I, 159.   6 *Ibid.* I, 160.
7 *Ibid.* I, 165.

PAGE 118

1 *Ibid.* I, 174.
2 *Ibid.* I, 188.

PAGE 119

1 *Ibid.* I, 17.
2 Butler, *Works*, vol. I, pp. 380–1.
3 *Ibid.* I, 170.

PAGE 120

1 *Ibid.* I, 212.   2 *Ibid.* I, 91.
3 *Ibid.* I, 246–7.   4 *Ibid.* I, 250–1.   5 *Ibid.* I, 185.
6 *Ibid.* I, 373–6.   7 *Ibid.* I, 222.   8 *Ibid.* I, 375.
9 *Ibid.* I, 238.
10 *Ibid.* I, 223.

PAGE 121

1 *Ibid.* I, 43.   2 *Ibid.* II, 98.   3 *Ibid.* I, 275.
4 *Ibid.* I, 155.
5 *Ibid.* I, 147.

PAGE 122

1 *Ibid.* I, 284.   2 *Ibid.* I, 261.   3 *Ibid.* I, 234.
4 *Ibid.* I, 209.   5 *Ibid.* I, 188.

Notes

PAGE 124

1 C. D. Broad, *Five Types of Ethical Theory*, p. 5.

PAGE 125

1 *Private Papers of James Boswell*, vol. xii, pp. 227–32, quoted by N. Kemp Smith in Hume's *Dialogues Concerning Natural Religion*, pp. 97–100.

PAGE 126

1 Hume, *A Treatise of Human Nature* (henceforth referred to as *Treatise*), Introduction, pp. xx–xxii.

PAGE 127

1 Hume, *Enquiry Concerning Human Understanding* (henceforth referred to as *Human Understanding*), p. 44.
2 *Treatise*, p. 415.

PAGE 128

1 *Human Understanding*, p. 30.
2 *Ibid.* p. 31.
3 *Treatise*, p. 1.
4 *Human Understanding*, p. 18.

PAGE 129

1 *Treatise*, pp. 98 ff.
2 *Human Understanding*, p. 22.

PAGE 130

1 *Human Understanding*, p. 165.
2 *Treatise*, p. 75.
3 *Ibid.* p. 77.
4 *Human Understanding*, p. 164.

PAGE 131

1 *Treatise*, p. 87.
2 *Ibid.* p. 134.
3 *Human Understanding*, p. 43.
4 *Treatise*, p. 132.
5 *Human Understanding*, pp. 45–7.

PAGE 132

1 *Treatise*, p. 252.
2 *Ibid.* pp. 180–3.

313

3 *Ibid.* p. 183.   4 *Ibid.* p. 185.   5 *Ibid.* p. 187; cf. p. 268.
6 *Human Understanding*, pp. 159–60.
7 *Ibid.* pp. 161–2.
8 *Treatise*, p. 268.

PAGE 133

1 *Ibid.* pp. 269–72. Cf. also Hume's essay on the Sceptic, *Essays*, vol. I,
  pp. 213–30.
2 *Treatise*, p. 457.
3 *Ibid.* p. 471.
4 *Ibid.* p. 589.   5 *Ibid.* p. 477.   6 *Ibid.* p. 532.

PAGE 134

1 Cf. Hume's essay, 'Of the Immortality of the Soul', *Essays*, II, 401.
2 Cf. B. M. Laing, *Hume*, pp. 191 f.
3 Hume, 'The Natural History of Religion', *Essays*, vol. II, p. 309.

PAGE 135

1 *Ibid.* II, 330.
2 *The Letters of David Hume*, vol. I, p. 154.
3 *Essays*, vol. II, p. 354.
4 *Ibid.* II, 362.
5 *Essays*, vol. II, p. 337.   6 *Ibid.* II, 399.

PAGE 136

1 Hume, *Dialogues Concerning Natural Religion* (henceforth referred to as
  Dialogues), p. 22.
2 *Essays*, vol. II, p. 348.
3 *Dialogues*, pp. 173, 276.
4 *Ibid.* p. 274.
5 *Essays*, vol. II, p. 309.

PAGE 137

1 *Dialogues*, p. 158.
2 *Ibid.* p. 264.
3 *Letters*, vol. I, p. 106.

PAGE 138

1 A good deal of ingenuity has been spent in identifying Hume with one or
  the other of the characters. Dr B. M. Laing contends that Hume is Cleanthes,
  holding the balance between scepticism and dogmatism, and many have
  agreed with him. I find Professor Kemp Smith's conclusion convincing:

Notes

no single character consistently represents Hume (though Philo is most frequently his spokesman), but the general trend of the argument, with its negative quality, accurately reflects his position.

2 *Letters*, vol. II, p. 334.
3 *Human Understanding*, section x.
4 *Essays*, vol. II, p. 107.

PAGE 139

1 *Human Understanding*, p. 146.

PAGE 140

1 *Dialogues*, p. 183.
2 *Ibid.* p. 184.
3 *Ibid.* p. 251.   4 *Ibid.* p. 260.   5 *Ibid.* p. 381.

PAGE 141

1 *Ibid.* pp. 260–1.
2 *Ibid.* p. 281.

PAGE 142

1 Adam Smith to William Strachan, in Hume, *Essays*, vol. I, p. ii.
2 Hume, 'My Own Life', *Essays*, vol. I, p. 8.
3 *Ibid.* p. 14.
4 Hume to Hutcheson, *The Letters of David Hume*, vol. I, p. 39.

PAGE 143

1 *Treatise*, p. 636.
2 Cf. B. Willey, *The Eighteenth Century Background*, p. 110.
3 Cf. *Letters of David Hume*, vol. I, pp. 348–51, 360–1.

PAGE 144

1 Reid, *An Inquiry into the Human Mind on the Principles of Common Sense*, p. 394.
2 *Ibid.* pp. 394–5.

PAGE 145

1 *The Letters of Edward Gibbon*, vol. II, p. 320.
2 J. Evans, *An Attempt to Account for the Infidelity of . . . Gibbon*, pp. 9, 5. Cf. R. Watson, *An Apology for Christianity*, p. 6.
3 Gibbon, *Letters*, vol. III, p. 216.

Reason and Authority

PAGE 146

1 Gibbon, *The Autobiographies*, p. 405.
2 Gibbon, *The History of the Decline and Fall of the Roman Empire* (henceforth referred to as *Decline and Fall*), vol. I, p. 299, vol. VI, p. 189.
3 *Ibid.* V, 244.   4 *Ibid.* VI, 110   5 Cf. *ibid.* I, 332; II, 77–9, 81.
6 Cf. J. B. Black, *The Art of History*, pp. 170–2.
7 *Decline and Fall*, end of ch. xxxviii.

PAGE 147

1 *Ibid.* II, I.
2 Cf. Priestley, *Letters to a Philosophic Unbeliever*, vol. II, p. 201.
3 Cf. W. Bagehot, *Works*, vol. II, p. 167.

PAGE 148

1 *Decline and Fall*, vol. V, p. 170.
2 Cf. G. M. Young, *Edward Gibbon*, p. 158.
3 C. Dawson, *Edward Gibbon*, pp. 18–22.

PAGE 149

1 Gibbon, *Letters*, vol. III, p. 118.
2 *Ibid.* III, 331.
3 Cf. D. M. Low, *Edward Gibbon*, p. 268.

PAGE 150

1 C. V. Wedgwood, *Edward Gibbon*, pp. 21, 28.
2 *Decline and Fall*, vol. V, p. 204.
3 *Ibid.* II, 30.   4 *Ibid.* V, 107.   5 *Ibid.* II, 63.
6 Gibbon, *The Autobiographies*, p. 137.
7 Porson, *Letters to Mr Archdeacon Travis*, p. xxviii.

PAGE 151

1 Sainte-Beuve, *Causeries du Lundi*, vol. VIII, p. 367.
2 Porson, *op. cit.* p. xxxi.
3 Gibbon, *The Autobiographies*, p. 312 n.
4 *Letters*, vol. II, pp. 100, 107, 117, 119, 120.
5 Gibbon, *A Vindication*, pp. 93–4; *The Autobiographies*, p. 316.

PAGE 152

1 Porson, *Letters to Mr. Archdeacon Travis*, p. xxviii.
2 Cf. Byron's comment in *Childe Harold*: 'sapping a solemn creed with solemn sneer'.

3 *The Autobiographies*, p. 143.
4 *Decline and Fall*, vol. II, pp. 43, 47; V, 107.

PAGE 153

1 *Ibid.* II, 28.
2 *The Autobiographies*, p. 221.
3 *Decline and Fall*, vol. II, pp. 29, 31.
4 *The Autobiographies*, p. 316; *Decline and Fall*, vol. I, p. 69.

PAGE 154

1 Porson, *Letters to Mr Archdeacon Travis*, p. xxx.
2 *Decline and Fall*, vol. IV, p. 66.

PAGE 156

1 Wesley, *Works*, vol. VIII, p. 483. Unless otherwise indicated, references are
to the collected *Works* (ed. of 1872). Where a title is specified, the reference
is to the edition indicated in the bibliography.
2 *Letters of Warburton to Yorke*, p. 51.
3 *Works*, vol. VI, p. 351.
4 *Ibid.* VIII, 11
5 *Standard Sermons*, vol. II, pp. 142–3.

PAGE 157

1 *Journal*, vol. V, p. 254.
2 *Works*, vol. VIII, p. 340.
3 *Ibid.* VIII, 249.   4 *Ibid.* VI, 200–1, 204.

PAGE 158

1 *Ibid.* IX, 329.
2 These words, which form the text of the sermon, are from II Kings x. 15.
3 *Standard Sermons*, vol. II, pp. 136–9.
4 *Works*, vol. VI, p. 337.
5 *Ibid.* VI, 360.
6 *Ibid.* VI, 353.   7 *Ibid.* VI, 354.   8 *Ibid.* VIII, 11–12.

PAGE 159

1 *Letters*, vol. V, p. 364.
2 *Works*, vol. VI, p. 360.
3 *Ibid.* VI, 359.   4 *Ibid.* VIII, 13.
5 *Standard Sermons*, vol. II, p. 216.
6 *Works*, vol. VIII, p. 14.
7 *Ibid.* VIII, 198.

PAGE 160

1 *Letters*, vol. III, p. 332.
2 *Ibid.* II, 117.
3 *Journal*, vol. V, p. 169.
4 *Works*, vol. XI, p. 484.

PAGE 161

1 *Standard Sermons*, vol. I, p. 208.
2 *Journal*, vol. I, pp. 471 ff.
3 Cf. R. N. Flew, *The Idea of Perfection*, p. 317.
4 *Letters*, vol. VII, p. 61.
5 *Ibid.* VIII, 190.
6 Cf. C. W. Williams, *John Wesley's Theology To-day*, p. 37.

PAGE 162

1 *Standard Sermons*, vol. I, p. 32.
2 *Journal*, vol. V, p. 492.
3 *Letters*, vol. II, p. 383.
4 *Works*, vol. XIV, pp. 267–8.

PAGE 163

1 Cf. H. Lindstrom, *Wesley and Sanctification*, pp. 7–14.
2 *Notes on the N.T.*, *ad loc.*
3 *Works*, vol. VIII, p. 277.

PAGE 164

1 *Ibid.* VII, 376–83.   2 *Ibid.* IX, 286.
3 *Standard Sermons*, vol. II, p. 225.
4 *Works*, vol. X, pp. 229 f.
5 *Ibid.* VI, 509.

PAGE 165

1 *Letters*, vol. VI, p. 297.

PAGE 166

1 *Standard Sermons*, vol. I, p. 45.
2 *Ibid.* II, 226–7.   3 *Ibid.* I, 299–300.
4 *Ibid.* I, 208.

PAGE 167

1 *Works*, vol. VIII, p. 472.
2 *Standard Sermons*, vol. I, p. 97.

3 *Ibid.* I, 410.
4 *Letters*, vol. III, p. 381.

PAGE 168

1 *Standard Sermons*, vol. II, p. 45.
2 *Ibid.* II, 66.　　3 *Ibid.* I, 152–3.
4 *Works*, vol. VIII, pp. 340–6.

PAGE 169

1 *Works*, vol. XI, pp. 366–466.
2 *Ibid.* XI, 374.

PAGE 170

1 *Preface to Hymns*, 1742, quoted *Works*, vol. XI, p. 383.
2 *Works*, vol. XI, p. 442.
3 *Ibid.* XI, 371.
4 *Ibid.* XI, 387.　　5 *Ibid.* XI, 396.
6 *Standard Sermons*, vol. II, p. 172.

PAGE 171

1 Flew, *The Idea of Perfection in Christian Theology*, pp. 327, 332–6.
2 *Letters*, vol. IV, p. 208.
3 *Works*, vol. XI, p. 384.

PAGE 172

1 *Letters*, vol. III, pp. 371–88.
2 *Works*, vol. VII, p. 378.
3 *Letters*, vol. III, p. 387.
4 *Works*, vol. VIII, p. 336.
5 G. Whitefield, *A Letter to the Rev. Mr John Wesley*, p. 12.

PAGE 173

1 A. M. Toplady, *Works*, vol. V, p. 325. Toplady's contribution can be judged by *A Letter to the Rev. Mr John Wesley*; *More Work for Mr John Wesley*; *An Old Fox Tarred and Feathered* (*Works*, vol. V). Many writings on the Arminian side were equally abusive; cf. *The Arminian Magazine*.
2 A. M. Toplady, *The Church of England Vindicated from the Charge of Arminianism*, vol. V, pp. 1–149.
3 A. M. Toplady, *Works*, vol. II, pp. 340–1. Cf. Thomas Scott, *The Force of Truth* (in *Theological Works*), vol. I, p. 13 and *Remarks on the Refutation of Calvinism*, vols. VI and VIII, *passim*.

Reason and Authority

1 R. Elliott, *A Summary of the Gospel Doctrine*, in a funeral sermon on his death; prefixed to G. Whitefield, *Select Sermons*.
2 W. Wilberforce, *A Practical View of the Prevailing Religious System of Professed Christians*, pp. 226–7.
3 Scott, *The Force of Truth*, vol. I, pp. 9 f.
4 H. Venn, *The Complete Duty of Man*, p. 68.

1 Wilberforce, *A Practical View*, p. 23.
2 *Ibid.* p. 235.

1 Toplady, *Works*, vol. I, pp. 16, 15, 28, 57, 49, 28. Cf. Wilberforce, *A Practical View*, p. 85.
2 Toplady, *op. cit.* vol. I, pp. 13, 16.

1 Wilberforce, *op. cit.* pp. 62–5.
2 Wordsworth, *The Prelude*, Bk. XI: *Works*, p. 318.
3 W. Cowper, *Table Talk*, Bk. II, ll. 734–9.

1 J. Hervey, *Meditations and Contemplations*, pp. 52, 55.
2 Doddridge, *Correspondence and Diary*, vol. V, p. 125.
3 Venn, *Complete Duty of Man*, Preface, p. xvii.
4 Wilberforce, *A Practical View*, p. 269.
5 *Ibid.* p. 288.

1 Toplady, *Works*, vol. I, p. 31.
2 R. Coupland, *Wilberforce*, pp. 232–4.

1 Hobbes, *Leviathan*, pp. 199, 175.

1 Locke, *Works* (ed. 1823), vol. VI, pp. 21, 54.

1 A. C. Vidler, *The Orb and the Cross*, p. 20.
2 N. Sykes, *Church and State*, pp. 286–9.
3 W. Kennett, *A Second Letter to the Lord Bishop of Carlisle*, p. 44.

Notes

PAGE 185

1 Leslie, *The New Association of those called Moderate Churchmen with the Modern-Whigs and Fanaticks*, pp. 1–2.
2 Leslie, *The Case of the Regale and the Pontificat stated, passim*; G. Hickes, *The Constitution of the Catholic Church*, pp. 62–3.
3 Leslie, *The New Association*, p. 15; *The Case of the Regale*, pp. 7 ff.
4 *The Case of the Regale*, p. 15.
5 *Ibid*. p. 25.
6 *Ibid*. p. 69; Hickes, *The Constitution of the Catholic Church*, p. 89.
7 Leslie, *The Case of the Regale*, pp. 161, 164.

PAGE 186

1 Tindal, *The Rights of the Christian Church Asserted*, p. 7.
2 *Ibid*. p. 16.

PAGE 187

1 *Ibid*. pp. xxi–xxii.   2 *Ibid*. p. xxviii.   3 *Ibid*. p. liii.
4 Cf. *The Rights*, ch. VIII, pp. 244–311.
5 *Ibid*. p. lxxxviii.

PAGE 188

1 The authorship has been a matter of dispute; it is generally conceded that Atterbury's share, if not exclusive, was decisive.
2 *A Letter to a Convocation Man*, pp. 2–3.
3 *Ibid*. p. 18.
4 *Ibid*. pp. 19, 21.

PAGE 189

1 *Ibid*. pp. 45, 50.
2 This was admitted by both Hurd and Warburton, *Letters from a Late Eminent Prelate*, pp. 230–3.
3 Wake, *The State of the Church and Clergy of England*, Preface, p. ii.
4 Wake, *The Authority of Christian Princes over their Ecclesiastical Synods Asserted*, p. 10.
5 Wake, *The Authority of Christian Princes over their Ecclesiastical Synods Asserted*, p. 56.

PAGE 190

1 *Ibid*. p. 64.   2 *Ibid*. p. 79.   3 *Ibid*. pp. 151 ff.   4 *Ibid*. p. 226.
5 *Ibid*. p. 336.
6 Atterbury, *The Rights, Powers and Privileges of an English Convocation*, p. 64.

PAGE 191

1 W. Kennett, *Ecclesiastical Synods and Parliamentary Convocations in the Church of England*, p. ix.
2 Wake, *The Authority of Christian Princes*, p. 342.
3 Burnet, *Reflections on a Book entitled the Rights, Powers and Privileges*, p. 2.

PAGE 192

1 W. Kennett, *An Occasional Letter on the Subject of the English Convocations*, p. 53.
2 Wake, *The State of the Church and Clergy of England*, Preface, p. i.
3 E. Gibson, *Codex Juris Ecclesiastici Anglicani* (1713).

PAGE 193

1 *Codex*, Ep. ded.
2 *Ibid.* p. i.   3 *Ibid.* p. xviii.
4 *Ibid.* p. xviii.   5 *Ibid.* p. ii.

PAGE 194

1 Foster, *An Examination of the Scheme of Church-Power laid down by the Codex Juris Ecclesiastici Anglicani*, p. 1.
2 *Ibid.* p. 5.
3 *Ibid.* p. 10.   4 *Ibid.* p. 15.   5 *Ibid.* p. 23.   6 *Ibid.* p. 74.

PAGE 195

1 Whiston, *Memoirs*, vol. I, p. 244.
2 Hoadly, *Preservative*, p. 33.
3 *Ibid.* p. 44; cf. also Sykes, *An Answer to the Non-Jurors' Charge of Schism upon the Church of England*.
4 Hoadly, *A Preservative against the Principles and Practices of the Non-Jurors*, p. 99.
5 *Ibid.* p. 55.   6 *Ibid.* pp. 61–6.

PAGE 196

1 *Ibid.* p. 100.
2 Cf. *ibid.* pp. 90–1.
3 *Ibid.* pp. 11 ff.   4 *Ibid.* p. 14.   5 *Ibid.* p. 18.   6 *Ibid.* pp. 20–4.
7 This was a point elaborated in the debates between John Rogers (*A Discourse of the Visible and Invisible Church*) and A. A. Sykes (*The Authority of the Clergy and the Liberties of the Laity*).

PAGE 197

1 Hoadly, *Preservative*, p. 98.
2 A point hotly debated was whether Hoadly had originally included 'absolute' in the text of his sermon, or whether it was a later insertion.
3 Balguy, *A Collection of Tracts*, Ded.

Notes

PAGE 198

1 *A Reply to the Representation of Convocation, Works*, vol. II, pp. 448–587.
2 Law, *Letters*, pp. 49 ff.; cf. pp. 318 ff.
3 Jackson claimed (*The Grounds of Civil and Ecclesiastical Government*, p. 58) that Law was less than honest in omitting vital parts of the quotations he took from Hoadly.
4 Hoadly, *The Nature of the Kingdom, or Church, of Christ*, p. 17.

PAGE 199

1 J. Jackson, *The Grounds of Civil and Ecclesiastical Government*, p. 34. Note Francis Hare's equally emphatic protest against those who treat 'all establishments of religion by the state' as 'utterly inconsistent with right reason, just liberty and true religion' (*Works*, vol. I, p. 120).
2 Rogers, *A Vindication of the Civil Establishment of Religion*, pp. 103–30.

PAGE 200

1 *Ibid.* pp. 7, 234.
2 In *The Dispute Adjusted about the Proper Time of Applying for a Repeal of the Corporation and Test Acts*.
3 *Ibid.* pp. 7–9.
4 Cf. Rogers' argument: the chief magistrate can give office to whom he likes (it is a matter of favour, not of right); he likes and trusts those who share his own religion. Others have no grievance. (*A Vindication*, pp. 88–91.)
5 Contrast the position of Sykes on this question: 'when the sacrament is made a qualification for civil office it is applied to ends for which Christ never designed it; for purposes which he never intended; it is perverted from spiritual to civil ends; from a religious end to make men better, to a support of one party of Christians against another; not as a symbol of friendship but of a party and division; not in remembrance of the death of Christ, but in memory of the grant of an office' (*The Corporation and Test Acts Shewn to be of No Importance to the Church of England*, p. 25).
6 Sherlock, *Works*, vol. III, p. 454.

PAGE 201

1 Sherlock, *A Vindication of the Corporation and Test Acts*: *Works*, vol. IV, pp. 431–91.
2 Gibson, *Codex*, p. 10.
3 R. Lowth, *Sermons*, p. 11.

PAGE 202

1 Sykes, *The Authority of the Clergy and the Liberties of the Laity*, p. 180.
2 This summary is based on works by Lowth, Rogers and Sherlock, on the

one hand, and of Jackson and Sykes on the other. On certain marginal points there are differences, but most of the statements in this paragraph could be supported by quotations from all these authors.

3 Warburton, *The Alliance between Church and State*, p. 1.

4 *Ibid.* pp. 4–5.

PAGE 203

1 *Ibid.* pp. 10–12.   2 *Ibid.* pp. 26–8.

3 *Ibid.* p. 33.   4 *Ibid.* p. 37.   5 *Ibid.* p. 53.

6 Hurd, *Life of Warburton* (prefixed to *The Divine Legation of Moses*), p. 10.

PAGE 204

1 Warburton, *The Alliance*, p. 88.

2 *Ibid.* pp. 117–19.

3 *Ibid.* p. 147.   4 *Ibid.* p. 166.   5 *Ibid.* pp. 168, 193.

6 *Ibid.* pp. 197–200.

PAGE 205

1 Horsley, *Review of the Case of the Protestant Dissenters*, Preface.

2 Warburton, *The Alliance*, p. 167.

3 *Ibid.* p. 257.

4 Cf. Gibbon's attitude: 'In the connection of church and state, I have considered the former as subservient only, and relative, to the latter' (*Decline and Fall*, vol. v, p. 244). Warburton would not have dissented.

5 Warburton, *The Alliance*, p. 118.

PAGE 206

1 S. Chandler, *The History of Persecution*, pp. iv–v.

2 *Ibid.* p. xxxv.

3 *Ibid.* pp. xxxviii–lxxii. Cf. J. Foster, *Discourses*, vol. II, p. 191.

PAGE 207

1 *Ibid.* p. 363.

2 Chandler, *The Case of Subscription*, p. 2.

3 *Ibid.* p. 179.

4 J. Foster, *Discourses*, vol. II, p. 173.

5 Watts, *Works*, vol. v, pp. 12, 44. Watts' important works in this area are *An Humble Attempt towards the Revival of Practical Religion among Christians* and *A New Essay on Civil Power in Things Sacred*.

PAGE 208

1 *Ibid.* IV, 172.

2 *Ibid.* IV, 180.   3 *Ibid.* IV, 189.   4 *Ibid.* IV, 196.

Notes

PAGE 209

1 *Ibid.* IV, 200.   2 *Ibid.* IV, 220.   3 *Ibid.* IV, 609.
4 White, *Three Letters to a Gentleman Dissenting from the Church of England,* I, p. 11.
5 *The Cambridge History of English Literature,* vol. X, p. 375.

PAGE 210

1 The title of Towgood's work is *A Dissent from the Church of England fully Justified, Being the Dissenting Gentleman's Letters . . . in answer . . . to the Rev. Mr White.* P. xxxvi.
2 *Ibid.* p. 135.   3 *Ibid.* p. 139.   4 *Ibid.* p. 67.
5 P. 140.
6 *Ibid.* pp. 134–5.

PAGE 211

1 *Ibid.* p. 98.   2 *Ibid.* pp. xxxvi–xxxvii.
3 *Ibid.* p. 10.   4 *Ibid.* p. 187.   5 *Ibid.* pp. 10, 242.

PAGE 212

1 *Ibid.* p. 24.   2 *Ibid.* p. 251.   3 *Ibid.* p. 245.   4 *Ibid.* p. 267.

PAGE 213

1 Paley, *Principles of Moral and Political Philosophy,* Preface, p. xv.
2 *Ibid.* III, 328.

PAGE 214

1 *Ibid.* III, 329.
2 *Ibid.* III, 329–37.   3 *Ibid.* III, 339.

PAGE 215

1 *Ibid.* III, 348.

PAGE 217

1 Hartley, *Observations on Man,* vol. I, Preface, p. iii.
2 *Ibid.* I, 6.   3 *Ibid.* I, 5.

PAGE 218

1 *Ibid.* I, iv.
2 *Ibid.* I, 1.   3 *Ibid.* I, 11.   4 *Ibid.* I, 13.   5 *Ibid.* I, 15.
6 *Ibid.* I, 22.

PAGE 219

1 *Ibid.* I, 56–64.   2 *Ibid.* I, 375.

PAGE 220

1 *Ibid.* I, 102.

PAGE 221

1 *Ibid.* I, 416.
2 Hartley, *Observations on Man*, vol. I, p. 425.
3 *Ibid.* I, 433.   4 *Ibid.* I, 433.   5 *Ibid.* I, 456.

PAGE 322

1 *Ibid.* I, 458.
2 *Ibid.* I, 465.   3 *Ibid.* I, 474.

PAGE 223

1 *Ibid.* I, 488.   2 *Ibid.* I, 497.

PAGE 224

1 *Ibid.* II, Introduction, p. ii.
2 *Ibid.* II, 347.   3 *Ibid.* I, Preface, p. iv.

PAGE 225

1 *Ibid.* I, 500.
2 *Ibid.* I, 501.   3 *Ibid.* I, 504.
4 *Ibid.* I, 507.

PAGE 226

1 *Ibid.* I, 510.
2 Cf. Copleston, *A History of Philosophy*, vol. v, p. 193.

PAGE 227

1 This position was further elaborated by Robinet, *Considérations Philosophiques de la Gradation Naturelle des Formes d'Être* (1767).
2 Hartley, *Observations on Man*, vol. II, p. 292.

PAGE 228

1 *Ibid.* I, Preface, v.
2 *Ibid.* I, 6.   3 *Ibid.* III, xvii.

PAGE 229

1 *Ibid. Prop.* 93.
2 Priestley, *Hartley's Theory of the Human Mind on the Principles of the Association of Ideas* (1775).

Notes

PAGE 230

1 Priestley, *Disquisitions relating to Matter and Spirit*, vol. I, p. 7.
2 Priestley, *Essay on the Principles of Civil Government*, pp. 296, 5.

PAGE 231

1 Priestley, *Letters to the Rt. Hon. Edmund Burke*, p. 145.
2 Priestley, *Disquisitions*, vol. I, p. 35.
3 *Ibid.* I, 46.   4 *Ibid.* I, 61–2.

PAGE 232

1 *Ibid.* I, 140.   2 *Ibid.* I, 144.   3 *Ibid.* I, 146.

PAGE 233

1 Priestley, *The Doctrine of Philosophical Necessity Illustrated*, pp. 150 ff.

PAGE 234

1 Priestley, *Disquisitions*, vol. II, p. 2.
2 *Ibid.* I, v.
3 *A Free Discussion of the Doctrines of Materialism and Philosophical Necessity.*

PAGE 235

1 Priestley, *Letters to a Philosophical Unbeliever*, vol. II, p. 33.

PAGE 237

1 Horsley, *Tracts in Controversy with Dr Priestley*, Preface.
2 Priestley, *Letters to a Philosophical Unbeliever*, vol. I, p. 126.

PAGE 238

1 *Ibid.* II, 34.

PAGE 239

1 Priestley, *An Appeal to the Candid and Earnest Professors of Christianity*, p. 15.
2 L. Stephen, *History of English Thought in the Eighteenth Century*, vol. I, p. 431.
3 Priestley, *A Sermon on the Subject of the Slave Trade*, Preface.

PAGE 240

1 Godwin, *Enquiry Concerning Political Justice* (henceforth referred to as *Political Justice*), vol. I, p. 308.
2 *Ibid.* I, 116, 400 n.   3 *Ibid.* I, ix.
4 W. Hazlitt, *The Spirit of the Age*, vol. I, p. 208.

Reason and Authority

PAGE 241

1 *Political Justice*, vol. I, pp. 368–9.
2 *Ibid.* I, 400 n. 3 *Ibid.* I, 402.

PAGE 242

1 *Ibid.* I, xxvi. 2 *Ibid.* II, 528.

PAGE 243

1 *Ibid.* I, 363. 2 *Ibid.* I, 364–5. 3 *Ibid.* I, 367. 4 *Ibid.* I, 371.
5 *Ibid.* I, 374–5.

PAGE 244

1 A. F. Rodway, *Godwin and the Age of Transition*, p. 28.
2 *Political Justice*, I, 384.
3 *Ibid.* I, 121. 4 *Ibid.* I, 201.

PAGE 245

1 *Ibid.* I, vii.
2 Godwin, *Thoughts Occasioned by the Perusal of Dr Parr's Spital Sermon*,
pp. 81–2. Quoted by D. Fleisher, *William Godwin*, p. 43. I am indebted
to Mr Fleisher throughout this paragraph.
3 *Political Justice*, vol. I, p. 75.

PAGE 246

1 *Ibid.* I, 86. 2 *Ibid.* I, 93. 3 *Ibid.* I, 49.
4 *Ibid.* I, xxiv, 22.
5 T. Paine, *Common Sense*, p. 1; quoted in *Political Justice*, I, 124.

PAGE 247

1 *Political Justice*, vol. I, p. 119.
2 *Ibid.* I, 104.
3 *Ibid.* I, 104.

PAGE 250

1 Cf. C. E. Vaughan, *Studies in the History of Political Philosophy*, vol. II, p. 4.

PAGE 251

1 F. Hare, *The Difficulties and Discouragements which attend the Study of Scripture*:
Works, vol. II, p. 21.

Notes

2 Whiston, *Memoirs*, vol. I, p. 147; *Athanasius Convicted of Forgery, passim*; *Primitive Christianity Revived, passim*; etc.
3 S. Clarke, *The Scripture Doctrine of the Trinity*, pp. viii–x.
4 D. Waterland, *The Case of Arian Subscription*, p. 25.
5 A. A. Sykes, *The Case of Subscription*; 'Phileleutherus Cantabrigiensis', *An Essay on Imposing and Subscribing Articles on Religion.*
6 Michaiajah Towgood, *Serious and Free Thoughts on the Present State of the Church and of Religion*, p. 275.

1 Gibbon, *Decline and Fall*, vol. VI, p. 128.
2 F. Blackbourne, *The Confessional*, p. 120.
3 *Ibid.* p. 22.   4 *Ibid.* p. 35.   5 *Ibid.* p. 189.
6 *Ibid.* p. 319.

1 *Ibid.* pp. 336–7.
2 *The Letters of Edward Gibbon*, vol. I, p. 305.
3 *Parliamentary History*, vol. XVIII, pp. 246 ff.

1 G. O. Trevelyan, *The Early History of Charles James Fox*, p. 414.
2 P. 7. I refer to the speech as given in *Works* (London, 1887), vol. VII.
3 Burke, *Works*, vol. VII, p. 10.
4 *Ibid.* pp. 10–11.   5 *Ibid.* p. 13.   6 *Ibid.* p. 16.   7 *Ibid.* p. 19.

1 Cf. *The Works of the Rev. A. M. Toplady*, vol. II, pp. 413 ff.
2 *The Works of Beilby Porteus*, vol. I, p. 39.
3 J. Priestley, *Letters to the Young Men at Oxford and Cambridge: Works*, vol. XVIII, pp. 346–7.
4 *Anecdotes of the Life of Richard Watson . . . written by himself*, pp. 255–6.
5 *Ibid.* p. 13.

1 *Ibid.* p. 105.   2 *Ibid.* p. 68.
3 *Ibid.* pp. 96, 71, 72, 89, 96, 255–6, 351, 368, 378, 503. Watson considered himself a disinterested reformer who had been most unjustly penalised. He has often been regarded as a prime example of many of the episcopal sins which he denounced; but his offences were less flagrant and the mitigating features were greater than his critics sometimes allowed. Cf. N. Sykes, *Church and State in England in the Eighteenth Century*, pp. 356 ff.

Reason and Authority

1 Watson, *Miscellaneous Tracts*, vol. II, pp. 102 ff.
2 Watson, *Anecdotes of the Life of Richard Watson*, p. 244; cf. pp. 241–2.
3 *Ibid.* p. 198.
4 *Ibid.* p. 39.   5 *Ibid.* p. 259. Cf. pp. 162, 256, 261.

1 *Ibid.* p. 163.
2 A. Lincoln, *English Dissent, 1763–1800*, p. 10.
3 R. Hall, *Christianity Consistent with a Love of Freedom: Works*, vol. III, p. 6.
4 *Ibid.* p. 12; cf. also p. 15.

1 R. Robinson, *Reflections on Christian Liberty, Civil Establishment and Toleration* (in Sparks' *Collection of Essays and Tracts*, vol. III, pp. 95–6). Cf. R. Price, *Observations on the Nature of Civil Liberty*, etc., pp. 3 ff.
2 P. Furneaux, *Letters to the Hon. Mr Justice Blackstone*, Pref. to 2nd ed.
3 R. Price, *Additional Observations on the Importance of the American Revolution*, pp. 3–4.
4 J. Priestley, *Sermon on the Slave Trade*, p. 31.
5 R. Robinson, *Arcana*, p. 33.
6 Priestley, *The Importance and Extent of Free Inquiry in Matters of Religion*, pp. 15–18, 23–4.
7 Cf. Robinson, *op. cit.* p. 13.
8 John Aikin, *Letters*, vol. I, p. 91, quoted by Lincoln, *Some Political and Social Ideas of English Dissent*, p. 62.

1 Priestley, *A Letter to the Rt. Hon. William Pitt*, pp. 32–3.
2 Cf. Hall, *Christianity Consistent with a Love of Freedom : Works*, vol. III, pp. 23, 26.
3 *Ibid.* p. 12.
4 Priestley, *A Letter to the Rt. Hon. William Pitt*, p. 16; Robinson, *Reflections*, pp. 92–3.
5 Priestley, *A History of the Corruptions of Christianity*, vol. II, pp. 226, 307.
6 Priestley, *A Letter to the Rt. Hon. William Pitt*, p. 23.
7 Cf. Hall, *op. cit.* pp. 23, 26.
8 G. Wakefield, *Memoirs*, vol. I, p. 339; Priestley, *View of the Principles*, p. 254.

1 Cf. J. Priestley, *Familiar Letters*, p. 89; *The Conduct to be observed by Dissenters in order to procure the Repeal of the Test Acts : works* vol. XV, p. 395.

Notes

2 *Ibid.* xv, 400.
3 Capel Lofft, *A History of the Corporation and Test Acts,* p. 16.
4 Priestley, *The Conduct:* works vol. xv, pp. 400, 398.
5 19 George III, c. 44.
6 B. L. Manning, *The Protestant Dissenting Deputies,* p. 218.

PAGE 262

1 Cf. the reports in *Parliamentary History,* vol. xxvi, pp. 786–832; vol. xxviii, pp. 387–452.
2 *The Anti-Jacobin,* vol. i, 362.

PAGE 263

1 Thomas Belsham, quoted by Lincoln, *op. cit.* p. 61.
2 J. Priestley, *The Importance and Extent of Free Inquiry,* p. 54.
3 R. Hall, *Christianity Consistent with a Love of Freedom*: *Works,* vol. iii, p. 30; *An Apology for the Freedom of the Press*: *Works,* vol. iii, pp. 158, 172.
4 Price, *A Discourse on the Love of our Country,* pp. 50–1.

PAGE 264

1 *European Magazine,* Sept. 1791.
2 Priestley, *A Letter to the Rt. Hon. William Pitt,* p. 17.

PAGE 265

1 *Life of Dr Thomas Newton,* by himself, vol. ii, pp. 240, 224.
2 R. Lowth, *Sermons,* p. 35.

PAGE 266

1 Watson, *A Defence of Revealed Religion,* pp. 400–1.
2 *The Letters of Edward Gibbon,* vol. iii, pp. 257, 258, 265, 287–8, 308.
3 *Ibid.* iii, 277.
4 Cf. Bishop Porteus' charges to the clergy of the diocese of London, 1790 and 1794, *The Works of Beilby Porteus,* vol. vi, pp. 225–86.

PAGE 267

1 Cf. Rowland Hill, *An Apology for Sunday Schools,* in which the various charges against the Sunday Schools are enumerated and answered.
2 Burke, *Works,* vol. vii, p. 30.
3 Burke, *Reflections,* vol. iii, p. 49.

PAGE 268

1 A. V. Dicey, *Law and Public Opinion in England,* p. 123.
2 *Reflections on the French Revolution*: *Works* (1792), vol. iii, p. 321; cf. also p. 28.

3 *Speech on a Plan for the Better Security of the Independence of Parliament* (1780): *Works* (1792), vol. II, pp. 189, 212.
4 *Reflections*, vol. III, p. 59.
5 *Ibid.* p. 320.

PAGE 269

1 Burke, *Reflections*, vol. III, p. 49.
2 *Ibid.* p. 94.
3 Cf. C. W. Parkin, *The Moral Basis of Burke's Political Thought*, p. 102.
4 Burke, *op. cit.* p. 28.

PAGE 270

1 *Ibid.* p. 124. 2 *Ibid.* p. 116. 3 *Ibid.* pp. 59, 60.
4 *Ibid.* p. 66.

PAGE 271

1 Vaughan, *Studies in the History of Political Philosophy*, vol. II, pp. 10–16.
2 Burke, *Reflections*, vol. III, p. 181.
3 Burke, *Letters on a Regicide Peace*, vol. V, p. 407.
4 Burke, *Reflections*, p. 136.

PAGE 272

1 *Ibid.* p. 140.
2 *Ibid.* p. 93. 3 *Ibid.* p. 320. 4 *Ibid.* p. 189.
5 Burke, *Letters to a Member of the National Assembly*, vol. III, p. 370.

PAGE 273

1 Burke, *Reflections*, vol. III, pp. 128–9.

PAGE 274

1 *Ibid.* pp. 144, 139, 130.
2 He also and equally elicited support. Cf. Gibbon's glowing praise of the *Reflections*, in *Letters*, vol. III, p. 216; *Autobiographies*, p. 342 n.
3 Priestley, *Letters to the Rt. Hon. Edmund Burke*, Preface.
4 Mackintosh, *Vindiciae Gallicae*, passim.
5 Burke, *Reflections*, vol. III, p. 172.
6 T. Paine, *The Rights of Man*, p. 26.
7 Cf. Acton on the vein of insincerity in Burke, H. G. Schenck, *The Aftermath of the Napoleonic War*, p. 7.

PAGE 275

1 Wordsworth, *The Prelude*, Book Seventh (*Works*, p. 287).

Notes

1 Cf. E. Troeltsch, *Gesammelte Werke*, vol. IV, pp. 353 ff.

PAGE 277

1 R. Watson, *A Defence of Revealed Religion*, p. 462.

PAGE 278

1 G. M. Trevelyan, *English Social History*, vol. III, pp. 57–8.

PAGE 279

1 *Preliminary Dissertation: Concerning the Fundamental Principle of Virtue or Morality*, in W. King, *The Origin of Evil*, translated by E. Law.

PAGE 280

1 *Ibid.* p. xxi.
2 J. Brown, *Essays on the Characteristics*, vol. II, iii, 137.
3 *Ibid.* II, ix, 210.
4 Tucker, *The Light of Nature Pursued*, vol. I, xxii, § 11.

PAGE 281

1 Bentham, *The Principles of Morals and Legislation*, vol. I, p. iii, § 10.
2 Cf. D. A. Winstanley, *Unreformed Cambridge*, p. 176.

PAGE 282

1 B. Porteus, *Works*, vol. I, pp. 20–1.
3 Watson, *Anecdotes*, pp. 38–9.
2 *Ibid.* p. 39.
4 J. Hey, *Lectures on Divinity*, vol. II, p. 360.

PAGE 283

1 Gibbon, *Decline and Fall*, vol. IV, p. 169. Gibbon added a footnote to show how signally this rule of progress had been exemplified in his own enlightened century.
2 R. Lowth, *Sermons and Other Remains*, p. 91.

333

INDEX

Abraham, 84
Addison, Joseph, 26
Affections, 222
Alciphron (Berkeley), 99, 107, 108
Alexandrians, 163
Altruism, 245
Ambition, 221, 222, 254
Analogy: Tindal confuses identity with, 96; Butler's *Analogy of Religion*, 112–24; Butler's analogical method, 115–19
Anarchism, 247
Andrewes, Launcelot, 1
Anger, 222
Annet, Peter, 62, 84
Antinomianism, 167
Apollonius of Tyana, 85
Archbishop of Canterbury, authority of, 192
Arianism: orthodoxy and, 33; Whiston and, 34; fostered by Clarke, 35, 36, 251; dissenters' adherence to, 37; supported by certain academies, 38; and Latitudinarianism, 40; Whiston and, 73; denies doctrine of reprobation, 172; Priestley and, 235; and demand for reform, 255
Arminianism: Presbyterians and, 37; strain of, in Wesley, 163, 164; Toplady condemns, 173; Thomas Scott and, 174; Priestley and, 235; and compulsory oaths, 251
Arrogance: of Warburton, 42–3, 202, 205; Law on, 94, 96; Hume on, 127: Hobbes and, 182; Locke and, 183
Art, 221
Articles, the Thirty-nine, 165, 189; revision of, 252, 253, 254, 255; exemption from, 261

Association: Hartley as a proponent of, 217, 219–24, 227, 228; Priestley's adaptation of Hartley's principle of, 229, 230, 231; Godwin and, 241
Association of ideas, 128, 129
Assurance, doctrine of, 166
Athanasian Creed, 257
Athanasianism, 34, 35, 38, 251
Atheism: natural religion leads to, 98; Berkeley on, 108; eighteenth-century attitude to, 137; Wesley on, 172; Atterbury on, 188; Priestley on, 232, 238
Atonement: attitude to, at Daventry, 38; Latitudinarian attitude to, 60; Tindal on, 95; Wesley on, 165, 171–2; Wilberforce on, 174, 175; Priestley on, 235, 236
Atterbury, Bishop F., 63, 90, 187–92
Authority: eighteenth-century preoccupation with, vii; suspicion of traditional forms of, 2–5, 18–19; of Locke and Newton (q.v.) 5; an issue at stake in religious controversy, 65; of the Bible, 83–4, 180; of natural law, 85; of reason, 89, 93; divine, 94; in the search for truth, 111; of religion, 137; Wesley's doctrine of, 159–60, 162; of experience, 162; of the Church, 185, 196; of magistrates, 186, 211; Atterbury on two kinds of, 188; of Christian Princes, 189–90, 191; Law and Hoadly on, 198; of Parliament, 211; Priestley on, 238; of Government, 265; Burke on, 268

Bacon, F., 1, 283
Balguy, John, 62, 75, 197

334

Index

335

Index

188–92; Gibson on, 192–3, 200, 201; Foster on, 194; Hoadly on, 194–9; Law on, 198; Sherlock on, 200–1; Warburton on, 201, 202–5; Chandler on, 206–7; Watts on, 207–9; White on, 209; Towgood on, 209–12; Paley on, 213–15

Church Missionary Society, the, 178

Citizen, rights of the, 210

Citizenship, duties of, 208

Civilization, Byzantine, 148

Clarendon, earl of, 187

Clarke, Samuel: realised implications of work of Locke and Newton, 16; set new standards of clarity and cogency, 29–30, 45; conciliatory tone of, in argument, 31; his doctrine and authority, 34–6, 44; in argument for 'self-motive principle' of morality, 59; on Deists, 63–4, 74, 87; on free thinking, 76; Hume on certain arguments of, 130; and subscription, 251

Clergy, Gibbon on, 146, 151; and Middleton, 153; Tindal's attitude to, 186, 187; lower, lack authority, 192; ecclesiastical law clarified for, by Gibson, 193–4; Paley's view on, 214, 215; Feathers Tavern Petition, on behalf of, 253; bishops and, 256, 266

Coleridge, S. T., 249, 277

Collins, A., 25; on Clarke, 64; his *Discourses*, 67–8; his method of argument, 73, 74–5, 76, 237; and the Bible, 83; statement by, of Deist position, 84–5; Burke on, 89; weakness of, 90

Common sense: Locke the apostle of, 8, 15; in Tillotson, 20, 22; a characteristic of best eighteenth-century writing, 22–3; Berkeley aspired to, 98; an ambiguous term in Reid, 144; Paley an exponent of, 213; and reason, 242; and Government, 247; in Whiston, 251; Brown on, 280

Common sense, Scottish School of, 143–4

Congregationalists, 38

Conscience: and the law, 201, 208; dominion over, is God's, 211; of the clergy, 214; noncomformist, 240; national, 256; natural right to freedom of, 258–9.

Consciousness, religious, 156, 157

Conservatism, 272, 274, *see also* Change

Constitution: power of bishops incompatible with, 194; of the Church, 198; Church an integral part of, 200, 209; aims of a religious, 215; supports accepted forms of religion, 254; attachment to, and public office, 257; nonconformists and, 258, 261, 262; Burke on, 270

Contract theory, 186, 203

Conversion, Evangelical preoccupation with, 180

Convocation, controversy in, 187–90

Conybeare, John, 80

Cornwallis, Archbishop, 255

Corporation Act, the, 200, 257, 261

Cosmological proof, of God's existence, 9, 13, 44

Cowper, William, 177

Creation, God revealed in, 140, 226

Cromwell, Oliver, 200

Crown, the, 193, 194, 256

Cyril of Alexandria, 152

d'Alembert, 5, 256

Daventry Academy, 38

Death: an intractable mystery, 27; Evangelical preoccupation with, 177

Defoe, Daniel, 206

Deism, Deists, vii, 2, 12, 31, 32, 33; claims, of, with regard to Locke, 12, 66–7; controversy concerning, vii, 40, 62–92, 93, 120; challenge of, 63; proclaimed purpose of, 63–4; in reaction against previous age, 64–5; essential beliefs of, 65–6; Collins' contribution to

Index

Index

Index

Index

Index

Index

343

Index

Index

Wesley, 156; on Hervey, 178; on Church and State, 202–5, 211, 214; tendency to be satisfied with externals, 277

Warrington Academy, 37, 38

Waterland, D., 36, 251

Watson, Bishop R.: Gibbon on, 151; his ideal of 'temperate reform', 255–8; in revolutionary excesses, 265; on reason, 277; representative of school of Cambridge divines, 281, 282

Watts, Isaac, 38–9, 207–9

Wesley, John, vii–viii, 30; his view of faith, 124, 167–8, 171; his appeal to emotion, 155–6, 238; theological framework of his ideas, 157–8, 162–7; on reason, 158–9, 276; his doctrine of authority, 159–62; his doctrine of Christian perfection, 168–71; his differences with other persuasions, 171–2

Whigs, the: and divine right of kings, 182; theories of, 185; Latitudinarian, 189, 213; pamphleteers among, 195; issues dividing Tories from, 197; and advocacy of toleration, 198; nonconformist loyalty to, 200, 261; Watson describes himself as one of, 255

Whiston, William: and revealed religion, 29; his confidence in own version of truth, 33–4; in controversy on reason and revelation,

68; on ridicule, 73–4; on free thinking, 76; on the authority of the Bible, 83; on Hoadly, 195; in issue of subscription to the Church, 251

White, John, 209, 210

Whitefield, George, 171, 172, 173

Wilberforce, William: on the defects in popular Christianity 174–5; and emotion in the service of religion, 176–7; on the relation of religion to life, 178, 179, 180

Wilkins, Bishop John, 13, 30

Will, 242, 243, 270

William III, 187

Williams, Bishop John, 52

Wisdom, 242, 269, 270, 272

Wit, 221

Wollaston, William, 32, 48, 80

Woolston, Thomas: on miracles, 68, 85–6; his lack of moderation in argument, 75, 76; on the literal meaning of Scriptures, 83, 84

Wordsworth, William, 249, 275, 283

Worship: uniformity of, 135; in the ancient world, Gibbon on, 152–3, 154; and unity in Christian witness, 158; and law, 202, 211; as an act of 'natural religion', 208; freedom of, 214; forms of public, and belief, 253

Zinzendorf, N. L. von, 165

349